Martha

MW00776098

1-11, 21-33

Lineages of Despotism
and Development

Lineages of Despotism
and Development

British Colonialism and
State Power

MATTHEW LANGE

The University of Chicago Press
Chicago and London

Matthew Lange is assistant professor of sociology at McGill University.

The University of Chicago Press, Chicago 60637
The University of Chicago Press, Ltd., London
© 2009 by The University of Chicago
All rights reserved. Published 2009
Printed in the United States of America

18 17 16 15 14 13 12 11 10 09   1 2 3 4 5

ISBN-13: 978-0-226-47068-9 (cloth)
ISBN-10: 0-226-47068-7   (cloth)

Library of Congress Cataloging-in-Publication Data

Lange, Matthew.
    Lineages of despotism and development : British colonialism and state
power / Matthew Lange.
        p. cm.
    Includes bibliographical references and index.
    ISBN-13: 978-0-226-47068-9 (cloth : alk. paper)
    ISBN-10: 0-226-47068-7 (cloth : alk. paper)
    1. Imperialism—Economic aspects—Great Britain—Colonies. 2. Great
Britain—Colonies—Africa—Administration—Case studies. 3. Great Britain—
Colonies—Africa—Economic conditions—Case studies. 4. Despotism—
Economic aspects—Africa. 5. Economic development—Political aspects—Africa.
6. Mauritius—Economic conditions. 7. Sierra Leone—Economic conditions.
8. Guyana—Economic conditions. 9. Botswana—Economic conditions. I. Title.
    JV341.L36 2009
    325'.3410967—dc22   2008042034

∞ The paper used in this publication meets the minimum requirements of the
American National Standard for Information Sciences—Permanence of Paper
for Printed Library Materials, ANSI Z39.48-1992.

CONTENTS

ACKNOWLEDGMENTS

This book investigates the developmental legacies of British colonialism and therefore analyzes complex processes over long periods of time in distant places. Paralleling the subject matter, the actual writing of the book was complex, occurred over several years, and brought me to diverse corners of the world. Along the way, I became indebted to a number of individuals and organizations, all of whom helped make possible this final product.

The Watson Institute of International Studies, Brown University, the National Science Foundation (grant number SES-0117514), and McGill University all provided the financial backing for two years of fieldwork. While overseas, a number of organizations gave me valuable resources and guidance. In particular, I thank professors and staff at the University of Botswana, the University of Guyana, the University of Mauritius, the National University of Singapore, the Public Records Office, the British National Library, the National Archives of Botswana and Mauritius, and the Mahatma Gandhi Institute for very generously giving me their time and insight.

In writing the book, a number of friends and colleagues provided invaluable assistance. Kubaje Adazu, Andy Dawson, Gebre Kiros, and Zewdu Woubalem prevented many a headache by generously assisting with my statistical analysis. Silvia Giorguli Saucedo, John A. Hall, Erik

Kuhonta, Matthias vom Hau, and Don Von Eschen helped out enormously through comments and conversations. Most notably, I am greatly indebted to Patrick Heller, James Mahoney, and Dietrich Rueschemeyer, three extraordinary mentors who provided detailed comments, amazing insight, needed critiques, and much support over the years.

Besides financial and professional assistance, I thank friends and family for their love and support. Ian and Joanne Taylor and Sharon Morgan befriended me in Botswana and helped make my fieldwork a wonderful experience. Seth Lieberman distracted me from data collection on a couple of occasions and thereby pushed me to open my eyes to present worldly wonders. Katie and Steve Andrzejewski were my best friends throughout the process yet always treated me more as a brother. My parents, Keith and Eileen Lange, are role models who have always provided unending love and guidance. Finally, I thank Clodine Loubert and Nicolas Lange, my wife and son, for providing my daily helping of joy and inspiration.

Introduction

British Colonialism and Developmental Legacies

1

Over sixty years after the wave of colonial independence began, a debate still rages over the developmental impact of British colonialism. On one side, neoliberals and British nationalists praise the many benefits of British rule. D'Souza (2002), for one, claims that British colonialism "was the transmission belt" that brought "the blessings of civilization" to much of the world (6). As a consequence, he states that the "descendants of colonialism are better off than they would be if colonialism had never happened" (4). In a best-selling book, Ferguson (2004) makes similar claims. He proposes that British colonial rule proliferated liberal political and economic institutions that made British colonialism a positive developmental force. In fact, Ferguson holds British colonialism in such high regard that he asks the United States to pick up where Britain left off and accept the proverbial white man's burden.

More left-leaning scholars see this procolonial view as misguided and downright delusional. Davis (2001) derides claims of British developmentalism and documents the self-serving and destructive effects of British colonial rule. Giving a real-world example that he believes exemplifies the colonial condition, Davis describes how British colonial officials left millions of Indians to starve to death during droughts while at the same time exporting record crops from other regions of the subcontinent. In a review of Ferguson's work, Blackburn (2005) argues that Ferguson overlooks the factors that "discredited" colonialism in the first place; lists slavery, mass starvation, ethnic violence, and economic dependence as common British legacies; and asks sardonically how anyone could view these outcomes as developmental.

So who is right? What is the developmental legacy of British colonialism? A glance at the developmental records of former British colonies provides some insight. Table 1.1 lists the Human Development Index scores and rankings of some fifty former British colonies; the index provides a general proxy for human development by combining indicators of educational attainment, societal health, and economic opportunity. According to the table, Australia, Singapore, and Barbados are among the most developed countries in the world, and their developmentalism lends support to D'Souza's and Ferguson's procolonial views. If one turns to the bottom of the list, however, Sierra Leone, Nigeria, and Bangladesh provide evidence in favor of the anticolonial perspective, as they have very low levels of development. In contrast, the development levels of Sri Lanka, Belize, and Egypt are mediocre, measuring up poorly against the likes of Singapore but very favorably when compared to Nigeria. Former British colonies can therefore be found at all levels of development—indeed, a close inspection of the list shows that British colonies are almost perfectly distributed throughout the world's developmental rankings.

Such an even distribution refutes strong claims made by both sides of the debate over British colonial legacies and suggests three possible scenarios. First, contrary to both the procolonial and the anticolonial perspectives, British rule potentially had little or no long-term developmental impact. According to this view, British colonialism might have affected development over the short run but did not transform the developmental trajectories of the colonies. Instead, whatever conditions promoted development prior to colonialism—human capital, agricultural technology, the environment, institutions, ethnic diversity, etc.—were relatively unaffected by colonial rule and continued to reinforce developmental trajectories both during colonialism and afterwards. Second, it is possible that postcolonial changes account for uneven development among former British colonies. This scenario downplays the role of colonialism and therefore appears contrary to both the pro- and anticolonial perspectives. Yet it potentially fits either side of the debate, as the wide range of postcolonial development might be caused either by the inability of several former colonies to retain the positive benefits of British colonialism or the ability of some former colonies to break free from British colonialism's

Table 1.1 Human Development Index among former British overseas colonies, 2004

Country	HDI score	HDI rank	Country	HDI score	HDI rank
Australia	0.957	3	Maldives	0.739	98
Canada	0.950	6	Guyana	0.725	103
United States	0.948	8	Jamaica	0.724	104
New Zealand	0.936	20	Egypt	0.702	111
Hong Kong	0.927	22	South Africa	0.653	121
Israel	0.927	23	India	0.611	126
Singapore	0.916	25	Solomon Islands	0.592	128
Cyprus	0.903	29	Myanmar	0.581	130
Barbados	0.879	31	Botswana	0.570	131
Malta	0.875	32	Pakistan	0.539	134
Brunei Darussalam	0.871	34	Ghana	0.532	136
Seychelles	0.842	47	Bangladesh	0.530	137
St. Kitts and Nevis	0.825	51	Sudan	0.516	141
Bahamas	0.825	52	Uganda	0.502	145
Trinidad and Tobago	0.809	57	Swaziland	0.500	146
Antigua and Barbuda	0.808	59	Lesotho	0.494	149
Malaysia	0.805	61	Yemen	0.492	150
Mauritius	0.800	63	Zimbabwe	0.491	151
Dominica	0.793	68	Kenya	0.491	152
St. Lucia	0.790	71	Gambia	0.479	155
Grenada	0.762	85	Nigeria	0.448	159
Jordan	0.760	86	Tanzania	0.430	162
St. Vincent & the Grenadines	0.759	88	Zambia	0.407	165
Fiji	0.758	90	Malawi	0.400	166
Sri Lanka	0.755	93	Sierra Leone	0.335	176
Belize	0.751	95			

negative developmental legacy. Finally, it is possible that the developmental impact of British colonialism varied from place to place. This third scenario suggests that British colonialism took different forms and intensities, transformed social structures in different ways, built a variety of institutions, and thereby left a wide range of developmental outcomes.

In this book, I assess the developmental legacy of British colonialism by analyzing the determinants of long-term development. Contrary to the first two scenarios, I find that precolonial and postcolonial factors account for little variation in development among former British colonies. In contrast, I find that British rule took diverse forms, that different forms of rule institutionalized different states, and that these dissimilarities led to radically different developmental outcomes. Specifically, the analysis highlights the importance of direct and indirect rule and documents how each institutionalized states with different capacities to promote broad-based development, with direct colonial rule laying the institutional foundations for development and indirect colonial rule laying the institutional foundations for despotism.

The Argument: Direct Rule, Indirect Rule, and Developmental Legacies

Direct and indirect rule were two fundamentally different systems of control used by the British in their vast overseas empire. Direct rule depended on an integrated state apparatus and resembled the form of state domination that developed in Western Europe over the previous five centuries. It required the dismantling of preexisting political institutions and the construction of centralized, territory-wide, and bureaucratic legal-administrative institutions that were controlled by colonial officials. Direct rule was therefore both transformative and intensive, being the British colonial version of Hobbes' *Leviathan*. Australia, Sri Lanka, and Barbados provide examples of former directly ruled British colonies.

Indirect rule, on the other hand, was a form of colonial domination via collaboration with indigenous intermediaries who controlled regional political institutions. It created bifurcated colonial states based on two radically different organizational principles. Like direct rule, the central legal-administrative institutions in indirectly ruled colonies were relatively bureaucratic, yet these institutions were usually minuscule and isolated in the colonial capital and areas of European settlement. In peripheral regions, chiefs, princes, sultans, and other indigenous leaders controlled "customary" legal-administrative institutions that were organized along patrimonial lines. Both patrimonial rulers and bureaucratic officials, in turn, depended on and collaborated with one another to maintain a decentralized and divided system of colonial domination. British Africa provides examples of colonies that were ruled through collaborative relations between the colonial administration and dozens—if not hundreds—of regional chiefs.

Although the British colonial doctrine and subsequent works on British colonialism suggest a stark division between direct and indirect rule, the line between the two was often blurred, and several former colonies combined both forms of domination to different extents and in different ways. Colonial India and Malaysia, for instance, were divided between directly and indirectly ruled regions, and each region experienced a different extent of direct and indirect rule, creating a kaleidoscope of domination in both colonies. In this way, the form of domination throughout the British Empire was more of a spectrum than a dichotomy, with former colonies possessing different extents of direct and indirect rule.

Throughout the twentieth century, most leading colonial officials, British politicians, and imperial scholars claimed that indirect rule was the superior mode of domination. One advantage was that it made colonialism relatively inexpensive. In addition, they believed indirect rule was more adaptive, participatory, and culturally sensitive than direct rule because it incorporated supposedly "traditional" institutions into the system of colonial control. Social anthropologist Bronislaw Malinowski (1929), for example, claimed that indirect rule was far superior to direct rule because it recognized that "social development is very slow, and that it is infinitely preferable to achieve it by a slow and gradual change coming from within" (23). By contrast, Malinowski and others believed that direct rule "would rapidly shatter the whole social fabric" of colonial societies, thereby reducing the colonized "to a disorganized mass of helots" (Low and Pratt 1960: 166).

Despite the demise of the British Empire, interest in the appropriateness of direct and indirect rule remains strong. Following the tradition begun by colonial anthropologists, Hechter (2000) believes direct rule is a disruptive force that sparks opposition and conflict between states and local populations. In fact, he believes the growing prevalence of direct rule caused the explosion of nationalist violence in the twentieth century. He sees indirect rule as inherently less confrontational and more collaborative and therefore as the preferred means of domination. Along these lines, Hechter and Kabiri (2004) suggest that American forces would have been most successful at establishing a stable and effective system of rule in occupied Iraq if they governed the country indirectly (22).

Others disagree strongly with Hechter's general conclusions. Mamdani (2001) describes how indirect rule institutionalized oppositional identities and inequality in Rwanda and ultimately caused ethno-national genocide. Analyzing all of sub-Saharan Africa in another book, he (1996) finds that indirect rule negatively affected development by institutionalizing "decentralized despotism," or a dispersed state dependent on local autocrats. By contrast, Kohli (2004) analyzes the state legacy of Japanese colonialism in South Korea and finds that direct colonial domination—despite colonial era atrocities—helped lay the state institutional foundations for the country's subsequent developmental success.

Similar to Mamdani and Kohli, my findings suggest that direct rule had a much more positive effect on broad-based development than indirect rule, and I provide evidence that the form of colonial rule helps explain much of the variance in postcolonial development among former British colonies. My argument focuses on the legal-administrative capacities of states and the ways in which these capacities affect the ability of states to provide developmental goods and impede developmental bads. The analysis offers evidence that three institutional differences caused directly ruled British colonies to have greater legal-administrative capacities and thereby superior developmental records. Consistent with Weberian theory, I find that direct rule institutionalized more bureaucratic states and that bureaucratic organization made possible corporate state action by helping to discipline and coordinate state agents. Next, I draw on the work of Mann (1984), provide evidence that infrastructural power was necessary for the provisioning of complex and territorially dispersed developmental goods, and show that the states of former directly ruled colonies were more infrastructurally powerful than their indirectly ruled counterparts. Finally, like Evans (1995, 1996), I show that inclusiveness—or the inclusion of societal actors in policy making and policy implementation—promoted development by making possible state-society synergy and increasing state accountability to the public.

These findings are based on both qualitative and quantitative insight. Using statistical methods and a new variable measuring the form of British colonialism, I find that the extent to which former British colonies were ruled indirectly is strongly and negatively related to numerous indicators of postcolonial governance and development. Then, through four detailed and eleven abbreviated case studies, I highlight different institutional mechanisms linked to state bureaucratization, infrastructural power, and inclusiveness that appear to underlie the relationship. In directly ruled Mauritius, for example, high levels of bureaucratization made possible corporate state action, and infrastructural power allowed state legal-administrative institutions to be present throughout the territory. Both state bureaucratization and infrastructural power, in turn, proved vital to state legal-administrative capacities and therefore the provisioning of law and order, clean water, health care clinics, sanitation systems, poor relief, public education, and a stable economic environment. In addition, high levels of state inclusiveness allowed state and societal actors to actively collaborate for the planning and implementation of development policy. This, in turn, increased the information, resources, and labor that could be used to promote broad-based development and allowed societal actors to hold state elites accountable for their interests.

In contrast, the case study of Sierra Leone shows that the more dispersed and patrimonial character of indirect rule impaired the state's legal-administrative capacities and thus had very negative effects on broad-based development. Extremely low levels of bureaucratization, infrastructural power, and inclusiveness made territorially dispersed, corporate state action practically impossible. And while low legal-administrative capacities effectively prevented the Sierra Leonean state from providing needed developmental goods both during and after colonialism, it also limited legal-administrative mechanisms of control and thereby encouraged state officials to turn to overt coercion as the means of regulating social relations and maintaining their positions. As a consequence, state officials were despotic and predatory and actively impeded the ability of Sierra Leoneans to pursue their well-being.

In showing that British colonialism had long-term effects on development by institutionalizing states with different legal-administrative capacities, the analysis suggests that state institutions are quite static, I do not find that they are unchanging, however. Instead, I provide evidence that state institutional change is common but tends to occur in a path-dependent fashion, thereby reinforcing the previous structure. The independence period, for example, coincided with major state reforms in directly and indirectly ruled colonies alike. These reforms greatly expanded the size of the state and promoted self-rule and local participation. Instead of scrapping previous state structures and starting anew, however, I find that the independence reforms reinforced the preexisting structure. By building on the state structure and promoting political participation, the states in directly ruled colonies usually became more bureaucratic, more infrastructurally powerful, and—especially—more inclusive as independence approached. The reforms in indirectly ruled colonies, on the other hand, almost always maintained minimal states with very limited legal-administrative capacities and therefore failed to build a state capable of promoting broad-based development.

Despite a high probability that direct rule institutionalized more effective states than indirect rule, a few exceptions exist, and I analyze two such cases—Botswana and Guyana—in order to investigate the causes of their break with the colonial norm. In both cases, the independence period was uncharacteristically transformative, radically changing the form of rule and thereby readjusting previous developmental trajectories. Both cases therefore show that independence had a heightened potential to be a critical juncture and are exceptions that help prove the general rule: states are important determinants of long-term development.

In Botswana, a chiefdom succession crisis and tension with South Africa combined to cause rapid centralization, infrastructural expansion, and bureaucratization during the final years of colonialism and the first years of independence. These changes, in turn, caused the construction of a more integrated and directly ruled state with relatively high legal-administrative capacities and thereby transformed the normal legacy of indirect rule. In contrast, Guyana's state became increasingly nonbureaucratic, noninclusive, and despotic during the independence transition despite a long history of direct rule. I find that conflict between British officials and local politicians, ethnic violence, and cold war politics impeded expansionary political reforms that usually occurred in directly ruled British colonies during the final years of colonialism. Instead, the strain of ethnic conflict promoted legal-administrative breakdown and the personalization and militarization of the state, factors that had very negative effects on subsequent development.

All in all, the analysis provides evidence that British colonialism left a lasting impact on developmental processes and that this impact varied from place to place depending on the extent of direct and indirect colonial rule. In so doing, the book also makes more general contributions to the literature on states and development. By tracing the lineages of developmental and despotic states, it sheds light on their historic origins. Moreover, the book provides valuable insight into which state structures promote development, which state structures promote despotism, and why. I find that state bureaucratization makes possible corporate state action, that infrastructural power allows states to act throughout their territories, and that inclusiveness promotes state accountability and synergistic relations between state and society. While these characteristics promote effective legal-administrative institutions and thereby enhance the state's capacity to provide developmental goods, their absence incapacitates states and encourages coercion and predation.

Literature on Colonialism, States, and Development

In focusing on colonial states and historical developmental trajectories, this book is situated within an ever-growing body of works. The preexisting literature includes comparative-historical analyses from the last two decades and recent quantitative works by institutional economists. Both traditions offer different yet broadly compatible evidence that colonialism shaped the developmental trajectories of former colonies, and both provide the base from which this book builds.

The earliest works on colonial state legacies are qualitative case studies and comparative historical analyses that emphasize the developmental consequences of state structures. Boone (1994), Mamdani (1996), and Migdal (1988), for example, describe how colonial states in Africa have impeded economic development and democratization. They focus on how colonialism created ineffective legal-administrative institutions, empowered local chiefs and notables, and thereby institutionalized decentralized and despotic systems of control. Amsden (1989), Wade (1990), Kohli (1994), and Huff (1994), on the other hand, find that colonial rule in Taiwan, South Korea, and Singapore left powerful states that successfully promoted rapid economic development after independence.

More recent comparative-historical analyses build on earlier case studies and document both positive and negative colonial state legacies. Kohli (2004) analyzes the origins of the Brazilian, Indian, Nigerian, and South Korean states and their subsequent impacts on industrialization. He finds that colonialism was a formative event that ultimately determined both the form of states and their ability to promote industrialization. Mahoney and vom Hau (2005) analyze the Spanish Empire and find that the intensity of Spanish colonialism affected the developmental capacity of postcolonial states. Whereas intensive colonialism institutionalized patrimonial states that implemented mercantilist policies, they show that more limited Spanish rule institutionalized states that were less afflicted by these characteristics. As a result, the more intensely ruled Spanish colonies have faced greater institutional constraints to broad-based development than those with only a limited colonial presence, and the authors argue that this difference is a major cause of the latter's superior postcolonial development.

More recently, the qualitative analysis of colonial legacies has been joined by quantitative works. Most of the latter are by economists who test the historical impact of institutions on economic development. These statistical analyses highlight the relationship between colonial institutions and development and make an effort to check whether endogeneity affects their findings. Overall, they provide strong evidence that colonialism was extremely transformative and radically readjusted developmental trajectories.

In a well-known analysis within this tradition, Acemoglu, Johnson, and Robinson (2002) find that a developmental "reversal of fortune" occurred among former colonies. They provide evidence that regions with relatively high levels of precolonial development transformed into developmental underachievers during the colonial period but that regions with low levels of precolonial development experienced relatively rapid economic development after the onset of colonialism. The findings therefore suggest that colonialism broke previous developmental trajectories and was an independent force shaping the developmental records of former colonies.

Subsequent statistical investigations by other economists also look into the developmental impact of colonialism. Feyrer and Sacerdote's (forthcoming) study of colonized islands instruments for length of colonial rule using wind direction and speed. They find that the number of years of colonialism is positively and significantly related to per capita GDP and negatively and significantly related to infant mortality. They also show that the instrumental variable results are substantively identical to the ordinary least squares (OLS) findings, providing evidence that endogeneity is not driving their findings. They therefore conclude that the institutions constructed during colonialism have had long-term effects on developmental processes. Instead of island colonies, Banerjee and Iyer (2005) investigate the causes of uneven development in the most populous territory ever colonized: India. They find that areas ruled through indigenous landlords during colonialism have had poorer postcolonial development than areas in which peasants owned land and claim that such uneven development was caused by the divergent effects of colonialism on property rights and policy choices.

In this book, I draw on insight from both research traditions. Most importantly, past qualitative analyses provide initial insight into the mechanisms linking states and development, past quantitative work provides powerful evidence that colonialism shaped long-term development, and both suggest that colonialism left diverse legacies. My analysis builds on and bolsters these findings. At the same time, I depart from the preexisting literature in several ways.

First, I analyze direct and indirect rule and their divergent effects on a state's legal-administrative capacities. This more sociological approach differs from works by economists, who almost without exception propose that colonialism shaped long-term development by affecting either property-right enforcement, policy decisions, or both.[1] By investigating the state's general capacity to provide any number of developmental goods (with the rule of law being only one of many), this book takes a more multifaceted approach to the study of colonial state legacies. In addition, its focus on capacities takes an important step back from policy-oriented *capacity*

analyses, recognizing that state elites do not always have the institutional means of implementing desired policy. In this way, state institutional capacity has an extremely powerful effect on policy.

Next, most analyses of colonial state legacies focus on a narrow aspect of development, usually either economic growth or democratization. Sen (1999) proposes a much broader conceptualization of development, which he calls "development as freedom" and defines as the general capacity of individuals to pursue their well-being. From this perspective, self-respect, law and order, education, democracy, health care, and productive economic opportunities all promote development. Accepting Sen's conceptualization of development as freedom, I analyze the impact of colonial rule on broad-based development. In order to limit the broad scope of this conceptualization, I focus on democratization, economic opportunity, education, and health.

This book also differs from nearly all previous analyses of colonial legacies because the latter focus strictly on general continuity and therefore downplay cases in which colonial legacies are weak or do not hold. Such a one-sided emphasis has generally occurred because the primary goal of past studies has been to provide evidence that colonialism has had enduring effects on social processes through institutional legacies. Thus, these studies have shown that colonialism mattered and have highlighted how its institutional legacies either promoted or obstructed social development. While a focus on institutional continuity is necessary to understand historical legacies, it limits insight into factors affecting institutional change. And from a policy perspective, the analysis of countries that experience radical institutional change is equally—if not more—important since it highlights factors that make possible state transformation and thereby the readjustment of developmental trajectories. Thus, in order to investigate how history matters as well as factors that limit history's hold on the present, I analyze cases in which colonial legacies have persisted over long periods of time and others in which developmental trajectories transformed.

Finally, this project combines quantitative and qualitative methods in a nested research design. Other analyses use one or the other. The quantitative analyses, for example, rely strictly on statistical relationships and therefore can do little more than speculate about potential mechanisms. On the other end of the methodological spectrum, the qualitative works investigate only a few cases and therefore are unable to provide generalizable insight into colonial legacies. As described below, I combine both methodological traditions in order to limit their respective deficiencies and maximize their strengths.

Methodology: A Three-Tiered Nested Research Design

Social scientists increasingly recognize that considerable leverage can be gained from both qualitative and quantitative methods. Many also note that each methodological tradition has its limitations and that each helps correct the limitations of the other. Because of this synergistic complementarity, there is growing agreement that qualitative and quantitative methods should be combined for macro-causal analysis whenever possible (Brady and Collier 2004; Huber and Stephens 2001; Rueschemeyer and Stephens 1997). I share this position and use both comparative-historical and multivariate statistical methods to investigate why former British colonies have diverse development records. Specifically, I use a three-tiered nested research design that includes a statistical analysis of thirty-nine former colonies, in-depth comparative-historical analysis of four former colonies, and abbreviated case studies of eleven former colonies. While the first step of the analysis provides insight into general causal processes, the second highlights particular causal mechanisms, and the third tests the generalizability of these mechanisms, thereby providing a systematic analysis of uneven development among former British colonies.

Tiers One and Two of the Nested Research Design

A nested research design always has two tiers: one quantitative and the other qualitative. Instead of simply exploiting the benefits of both methodological traditions, this strategy attempts to integrate them by selecting cases for qualitative analysis based on their fit with the statistical findings. The major benefit of a nested strategy is the minimization of selection bias for the qualitative analysis, which, in turn, increases the chances of pinpointing general causal mechanisms and heightens the possibility that the qualitative findings provide insight into the statistical relationships.

According to Lieberman (2003, 2005), nested research designs have two primary strategies for case selection. The first strategy involves using residuals to choose non-outlier cases for in-depth analysis.[2] As represented by the x in Figure 1.1a, the non-outlier strategy investigates one or more cases that are near the regression line, or on-line cases. This strategy optimizes the possibility of discovering general processes and mechanisms that underlie statistical relationships. Alternatively, one might select a case, as represented by the o in the same figure, that does not conform to the statistical findings. This off-line strategy provides two potential benefits: it tests the statistical findings more rigorously by analyzing excep-

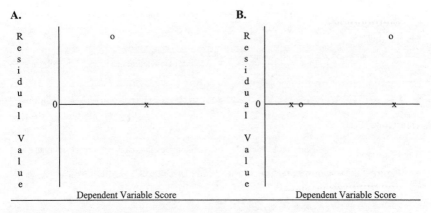

Figure 1.1a and 1.1b Nested Strategies for Case Selection

tions and provides an opportunity to discover additional factors affecting the dependent variable.

While nested research designs might be used to select individual cases for qualitative analysis, they can also guide the selection of multiple cases for structured comparison. Again, two main strategies exist. The first selects multiple cases that conform to the statistical findings but have different scores on the dependent variable. As depicted by the x's in Figure 1.1b, this strategy compares two or more on-line cases and allows researchers to investigate general causal mechanisms underlying the statistical findings. A comparative analysis has a greater chance of discovering causal mechanisms than a single on-line case study and provides an initial means of testing the generalizability of these mechanisms.

The second strategy compares on-line and off-line cases and is depicted by the o's in Figure 1.1b. Similar to individual case studies of off-line cases, this comparative strategy helps highlight additional factors affecting the dependent variable and provides a check on the findings of the on-line case study. The outlier case might provide evidence that the mechanisms highlighted in the non-outlier case study are incorrect or peculiar to a particular situation. Also, similar to Lipset, Trow, and Coleman's (1956) classic analysis of the International Typographical Union's vibrant democracy, it might clarify and confirm general mechanisms through the analysis of cases with exceptional circumstances.

In this book, I analyze both on-line and off-line cases and combine both strategies of structured comparison. Finding that the extent of indirect colonial rule is strongly and negatively related to both the effectiveness of postcolonial states and postcolonial development, I select two directly

Figure 1.2 Developmental Trajectories of the In-Depth Case Studies

ruled colonies and two indirectly ruled colonies for comparative-historical analysis. Within each pair, one case conforms to statistical findings while the other does not. As depicted in Figure 1.2, Sierra Leone is a former indirectly ruled colony, Mauritius is a former directly ruled colony, and both have levels of postcolonial development that are consistent with their forms of colonialism. Botswana, on the other hand, has levels of postcolonial development that are considerably higher than its indirect form of colonialism predicts, and Guyana has postcolonial levels of development that are lower than expected given its direct form of colonialism. Analysis of Mauritius and Sierra Leone—the two non-outlier cases—therefore provides an opportunity to investigate causal mechanisms underlying the general statistical findings, while analysis of the two outlier cases tests more rigorously both the statistical results and the findings of the Mauritian and Sierra Leonean case studies.

In addition to individual case studies, the structured comparison of cases also provides potential insight into my research question, and case selection based on statistical residuals increases potential insight gained from cross-case comparison. Figure 1.3 depicts the six sets of structured comparison that I use, three of which highlight differences and three of which highlight similarities.

The comparison of cases with *different* outcomes helps pinpoint factors or processes that caused their divergent developmental trajectories. The first difference-oriented comparison involves Mauritius and Sierra Leone, two conforming (non-outlier) cases that had very different developmental trajectories. This comparison helps highlight potential causal mechanisms underlying the general statistical findings. Two additional difference-oriented comparisons pair on-line and off-line cases—Botswana-Sierra Leone and Guyana-Mauritius. These comparisons are structured to test

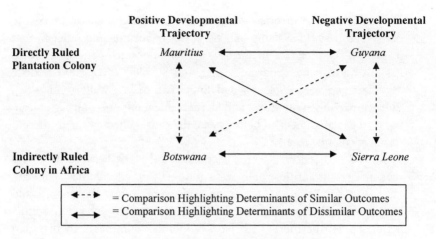

Figure 1.3 Focused Comparisons among the In-Depth Case Studies

the accuracy of the causal mechanisms highlighted in the on-line cases and to investigate additional factors that might have caused Botswana and Guyana to have unexpected developmental trajectories over the past half century.

Along with these three difference-oriented comparisons, I compare three sets of cases with similar developmental trajectories to see if they have similar causal determinants. Comparison of Botswana and Mauritius helps highlight common factors that promoted each former colony's relatively positive developmental trajectory. Qualitative comparison of Sierra Leone and Guyana, on the other hand, provides insight into why each has had a low level of development since independence. Finally, comparison of Botswana and Guyana helps highlight why neither former colony has postcolonial developmental trajectories that coincide with their forms of British colonialism.

Although case selection based on statistical residuals allows researchers to increase the likelihood that their findings are generalizable, it does not necessarily increase a researcher's ability to test rival hypotheses. As a consequence of this analytic weakness, I also consider individual case characteristics for case selection. The comparison of Mauritius and Sierra Leone, for example, is particularly insightful because neither was expected to be a successful postcolonial developer. Indeed, while the superior development of the directly ruled white settler colonies (Australia, Canada, New Zealand, and the United States) and the trade-based colonies (Hong Kong and Singapore) might have been expected for a number of reasons, several theories—ranging from environmental to Marxist to neoliberal to world systems—all claim that Mauritius and other former plantation colonies face major developmental obstacles (Beckford 1983; Easterly and Levine 2002; Engerman and Sokoloff 1997; Herbst 2000; Mandle 1974, 1982; Sokoloff and Engerman 2000; Wallerstein 1974). The comparison of Mauritius and Sierra Leone therefore controls for leading rival explanations and helps isolate the causal effect of their different forms of colonial rule.

Next, I have selected Sierra Leone and Botswana because they have several key similarities: both were indirectly ruled colonies, both are located in sub-Saharan Africa, and both were among the poorest and least developed countries in the world shortly after gaining colonial independence. Furthermore, both have economies dominated by diamond mining, and recent studies find that economic dependence on natural resources impedes economic growth and promotes state predation (Collier 2000; Fearon and Laitin 2003; Reno 1995; Snyder and Bhavnani 2005). Comparison of the two therefore helps to isolate the factor or group of factors that caused Botswana to be an exceptional developmental success through the exploitation of diamond reserves but caused Sierra Leone to be a developmental nightmare torn apart by fights over the diamond trade.

Finally, I have selected Mauritius and Guyana because each had similar colonial state institutions, levels of development, and populations during late colonialism. In addition, both had economies based on the production of sugar on large plantations, and their plantation economies affected all social institutions. Despite these similarities, each has had a sharply different developmental trajectory over the past fifty years. Thus, the focused comparison of the two helps highlight the determinants of their different outcomes and tests the findings of the Mauritius case study more thoroughly.

Tier Three of the Nested Research Design

While a two-tiered nested research design helps limit selection bias and thereby allows the quantitative and qualitative findings to guide one another, it cannot guarantee that the mechanisms highlighted in the case studies actually account for the statistical relationships among a much larger number of cases. Indeed, it is possible that the statistical findings are spurious, that the qualitative case studies provide incorrect inference, that the case studies are unique, or that the case studies highlight only one of several mechanisms underlying the statistical relationships.

In order to increase confidence in the qualitative findings, two methodological strategies are possible. First, one can simply increase the number of case studies in the second tier of the nested analysis. Alternatively, one can employ only a few case studies in the second tier of the nested analysis and supplement them with an additional tier of more abbreviated case studies. Notably, case studies in the third tier differ from those in the second tier in that they are more cursory and attempt to corroborate rather than explore. In particular, they test the accuracy and generalizability of the in-depth case study findings by applying them to additional cases.

Each strategy has its own strengths and weaknesses. Expanding the number of cases in the second tier of the nested analysis allows researchers to go into considerable detail for a larger number of cases and therefore increases analytic rigor. This strategy, however, requires a tremendous amount of work, can result in overly repetitive or incoherent analysis, and likely limits the analytic depth of any single case. The use of several abbreviated case studies, on the other hand, is disadvantaged in that the more limited length and detail of the abbreviated cases reduce the inference that can be gained from each case. The strategy is advantaged, however, in that it requires a more manageable workload, is less repetitive, and allows the in-depth case studies to go into greater detail.

In this book, I employ abbreviated case studies. Thus, while the second tier of the analysis provides detailed descriptions of causal processes in order to explore mechanisms that potentially underlie the statistical findings, the third tier uses several abbreviated case studies to test whether the findings of the second tier are applicable to additional former colonies. In this way, the abbreviated case studies help integrate the first two tiers by providing insight into whether or not the mechanisms uncovered in the in-depth case studies underlie the statistical findings.

Unlike the in-depth case studies analyzed in this book, case selection for the more abbreviated cases is based simply on variation in the extent of direct and indirect rule. Cases are selected to cover the entire range of direct/indirect rule, with some having experienced very direct forms of rule, others very indirect forms of rule, and still others mixed forms of colonial domination. The abbreviated case studies examine Barbados, Ghana, Hong Kong, India, Malaysia, Myanmar, Nigeria, Singapore, the Solomon Islands, South Africa, and Sri Lanka.

The Organization of the Book

Throughout the remainder of this book, I investigate the causes of the different developmental trajectories within the British Empire. In Chapter 2, I explore the possibility of British colonial state legacies through empirical and theoretical discussions. I provide a history of British colonialism, describe the institutional bases of both direct and indirect rule, and outline a model of development that focuses on differences between direct and indirect rule. Finally, I examine the possibility of state-enforced, path-dependent development.

I begin the empirical analysis in Chapter 3 by testing the relationship between the form of British rule and several measures of postcolonial development. I operationalize the extent of indirect rule and find that the variable is negatively and significantly related to different measures of development, thereby supporting claims that colonial state legacies have reinforced long-term developmental trajectories. In the final section of the chapter, I set up the nested research design used in subsequent chapters by showing the extent to which Botswana, Guyana, Mauritius, and Sierra Leone conform to the statistical relationships.

Chapters 4 and 5 analyze cases that conform to the statistical findings and therefore provide insight into potential mechanisms underlying the relationship between the form of British colonialism and development. In Chapter 4, I analyze Mauritius, a former directly ruled colony located off the east coast of Africa. I describe how the relatively bureaucratic, infrastructurally powerful, and inclusive state made possible broad-based development during late colonialism and after independence and provide evidence that direct rule caused these state characteristics. In Chapter 5, I describe how indirect colonial rule in Sierra Leone institutionalized a more patrimonial state with extremely limited legal-administrative capacities. These characteristics, in turn, promoted state-led predation instead of development.

Chapters 6 and 7 investigate cases that have had unexpectedly high or low development levels given their forms of colonialism and, in doing so, provide checks on the accuracy and generalizability of both the statistical findings and the institutional mechanisms highlighted in Chapters 4 and 5. Like the previous case studies, both Botswana and Guyana show that states have influential effects on development and highlight the importance of bureaucracy, infrastructural power, and inclusiveness. Yet both chapters also show that the structure of the state is not set in stone and provide evidence that colonial independence was a critical period during which state institutional changes readjusted development trajectories in ways that did not coincide with the form of colonial rule. The cases therefore show that the institutional legacies of colonialism are not permanent and rapidly transformed in a few exceptional cases.

Chapter 8 provides the final tier of the nested research design. It explores the generalizability of the findings from the in-depth case studies through several more abbreviated case studies of former British colonies. Finally, in Chapter 9, I summarize the findings, describe their fit with previous works, and make a preliminary attempt to apply them to former colonies outside of the British Overseas Empire.

The Developmental Legacies of British Colonialism

2

A State-Centered Framework for Analysis

This chapter frames the subsequent analysis of the British imperial behemoth—the largest, most dispersed, and most diverse overseas empire the world has ever seen. To begin, I review the rise and fall of the British Empire, focusing on three different periods of colonial expansion and the different forms of rule that coincided with each. Next, I describe and compare the two general systems of colonial control employed by the British: direct and indirect rule. Finally, I outline a theoretical framework proposing that direct rule promoted state bureaucratization, infrastructural power, and inclusiveness to a greater extent than indirect rule and thereby had more positive effects on development. The framework also discusses the possibility that direct and indirect rule reinforced developmental trajectories both during colonialism and afterwards. Overall, the chapter suggests that different forms of colonial rule potentially account for uneven development within the former British Empire.

The British Empire: A Brief History[1]

With territories in the Mediterranean, Middle East, North America, Central America, the Caribbean, Africa, South Asia, East Asia, and the Pacific, the sun most definitely never set over the British Empire. Its construction took several hundred years and did not occur evenly. There were three main periods of colonial conquest, and time and geographical location are strongly related. The empire began with New World conquests between 1600 and 1750, expanded into Asia and Australasia between 1750 and 1850, and spread into Africa and the Middle East between 1850 and 1920. Besides region, the different periods of British colonial conquest generally coincide with different forms of domination, as colonial rule was usually direct during the first period, indirect during the third, and a mixture of the two during the second.

Phase I: Direct Rule in the Americas

The English looked beyond the British Isles and previous claims to northern France and established their first overseas colonies in Virginia and Newfoundland in the early seventeenth century. Within a century and a half, the British Empire had spread throughout eastern North America and expanded to include Barbados (1627), Jamaica (1655), and other Caribbean islands. Wherever it occurred in the New World, colonial contact quickly decimated and marginalized indigenous peoples, making rule through indigenous collaborators an impossibility. Colonialism therefore depended on the settlement of a large number of Europeans and the establishment of legal-administrative institutions similar to those in Great Britain. The first phase of British colonialism was therefore extremely transformative and direct in form.

Up until the mid-seventeenth century, all of Britain's possessions in the Americas were settler colonies. At this time, however, plantation systems were established in the Caribbean and the American South, resulting in the importation of over a million slaves into Anglo-America. With this influx, the African population in the British West Indies increased from 25 percent of the total population in 1650 to 90 percent in 1770 (Abernethy 2000: 54).

The settler colonies differed from the plantation colonies in several ways (Beckford 1983: 813; Ferguson 2002: 60–113). Although more rugged than and quite independent from their motherland, the settler colonies were for all intents and purposes British transplants. With the Native American population declining and pushed westward, peoples of European origins soon dominated all aspects of life in Canada and the United States. Seeking economic opportunity, freedom of religion, or both, they established farming and trading communities characterized by economic differentiation, production for local consumption, and greater equality than back in Europe. They also established and participated in local government.[2]

In plantation colonies, on the other hand, life was far removed from that in Great Britain. African slaves usually comprised the overwhelming majority of the population and were forced to work on large plantations that produced one of three cash crops geared toward the European and North American markets: tobacco, cotton, and sugar. With an institution that allowed some humans to be free and others chattel, the plantation societies were obviously highly unequal. Even after emancipation, former slaves and their descendents continued to face severe economic and political obstacles at the hands of the plantation elite. The plantation colonies therefore had higher levels of stratification and institutionally enforced inequality than the settler colonies.

Phase II: A Mixed Legacy

Over the next century (1750–1850), several new British colonies were added during a second wave of British colonial conquest, and many continued to be either settler (Australia and New Zealand) or plantation (the Bahamas, Belize, Mauritius, Guyana, and Trinidad and Tobago) colonies. In addition, new colonies were conquered that fit neither the settlement nor the plantation model but that were still ruled directly. Singapore and Hong Kong, for example, did not attract settlers, were not suited for plantation-based production, and had strategic trade locations. As a result, the British invested heavily in order to construct intrusive and effective institutions underpinning the colonies' economies.

Although less intensive than in Hong Kong and Singapore, Ceylon (modern Sri Lanka) also experienced direct colonial rule. It differed, however, in that plantations were introduced and that the colony was much larger in terms of territory and indigenous population. Because the majority of the population lived outside of the plantations, the plantations evolved as economic enclaves within a larger system of socioeconomic relations, not totalizing institutions that shaped nearly all aspects of life as in the Caribbean (Beckford 1983).

Formal colonial domination of the Indian Raj, the preeminent jewel within the British Empire, also began during this period and took a novel and eclectic form. Its conquest was a long process during which trade turned into political domination. The East India Company was formed in 1600 to allow Britain to control some of the lucrative trade between India and Europe. By the mid-eighteenth century, British control of trade within a few port cities had transformed into political domination of the cities and their surrounding areas. The Indian Mutiny of 1857—also known as the first war of independence—sparked the beginning of formal British colonialism by forcing the transfer of power from the East India Company to the British Crown. After the conflict, the British attempted to prevent future disturbances by strengthening indigenous elites in some regions of the colony and allowing them to rule local lands along supposedly traditional lines. This form of rule became known as indirect rule.

The British also conquered South Africa during the second period of colonial expansion. It began as a Dutch settler colony, was conquered by the British during the late eighteenth century, and subsequently became a British settler colony with large Dutch and African populations. The British colony was at first limited to the Cape and was ruled directly. As the colony expanded into the surrounding hinterlands, however, the British found it increasingly difficult to control the Boers and the indigenous Africans and therefore began to devise new modes of control. In the peripheral areas of Boer settlement, the British attempted to exert some influence but ultimately gave the communities considerable autonomy. In the African territories surrounding the Cape Colony, the British began to organize indirect forms of rule through chiefs.

Phase III: The Dominance of Indirect Rule

The final phase of British colonial conquest began during the mid-nineteenth century and included new acquisitions in the Australasian archipelago, the Middle East, and Africa. Although a few of these colonies attracted European migrants, none experienced large-scale European settlement, as European migrants preferred to move to the original settler colonies, especially the United States. In addition, only Malaya, Fiji, and the Solomon Islands developed plantations. As in Ceylon, the plantations were only enclaves within a larger social system, not total institutions dominating all aspects of life. Consequently, the colonizers in this third phase continued to devise new ways of controlling the indigenous population. And due to the acute personnel shortages caused by the dramatic expansion of the British Empire, concomitant domestic concerns over a burdensome Empire, pressure from humanitarian groups to respect indigenous culture, deadly disease environments, and the existence of large indigenous populations spread over extensive territories, the new strategies of colonial domination were almost always some form of indirect rule.

Although the British began colonizing present-day Malaysia during the second phase of colonial expansion by establishing small and directly ruled trading posts known as the Straits Settlements, the overwhelming majority of the region was conquered during the final phase. Unlike the Straits Settlements, the regions that were added to the British Empire during the late nineteenth and early twentieth centuries combined direct and indirect rule. In the Federated Malay States, which were conquered during the 1870s, indigenous sultans were recognized as traditional authorities, although the British built relatively large legal-administrative institutions and usurped nearly all of the sultans' formal powers. In this way, they were for all intents and purposes directly ruled colonies. The Unfederated Malay States, on the other hand, were added to the empire even later, and their sultans retained greater formal powers (Brown and Ampalavanar 1986: xxvii; Heussler 1981; Ibrahim 1998: 12–13; Ryan 1976). Thus, Malaya had several different forms of colonialism, ranging from highly direct, to direct rule in the guise of indirect rule, to relatively indirect (Welsh 2001).

The British also experimented with indirect rule in their new colonial acquisitions in the Pacific Ocean. In Fiji, the British recognized precolonial chiefdoms and collaborated with indigenous chiefs in order to control the entire colony. Yet the British also established large plantations and imported tens of thousands of Indian laborers to work on them. Because the plantations and their workers did not fit into the system of indirect rule, the British ruled them directly, thereby creating a hybrid form of colonialism that separated ethnic Indians from Fijians. A similar combination occurred in the Solomon Islands, yet the colony differed from Fiji in that the plantations were fewer and smaller, foreign laborers were not imported, and the British ruled through headmen and native councils because of the absence of powerful precolonial chiefs.

Although the British controlled the Cape Colony and small outposts along the African littoral since the eighteenth century, full-scale colonization of the "Dark Continent" did not begin until the end of the nineteenth century. Once begun, however, large chunks of Africa quickly fell under British rule, including modern Botswana, Gambia, Ghana, Kenya, Lesotho, Malawi, Nigeria, Sierra Leone, Sudan, Swaziland, Tanzania, Uganda, Zambia, and Zimbabwe.

All British colonies in Africa were indirectly ruled and therefore experienced a bifurcated system of collaborative rule, with a small administration staffed by Europeans and located in the colonial capital and patrimonial chiefs in the peripheral areas of the colony. The chiefs were supposedly

traditional although frequently had little or no precolonial authority, and
their powers always depended on British recognition and support. For
their part, the small size and limited geographical scope of the central
legal-administrative institutions caused the British to be very dependent
on the chiefs, who were given considerable autonomy to perform legislative, executive, and judicial functions for the colonizers. Thus, the relationship between the British and the chiefs was one of mutual dependence,
with the chiefs dependent on the colonizers for their positions and the
colonizers dependent on the chiefs for some semblance of control.

In a few exceptional cases—Zimbabwe and Kenya and to a lesser extent
Swaziland, Botswana, and Zambia—the British established a form of indirect settler colonialism somewhat akin to that in South Africa. Similar to
the full-blown settler colonies, which excluded the indigenous population
from settler institutions (such as the Native American reserve system in
the United States), most of the indigenous population lived in territories
ruled by chiefs. Different from the settler colonies, however, the number of European settlers was much smaller, the number of indigenous
peoples was much larger, and many Africans lived in directly ruled areas
because of settler dependence on their labor.

Egypt, Iraq, Palestine, and Transjordan were among Great Britain's last
colonial acquisitions and provided it with a formal colonial footing in the
Middle East. Each of these colonies had been part of the Ottoman Empire
for hundreds of years before their incorporation into the British Empire
for only a brief stint. Although important changes occurred during British
rule, the British left the preexisting state structures intact whenever possible while adding a new colonially controlled level to the administrative
hierarchy. Thus, the Middle Eastern colonies were ruled through a unique
and informal type of foreign domination in which the British usurped
relatively developed state structures and simply added or replaced upper-
level officials.

The End of Empire

While the British Empire was being built, struggles were already under
way to tear it asunder. The thirteen American colonies were the first casu-
alty, with the settlers having fought for and won their independence before
most of the British Empire had been conquered. Having learned from the
American experience, the British granted greater rights and autonomy to
the remaining settler colonies and eventually granted them self-rule by
the late nineteenth and early twentieth centuries. Next, the Middle East-

ern colonies gained their independence in the 1920s and 1930s and, in doing so, became the first nonsettler colonies to become independent.

Although colonial attrition was relatively slow up until the Second World War, the latter was a cataclysmic event that began the full-scale dismantling of empire. Indeed, after this massive and diverse empire had been built up over three and a half centuries, it crumbled with remarkable speed. First, Palestine and the British colonies in South Asia—Bangladesh, India, Myanmar, Pakistan, and Sri Lanka—received their independence in the late 1940s. By the 1950s, several factors prompted other regions to demand independence, including knowledge that other colonies had already received independence, various war-induced transformations, the rise of the United Nations and its Declaration of Human Rights, and increased political participation by indigenous populations. The second wave of postwar independences therefore began faster than the British anticipated, with Sudan and Ghana freeing themselves from British rule in 1956 and 1957 respectively. It continued over the next decade and a half, with a few tiny stragglers not receiving their independences until the 1970s and 1980s.[3] Thus, after nearly four centuries, British colonial red had finally been erased from the world's maps.

Direct and Indirect Colonial Rule

As is evident in the brief account of British colonialism, one important point of differentiation among British colonies is the extent to which colonial state institutions were either "direct" or "indirect." Yet these concepts were part of a British colonial doctrine that sometimes overlooked the difference between colonial ideals and real-world forms. As a consequence, confusion over which colonies were direct and which were indirect is common, and direct and indirect rule have become contested concepts. Rather than simply disregarding the terms altogether as some suggest (Newbury 2003), I attempt to provide clearer conceptualizations.

Defining Direct and Indirect Rule

Most analyses of colonialism suggest that the primary difference between direct and indirect rule concerns the origin of the colonial state officials. Doyle (1986), for instance, claims that direct rule occurs when only the lowest levels of the colonial administration are run by locals while the remaining positions are run by European officials. He writes that indirect rule, on the other hand, occurs when "the governance of extensive districts of the colony is entrusted to members of the native elite under the supervision of the imperial governors" (38). Although conforming to popular ideas, this origins-based definition becomes problematic when placed under empirical scrutiny, as nearly all former colonies employed indigenous peoples in mid- and high-level positions and should therefore be classified as indirect rule.

Alternative definitions of direct and indirect rule focus on differences in their structures of domination instead of the origins of colonial officials. Hechter (2000), for example, suggests that indirect rule allows local political officials greater autonomy from the central state apparatus. Here, the distinction revolves around the decentralization of power from the central state to local officials, not the origins of the state officials. While capturing an important characteristic of indirect rule that is usually ignored by the origin-oriented conceptualization, this definition appears overly general for the present study. Federated states such as Canada and Switzerland, for example, must be categorized as indirect systems of rule under this definition.

Following Lugard's (1922) doctrine more closely, Fisher (1991) provides an alternative definition that incorporates both indigenous and autonomy components into a conceptualization of direct and indirect colonial rule, and I employ a similar conceptualization throughout the remainder of this analysis. Fisher describes indirect rule as a system of collaborative rule that incorporates local institutions—not simply individuals—into an overall structure of colonial domination. While linked to the dominant central legal-administrative institutions, the local institutions are run by indigenous elites and based on different organizational and authority systems—usually some form of supposedly customary patrimonialism in the peripheral areas and bureaucratic legalism in the center. This bifurcated state structure, in turn, increases the autonomy of the local peoples and creates a division between indigenous and colonial institutions. I therefore define indirect rule as *domination via collaborative relations between a dominant colonial center and several regionally based indigenous institutions.* Direct rule, on the other hand, entails *the construction of a complete system of colonial domination in which both local and central institutions are well integrated and governed by the same authority and organizational principles.*

Notably, the distinction between direct and indirect rule is more of a spectrum than a strict dichotomy, as colonial states were only occasionally complete colonial constructs with integrated systems of rule—the ideal type of direct rule—and were never completely bifurcated systems of domination via collaboration—the ideal type of indirect rule. The European settlement colonies, for example, are among the most extreme cases of direct rule, and British colonialism in northern Nigeria provides one of the most extreme cases of indirect rule. Colonial rule in India, Malaysia, and elsewhere combined colonial and indigenous institutions in different ways and to different extents, creating hybrid forms of rule.

Direct Rule within the British Empire

When pursuing direct rule, the British constructed centralized and territory-wide legal-administrative institutions. These states usually approximated what Migdal (1994) calls "integrated domination," or the projection of state power throughout an entire territory (9). They were organized bureaucratically, with formal rules delimiting the duties of officials according to their position, salary-based compensation, and a formal chain of command that linked the diverse state actors throughout the colony. In most directly ruled colonies, the secretariat controlled communication between all other departments and was therefore the departmental nerve center of the colonial state. It served the colonial governor, who was the highest authority in the colony, controlled the highly centralized administration, and reported either to London or to a higher regional authority. Like the administration, the legal institutions were also rule-based, centralized, and colony-wide. Large police forces and courts based on British law were constructed, and they collaborated to create a broad legal framework regulating all societal and state-society relations.

Colonial Singapore provides an example of a directly ruled colony. By the late nineteenth century, it had developed an extremely centralized, large, and bureaucratic state that was highly integrated and controlled by a colonial governor. Although the colonial state was not evenly spread throughout the territory, it had a strong presence in all regions and was able to shape social relations in a variety of ways. The maintenance of law and order provides one example, as the state had a large and relatively effective law enforcement system. Indeed, there were 3.2 police officers per 1,000 civilians in colonial Singapore in 1955 compared to only 1.4 police officers per 1,000 civilians in Great Britain itself.

As Mann (1984) and Tilly (2005) note, direct rule not only affects intrastate relations but also shapes relations between state and society. Because direct rule in British colonies extended down to the grassroots level, it offered several avenues of access to the colonial state and incorporated local communities into the political system, especially after post–World War II political reforms. The large and territory-wide administration, for example, provided numerous points of interaction between the colonized and the colonizers while effectively limiting the autonomy of local communities. The most common form of interaction was between the police, district officials, teachers, and the local population and involved tax collection, public works and services, and law enforcement. In addition, many subjects in directly ruled British colonies were actually employed within the colonial administration, thereby opening many formal and informal avenues to the state.

Despite the relatively high levels of interaction between colonized and colonizer in directly ruled colonies, all systems of foreign domination are one-sided and exclusionary, characteristics that affect the inclusiveness of the colonial state and its active incorporation of local communities into national political institutions. Among directly ruled colonies, the extent to which the colonial state institutions excluded the local populations varied considerably depending on the type of direct rule. Direct colonial rule was the most inclusive in the settler colonies, although this depended on one's race.[4] As mentioned above, settler colonies were neo-Europes, in which settlers and officials established institutions very similar to those in the homeland. Because the settlers helped create the institutions and generally shared a common national identity with the officials, they were allowed to participate in colonial politics.

Plantation colonies, on the other hand, had lower levels of European settlement and established strict racial hierarchies and coercive labor systems. Planters often had their own informal police forces and maintained high levels of influence within the colonial regime. With the help of the colonial state, they exploited and isolated the colored laboring classes (Stinchcombe 1995). After the abolition of slavery and the declaration of Crown Colony status in the nineteenth century, however, the planters lost considerable power, and British rule in the plantation colonies increasingly and even actively incorporated non-Europeans into the political system, especially after World War II (Rueschemeyer, Stephens, and Stephens 1992).

Finally, directly ruled colonies with large indigenous populations lacked both European settlers and coercive plantation systems. The purest form of this type of rule occurred in colonies with strategic economic or geopolitical locations, such as Singapore and Cyprus. Colonialism created free and colony-wide markets and integrated legal-administrative institutions, and both incorporated the local population to a greater extent than in plantation colonies. Yet the different ethnic backgrounds of colonized and colonizer combined with a colonial superiority complex caused greater divisions and social distance than in the settler colonies.

Indirect Rule within the British Empire

Prior to the colonization of India, British colonial rule had been on the direct side of the dichotomy. Yet the geographic size and gigantic population of the Indian subcontinent, the lack of settlers, and the violent anticolonial uprising in 1857 all forced colonial officials to devise a more cost-efficient means of rule that would not spark violent indigenous opposition. The result was an early form of indirect colonialism that would soon be established in various guises elsewhere in Asia, the Middle East, the Pacific, and Africa and would be referred to in any number of ways: "'paramountcy', 'protection', 'subsidiary alliance', 'collaboration'" (Newbury 2003: 1).

On paper, indirect rule was supposed to create a relatively integrated form of colonial control. According to Lord Frederick Lugard (1922), the acclaimed theorist and practitioner of indirect rule,

> The essential feature of the system . . . is that the native chiefs are constituted as an integral part of the machinery of the administration. There are not two sets of rulers—the British and the native—working either separately or in co-operation, but a single Government in which the native chiefs have well-defined duties and an acknowledged status equally with British officers. Their duties should never conflict, and should overlap as little as possible. They should be complementary to each other, and the chief himself must understand that he has no right to place and power unless he renders his proper services to the State. (203)

The material reality, however, was usually far from a unified system of rule, as the states in indirectly ruled colonies approximated Migdal's (1994) "dispersed domination," or a fragmented state unable to achieve countrywide domination over local power holders. According to Mamdani (1996), indirect rule created a "bifurcated state" in which two separate and incompatible forms of rule existed—one dominated by colonial officials, the other by numerous indigenous authorities. This form resulted from the uneasy combination of colonial institutions based on bureaucratic principles and more patrimonial institutions at the local level, which limited state integration and increased the autonomy of the peripheral institutions.

Similar to directly ruled colonies, the central state institutions of indirectly ruled colonies were organized bureaucratically. The collaborating indigenous elites, on the other hand, controlled patrimonial institutions in peripheral regions. The British selected the indigenous collaborators based on their status as well as their willingness to collaborate. Moreover, although often receiving a salary, indigenous collaborators earned most of their livelihoods through the control of land and by taxing their subjects. They were given executive, legislative, and judicial powers to regulate social relations in their chiefdoms, vast authority that was supposed to be grounded in preexisting customs. Thus, indirect rule took the form of numerous patrimonial kingdoms linked together only weakly by a foreign and tiny central administration.

Sierra Leone provides an example of indirect colonial rule. It possessed a tiny colonial state that was extremely concentrated in the capital, Freetown, which was ruled directly throughout the colonial period. The remainder of the colony contained the overwhelming majority of the population and was ruled by a dozen district officers, each of whom had a few assistants and controlled a small police force. Such a small and uneven state was able to maintain some semblance of order only because the administration collaborated with indigenous chiefs. Under this indirect form of rule, the colonial state recognized and supported over a hundred chiefs, used them as local colonial agents, and endowed them with immense powers to rule their subjects along supposedly customary lines.

While the British Colonial Office and media romanticized indirect rule as a gentle and respectful means of foreign domination, recent qualitative works claim that indirect rule institutionalized despotic rule and ineffective states. According to this view, far from being traditional, indirect rule adulterated or even created local institutions in order to control rural areas more easily (Laitin 1986; Mamdani 2001). And three common characteristics of indirect domination frequently promoted misrule.

First, the central state apparatus in indirectly ruled colonies was infrastructurally weak. That is, the central legal-administrative institution was minuscule, concentrated almost exclusively in the colonial capital, and had very little interaction with the colonial population, characteristics that prevented it from acting corporately or regulating society. As a result of both, the colonial state in indirectly ruled colonies lacked the capabilities to implement policy successfully in large regions of the colonies (Migdal 1988; Phillips 1989).

Next, indirect rule endowed chiefs with great institutional powers that frequently enabled them to dominate their subjects at will (Boone 1994; Chanock 1985; Mamdani 1996; Merry 1991; Migdal 1988; Roberts and Mann 1991). Chiefs were given control of "customary law" and, because it lacked formalization, were able to mold and wield it for personal benefit. Customary law also endowed chiefs with control over communal lands and chiefdom police, both of which could be coercively employed to dominate local inhabitants. Their powers were also augmented by the weakening of precolonial forms of constraint, which were almost always undermined by indirect rule.

Finally, the intermediary positions of chiefs further enhanced their powers by increasing their control over information and resource flows between the colonial administration and the local population (Clapham 1982; Lange 2003b; Reno 1995; Scott 1972). Consequently, chiefs were often able to avoid supervision and pit administrators and local subjects against one another, both of which allowed them to retain considerable autonomy and to be rent seekers extraordinaire (Lange 2003b). This intermediary network structure had important implications on the interaction between the colonial state and society. The central colonial state in indirectly ruled colonies was hardly embedded in local society, leaving the majority of the local population completely excluded from national-level politics.

A Theory of British Colonial State Legacies

Direct and indirect rule therefore created very different states, with integrated domination, bureaucratic organization, and high levels of infrastructural power in the former and dispersed domination, a bifurcated state that combined bureaucracy and patrimonialism, and low levels of infrastructural power in the latter. And because states have important effects on a variety of developmental processes, direct and indirect rule quite possibly had different effects on broad-based development. In this section, I review literature of states and development, describing how state bureaucratization, infrastructural power, and inclusiveness affect the possibility of state-led development. Then, I apply this theoretical insight to British colonialism and create a model proposing that direct rule had more positive effects on development than indirect rule. I argue that indirect rule built legal-administrative institutions with very limited capacities to provide goods that allow individuals to pursue their well-being. In addition, the ineffectiveness of the legal-administrative institutions promoted despotic and predatory rule. Direct colonial rule, on the other hand, institutionalized states with greater legal-administrative capacities, and the latter allowed state officials to both provide developmental goods and limit developmental bads.

States and Development

In *The Logic of Collective Action*, Olson (1965) suggests that the provisioning of nonrival and nonexcludable public goods is often difficult, if not impossible, because of the free-rider problem. This dilemma occurs when individuals choose not to participate in the construction or maintenance of public goods, waiting instead for others to provide them before using the goods at no cost. Although Olson discusses potential ways for individuals to overcome this problem, he largely ignores the important historic role that states have played in providing public goods. Through their various powers, states are able to convince individuals to give the state resources. Then, through their capacity to act collectively, states can use these resources to create public goods. Similarly, states frequently provide diverse collective goods, which differ from public goods in that they do not suffer from the free-rider problem; nevertheless, states frequently create them either because the market has difficulty providing them or because large segments of the population cannot purchase them through the market.

In providing collective and public goods, states have important effects on broad-based development. Education, health care, transportation, law and order, and sanitation and waste management are all important developmental goods that states can and do provide. Although each of these examples enhances the ability of individuals to pursue their well-being and is therefore developmental, most of the literature on states and development focuses on another developmental good: economic management, which, in fact, requires the provisioning of several developmental goods that make possible a favorable economic environment, including a stable currency, the regulation of macroeconomic indicators, and a legal system enforcing property rights and contracts. In addition, active state intervention in the economy can help spur economic growth by providing protection, resources, and guidance (Amsden 2001; Evans 1995; Johnson 1982).

Unfortunately, not all states have the capacity to provide developmental collective and public goods. Furthermore, because state intervention can be poorly implemented and expands possibilities for rent seeking, it is a double-edged sword that can have very negative developmental consequences (Bates 1981; Callaghy 1984; Lange and Rueschemeyer 2005). Indeed, state officials can abuse their powers to extract resources and services from the public for personal use, thereby limiting the ability of the public to pursue their personal well-being. Most obviously, states can—and sometimes do—use their coercive powers not to protect their citizens but to mutilate and kill them. Even in less extreme cases, state coercion can harass people to such extents that it prevents them from accessing goods, working, traveling freely, participating in civil societal associations, and using personal resources.

As the providers of both developmental goods and developmental bads, states can have either profoundly positive or profoundly negative effects on development. Although the ultimate developmental impact of states is shaped by the desires of those who steer them and the policies the leaders implement, more structural factors are also influential. In the pages that follow, I propose that effective legal-administrative institutions make possible the provisioning of developmental goods, help to impede coercive and destructive state action, and therefore shape the developmental impact of states. In turn, I propose that three state characteristics help determine a state's legal-administrative effectiveness: bureaucracy, infrastructural power, and inclusiveness.

States and the Provisioning of Developmental Goods
From the Weberian perspective, the extent to which a state's legal-administrative institutions are bureaucratic is the most important factor affecting its general capacity to successfully create developmental goods. For one thing, bureaucracy provides the organizational means of supervising and controlling agents. As a result, it limits rent seeking and insubordination among state actors. In addition, bureaucracy provides an effective means of coordinating diverse and multiple actors within the state and therefore makes possible corporate action on a grand scale. Both the control and coordination of state actors, in turn, are necessary conditions for the provisioning of large, complex, and expensive developmental goods (Chibber 2002; Evans 1995; Evans and Rauch 1999).

In order for collective and public goods to be developmental, the population must have access to them. Accessibility, in turn, requires that the state's legal-administrative institutions be physically present and able to provide goods throughout its territory, which, according to Mann (1984), requires "infrastructural power." Infrastructural power is therefore a second structural characteristic that makes possible effective legal-administrative institutions.

While some developmental goods such as roads require little more than the provisioning of physical infrastructure and its maintenance, others depend on and occur through the interactions between state and societal actors. Because they require the presence of both physical infrastructure and state personnel, infrastructural power is doubly important for the provisioning of these more interactive developmental goods. Law and order is one example of a developmental good that depends heavily on state infrastructural power. As Weber (1968) stressed long ago, a rule of law is vital to the functioning of capitalist markets because it increases the relative calculability of law and enforces property rights and freedom of contract (668). More recently, sociologists and political scientists recognize that a rule of law also helps diminish hierarchical relations of dependency and therefore promotes a vibrant civil society (Evans 1996; Mendez, O'Donnell, and Pinheiro 1999). For the legal system to promote development, however, the state must actually be capable of enforcing a rule of law, for which infrastructural power is vital. When infrastructural power is low, state agents cannot regulate society because they are not physically present throughout large stretches of the territory. As a consequence, laws are unenforceable, and individuals are free to pursue their interests in violent and self-serving ways, which encourages the violation of property rights and promotes dependent and exploitative social relations (O'Donnell 1993). When the state is present throughout the territory, on the other hand, state agents are able to interact with the population, monitor their actions, and sanction individuals who break laws.

Along with bureaucracy and infrastructural power, numerous works provide evidence that a state's inclusiveness—that is, its inclusion of diverse societal actors in policy formulation and implementation—is another key attribute determining a state's legal-administrative capacities. Although allowing societal actors to participate in state activities, inclusiveness should not be equated with the lack of state autonomy. Indeed, inclusive states can act contrary to strong societal interests, especially when societal actors pursue diverse and oppositional interests and when states have high organizational capacities (Evans 1995). Equally important, inclusiveness refers to broad ties between the state and diverse societal communities and actors. In this way, a state that is dominated by a particular societal group and therefore lacks autonomy in the Marxist sense of the concept has low levels of inclusiveness.

Inclusiveness enhances the state's capacity to provide developmental goods by making possible synergistic relations between state and society. Many works focus on the effects of state-society synergy on economic development (Amsden 2001; Evans 1995; Onis 1991; Stiglitz 2002; Wang 1999). These analyses find that states are not omnipotent demiurges that can promote economic development at will. Instead, they depend on societal actors, and positive-sum relations between state and economic actors make possible economic expansion by exploiting the state's central control and permanence to guide economic production and the market's ability to discipline and engage economic actors. Other scholars recognize that active relations between the state and societal actors can promote development in noneconomic ways as well (Esman and Uphoff 1984;

Evans 1996; Hadenius and Uggla 1996; Heller 1999, 2001; Tendler 1993; Tendler and Freedheim 1994; Uphoff and Esman 1979). They focus on relations between the state and local associations and find that inclusiveness promotes democratization, public health, and education by combining the centralization, resources, and permanence of the state with the adaptability, participation, and low maintenance costs of local groups.

States and the Suppression of Developmental Bads

Besides promoting the provisioning of developmental goods, effective legal-administrative institutions can improve the ability of individuals to pursue their well-being by impeding state coercion and predation. Indeed, while states can use their powers to benefit the public, one of their defining traits is coercive force, which, when directed domestically and poorly controlled, can have devastating developmental effects. In allowing state officials to govern through legal and administrative means, controlling officials, increasing state accountability to the public, and facilitating state control over the military, bureaucracy, infrastructural power, and inclusiveness all help limit destructive state coercion.

Despite a state's monopoly over the legitimate use of coercion, Weber (1968) recognizes that states do not usually need to employ coercion domestically. His explanation for its infrequent use focuses on how ideas of legitimate authority cause people to accept state domination and willingly follow state directives. In this way, he emphasizes that the way civilians act affects whether or not the state must resort to coercion. Although legitimacy undoubtedly affects the state's use of coercion, the structure of states can also influence the propensity of officials to rule through brute force. I propose that the level of state legal-administrative effectiveness helps limit destructive state coercion in four general ways.

First, the ability of states to govern through noncoercive means affects whether state officials employ coercion. If the state possesses effective legal-administrative institutions, officials can—and almost always prefer to—employ noncoercive methods to implement policy. If, however, the legal-administrative institutions are incapable of implementing policy, officials might have no other option than to implement policy through overtly violent means. And once state coercion is employed against the public, state legitimacy declines, thereby increasing the future need for coercion and potentially initiating a vicious circle of ever-increasing state violence.

Second, Evans (1995) notes that state bureaucratization helps discipline state actors and thereby limits their abilities to abuse their positions in self-serving ways. Salary-based compensation, formal duties, supervision, and record keeping work together to pressure officials to pursue state interests. In so doing, bureaucratic organization impairs the ability of state officials to use their coercive powers to prey on society for personal gain.

Inclusiveness increases state accountability to broad segments of the public and is thereby a third structural characteristic limiting excessive and destructive state coercion. Lipset, Trow, and Coleman (1956) and Heller (1999), for example, provide evidence that inclusive political structures help prevent the iron law of oligarchy from setting in by keeping political elites from gaining a stranglehold on organizational resources. In addition, state inclusiveness empowers those actors who are actively engaged with the state, thereby increasing their ability to hold the state accountable. Furthermore, by expanding the state's capacity to engage diverse societal actors in active relations, inclusiveness prevents any societal group from using the state as an instrument to pursue its particular interests. In so doing, inclusiveness enhances the state's ability to promote compromises between competing societal groups and thereby to respect diverse interests simultaneously.

Finally, the military is the state's ultimate coercive apparatus, and effective state institutions help control it. The military must be effectively organized and coordinated in order to prevent individuals within it from abusing their power. Just like legal-administrative institutions, bureaucratic organization helps limit insubordination within the military. Moreover, the organizational structure linking the military to legal-administrative institutions affects how military power is exercised. Specifically, effective legal-administrative institutions can provide checks on how the military is used domestically, thereby helping to maintain civilian control over it. This is particularly the case when legal-administrative institutions are inclusive, as civilian control promotes legal-administrative accountability to the public instead of the military.

A Model of British Colonial States and Development

Having described the differences between direct and indirect rule and the effects of state bureaucratization, infrastructural power, and inclusiveness on development, I now combine them to construct a model of British colonial state legacies. As Figure 2.1 depicts, I argue that the form of British colonial rule shaped state bureaucratization, infrastructural power, and inclusiveness. In particular, it had either positive or negative effects depending on whether colonial rule was direct or indirect, with direct rule having more positive effects than indirect rule. I also propose that bureau-

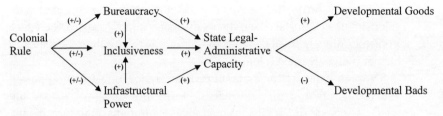

Figure 2.1 Model of the Developmental Legacies of British Colonialism

cratization, infrastructural power, and inclusiveness all positively affect a state's legal-administrative capacities, which in turn enhances the state's ability to both provide developmental goods and limit developmental bads. Combining both propositions, I propose that former directly ruled colonies should have developmental trajectories superior to those of former indirectly ruled colonies.

Colonialism had direct effects on bureaucracy and infrastructural power, yet these effects depended on the form that colonialism took. Directly ruled colonies had relatively integrated and bureaucratic legal-administrative institutions that were present throughout much of their territories, while indirectly ruled colonies had dispersed states that combined a bureaucratic center with regional patrimonialism and had very limited control over most of their territories. On average, former directly ruled countries should therefore have more bureaucratic and infrastructurally powerful legal-administrative institutions than former indirectly ruled colonies.

Next, although all British colonial states had relatively low levels of inclusiveness throughout the majority of the colonial period, indirect rule obstructed inclusiveness to a greater extent than direct rule, and direct rule created the institutional foundations for the subsequent expansion of inclusiveness. Because of its bifurcated structure, indirect rule separated the central state from the public, limited its relations to local elites, and thereby directly impeded state inclusiveness. Direct rule, on the other hand, did not restrict inclusiveness as much as indirect rule. In addition, direct rule created the institutional underpinnings for the subsequent expansion of inclusiveness through its positive effects on state bureaucratization and infrastructural power: bureaucratic organization limits state predation and therefore increases the likelihood of two-sided exchanges between state and society (Evans 1995), and infrastructural power allows state officials to interact and communicate with societal actors on a regular basis and thereby creates the structural foundation for inclusive relations (Evans 1996; Tilly 2005). Because British officials attempted to increase inclusiveness during the final years of colonialism in an effort to prepare colonial subjects for self-rule, these differences likely caused the states in former directly ruled colonies to be more inclusive than the states in former indirectly ruled colonies.

Through its effects on state bureaucratization, infrastructural power, and inclusiveness, I propose that the form of colonialism shaped the effectiveness of the legal-administrative institutions and thereby the state's ability to promote development. Because direct rule positively affected bureaucratic organization, infrastructural power, and inclusiveness, the legal-administrative institutions of former directly ruled colonies were more capable of both providing developmental goods and limiting destructive state action. Indirect rule, on the other hand, institutionalized relatively ineffective legal-administrative institutions. Not only did this impair the state's capacity to provide developmental goods, but it also promoted coercive and personal rule that encouraged state predation. In this way, British colonialism potentially laid the institutional foundations for both despotism and development, with indirect rule causing the former and direct rule the latter.

Although proposing that British colonialism was an important determinant of long-term developmental trajectories, my argument is probabilistic for three reasons. First, states are only one of *many* causes of development, and other factors might counteract the developmental effects of states. Next, the capacity to construct developmental goods and limit developmental bads does not mean that such policy is actually implemented. Indeed, a developmental will must go along with a developmental capacity. Third, state institutions are not static, and postcolonial institutional change might reduce or even terminate the long-term impact of colonial states. There are, however, compelling reasons to believe that the form of colonial states usually persists long after independence and therefore reinforces long-term developmental processes, a topic to which I now turn.

Continuity, Change, and the Possibility of Colonial Legacies

Many social processes occur over long periods of time and must be analyzed historically (Tilly 1984; Pierson 2003, 2004). These historical processes are sometimes characterized by asymmetric causality (Lieberson 1985). That is, once an asymmetric causal process begins, it creates or transforms structures as to perpetuate the process even after the initial causal conditions have been removed. For example, Weber's (1992)

Protestant Ethic and the Spirit of Capitalism suggests that capitalist development is an asymmetric process because one of the initial conditions causing its rise—the Protestant ethic—was not necessary for its continued development given that, once established, capitalism shaped individual norms and cognitions and thereby created "mechanical foundations" that reproduced capitalism (181–82). As this example shows, asymmetric causal processes must be analyzed temporally, with a focus on the period in which the process begins, since the initial cause might not be present after the process is set in motion.

Because some agent or driving force is needed to perpetuate the process after the initial cause is removed, asymmetric processes are generally self-reinforcing and occur over long periods of time. As a consequence, many asymmetric processes are also path-dependent. Mahoney (2000) defines path dependence as having two components: (1) a critical juncture period initiating the causal process and (2) the establishment of mechanisms reinforcing the process begun during the critical juncture. Thus, path dependence might simply result from irreversible causal chains. That is, a critical event sparks a chain of events that, in turn, prevents the return to the initial condition. In addition, path-dependent processes can be perpetuated by institutional legacies. For this second scenario, an institution is created during the critical juncture, reproduces itself over a long period, and exerts continuous effects that reinforce a long-term process.

British colonialism quite possibly began developmental processes that are simultaneously asymmetric and path-dependent. No matter where or when it occurred, British colonial domination was always a transformative force that destroyed social institutions and created new ones, and it must therefore be viewed as a critical juncture (Abernethy 2000; Kohli 2004; Mamdani 1996; Newbury 2003; Wallerstein 1966). Settlers, slaves, and indentured workers arrived; new modes of economic production were initiated; Christianity was introduced; and alien political organizations were constructed. In many places, wars of conquest and the spread of contagious diseases decimated the indigenous population or forced them into peripheral territories. In others, indigenous social structures survived, albeit in greatly adulterated forms. By themselves, these transformations prevented any return to precolonial conditions after the end of colonial rule. In addition, many analyses find that postcolonial state institutions strongly resemble their colonial precursors and have profound effects on social relations (Boone 1994; Kohli 1994, 2004; Mamdani 1996; Migdal 1988). British colonialism might therefore have begun path-dependent processes that were reinforced by continuous state institutional effects.

In this way, direct and indirect rule potentially had long-term effects on developmental processes, and colonialism might continue to affect developmental processes despite its demise.

One must be careful not to simply focus on historical continuity, however, as change is obvious and inevitable. Although important changes occurred within the British Empire both during and after colonialism, the independence period was a common period of instability that potentially transformed state legacies. Indeed, not only were political reforms implemented during the independence transition but the transfer of power frequently readjusted power relations by sparking conflict.

As political scientists recognize, regime change is often unstable. Within the British Empire, such instability was compounded by institutional reforms that prepared the colonies for self-rule. Between 1850 and World War II, British colonial rule focused almost exclusively on the task of establishing and maintaining colonial control on a shoestring—balanced budgets were the norm, and stability was the goal. Colonial officials therefore hoped to restrain revolts against colonial rule and maintain the status quo. Beginning in the 1930s and accelerating rapidly after the Second World War, however, a new and more proactive colonial position was taken and stressed social welfare development and political participation as a necessary means of preparing colonies for independence (Lee 1967). Local, district, and legislative councils were created to engage the local population in political activities and "train" them to run the colonies after independence. The colonial state helped organize co-ops, unions, and other associations in order to get locals to pursue developmental activities. The colonial provisioning of health care, education, transportation, a rule of law, and clean water and sewage all increased. In order to do all of this, colonial officials expanded and restructured the state during the final years of colonialism. Although these reforms usually built on previous state structures, they had the potential to initiate radical institutional change.

The transfer of power from foreign to local hands also created an opening for state institutional change by instigating conflict, as indigenous actors struggled with one another and with colonial officials in an attempt to influence the reforms and to place themselves in a position to usurp power after independence. Because British colonialism was exclusionary, conflict between the colonizers and the colonized was almost always present in some form or another. In a few cases within the British Empire, such as the United States and Malaysia, anticolonial conflict turned violent and resulted in prolonged wars. Elsewhere, struggles between different indigenous groups erupted and were instigated by competition over control of the state. The resolution of conflict between colonial and indigenous actors and between opposing indigenous actors had important effects on institutional legacies. Such conflict sometimes created instrumental states and sometimes created states with high levels of inclusiveness, sometimes created deep-seated cleavages among groups and sometimes helped to integrate them, sometimes personalized power and sometimes helped to strengthen a rule of law.

Thus, colonialism constructed state institutions, and these institutions have generally persisted since independence. As a consequence, colonial rule potentially began developmental processes that are both path-dependent and asymmetric. Despite a high probability of state structural continuity over extended periods of time, analyses of colonial legacies must still recognize that state institutional change is possible. In particular, the independence transition had a heightened potential to transform colonial state legacies because colonial officials usually implemented political reforms during the late colonial period and because the transfer of power frequently sparked conflict and readjusted power relations.

Summary

In this chapter, I lay the foundations for the subsequent empirical analysis of British colonial legacies by sketching a history of the British Empire, conceptualizing direct and indirect rule, and outlining a theoretical framework. I review the rise and fall of the British Empire, document the use of both direct and indirect rule, and describe the structural characteristics of both direct and indirect rule. Because of their differences, I propose that direct rule institutionalized more bureaucratic, more infrastructurally powerful, and more inclusive states than indirect rule. These characteristics, in turn, potentially caused the states of directly ruled colonies to have greater developmental capacities and lower propensities to be coercive and predatory. Throughout the remainder of this book, I look into these possibilities.

A Statistical Analysis of British Colonial Legacies

3

In this chapter, I begin the empirical analysis of the divergent developmental trajectories among former British colonies through a cross-national statistical analysis. Statistics are advantaged over qualitative methods because they provide formal techniques to test rival hypotheses. Using postcolonial measures of per capita GDP, infant mortality rate, average years of educational attainment, democracy, and governance as dependent variables, I employ different independent variables and test three general hypotheses of uneven development among former British colonies.

According to the colonial hypothesis, colonialism transformed developmental trajectories but did so in different ways. Of particular interest to this analysis, colonialism institutionalized different states that might have had very different effects on developmental processes. To test this hypothesis, I construct a new variable measuring the extent of direct and indirect colonial rule.

The precolonial hypothesis, on the other hand, claims either that postcolonial development is the continuation of precolonial developmental trajectories, that postcolonial development is determined by factors that preceded colonialism, or both. It therefore takes an extremely historic view, suggesting that the factors determining developmental processes over the past half century were already in place hundreds if not thousands of years ago. To test this hypothesis, I include variables measuring latitude, precolonial population density, history of precolonial statehood, and onset of settled agriculture.

Finally, the postcolonial hypothesis argues that more proximate factors from the postcolonial period account for uneven development. Such factors are diverse and potentially influential, yet often difficult to operationalize. Examples include war, development policy, leadership, and the AIDS epidemic. For this final hypothesis, I use dependent variables from both 1970 and 2000 and see whether the predictive power of precolonial and colonial factors diminishes over time.

Operationalizing the Form of British Colonial Rule

To test the colonial hypothesis, one needs to operationalize colonially induced differences among British colonies. For this analysis, I create variables measuring (1) the duration of British colonialism, (2) colonial police officers per capita, (3) the presence of plantation economies, and (4) the extent of indirect rule. Through subsequent analysis, I discover that police officers per capita and the extent of indirect rule are much better predictors of postcolonial development than either the duration of colonialism or the presence of plantation economies. The indirect rule and police variables are highly correlated with one another, however, and therefore might provide inaccurate results if included in the same models. Because the indirect rule variable is consistently the best predictor of postcolonial development, because it operationalizes the most central element of Chapter 2's theoretical framework, and because a few former colonies lack comparable data on police officers per capita, I exclude police officers per capita and use the indirect rule variable as the sole measure of colonialism.

To gauge the extent of indirect rule, I use archival sources to construct a new variable measuring the extent of colonial dependence on supposedly customary institutions for the regulation of societal relations. Specifically, I measure the percentage of total colonial court cases heard in "customary" courts.[1] Within British colonies, customary courts were formerly recognized by colonial officials and were supposed to enforce local custom. Indigenous leaders ran the customary courts, collaborated with colonial officials, and based their authority on precolonial tradition. While some British colonies lacked customary courts, all possessed magistrate courts, which enforced some form of Common Law and were run by colonial officials. Based on this operationalization, the variable directly measures the extent to which the colonial state depended on customary courts—as opposed to magistrate courts—to regulate social relations, and the colonial dependence on customary courts was the telltale sign of indirect rule. Thus, Nigeria's high score (93) shows that the colonial state depended very heavily on customary courts and that colonial rule was very indirect. In contrast, Barbados' low score (0) shows that colonial rule was purely direct, as all courts were heard in magistrate courts. Finally, Fiji's moderate score (55) demonstrates that colonial officials used customary and magistrate courts equally in their attempt to control the population, suggesting a hybrid form of colonialism that mixed direct and indirect techniques. The scores of the variable are listed in Table 3.1.

The customary court variable is usually measured in 1955, and the variable therefore measures the extent of indirect rule during the late colonial period. In a few cases, however, data are unavailable in 1955, so I gather scores as close to that year as possible. In a few additional cases, colonies received independence prior to 1955, and I employ the latest available colonial-era data for these cases. The data for the variable were collected from annual colonial reports, annual judicial reports, and other primary documents and are an updated version of those presented in Lange (2004, 2005a).[2]

As described in Chapter 2, direct and indirect rule created very different states. As a measure of the extent of indirect rule, the customary court variable captures additional state characteristics beyond colonial dependence on indirect institutions. In particular, the variable provides a general indicator of the colonial state's organizational capacity, as it measures three characteristics that affect the state's ability to act corporately and implement policy.

First, the customary court variable provides a negative proxy for the extent of state bureaucratization. Within the British Empire, central legal-administrative institutions were almost always highly bureaucratic. At the local level, however, there was considerable variation in the level of bureaucratization. Under direct rule, colonial officials governed the peripheral regions of the colony via institutions that were generally organized along the same lines as the center, and the state was therefore bureaucratic through and through. When colonies were indirectly ruled, on the other hand, the central legal-administrative institutions were tiny, and colonial dependence on customary authorities left large regions of the country under much more patrimonial institutions. A low score on the customary court variable therefore demonstrates relatively high levels of state bureaucratization whereas a high score represents lower levels of state bureaucratization.

Table 3.1 Legal-administrative indicators for British colonies

Colony	Customary court cases (% of total)	Colonial police officers per 1,000 people	Colony	Customary court cases (% of total)	Colonial police officers per 1,000 people
Australia	0	—	Malaysia[a]	6	2.3
Bahamas	0	2.7	Mauritius	0	2.1
Bangladesh	50	0.5	Myanmar	16	1.0
Barbados	0	2.8	New Zealand	0	—
Belize	0	2.7	Nigeria	93	0.3
Botswana	43	1.2	Pakistan	50	1.1
Brunei	1	3.2	Sierra Leone	81	0.6
Canada	0	—	Singapore	0	3.2
Cyprus	0	3.5	Solomon Islands	52	2.1
Egypt	0	—	South Africa	39	—
Fiji	55	1.5	Sri Lanka	0	0.6
Gambia	37	1.0	Sudan	73	0.7
Ghana	65	1.1	Swaziland	49	0.9
Guyana	0	3.3	Tanzania[a]	75	0.6
Hong Kong	0	2.2	Trinidad	0	2.5
India	49	0.4	Uganda	80	0.7
Jamaica	0	1.3	United States	0	—
Kenya	59	2.2	Zambia	60	1.6
Lesotho	50	0.7	Zimbabwe	40	0.4
Malawi	82	0.6			

Sources: British Colonial Office (1947, 1951, 1953, 1955a, 1956, 1958); Colony of Fiji (1955); Colony of Kenya (1952); Colony of Nigeria (1953); Colony of Northern Rhodesia (1955); Colony of Sierra Leone (1955); Colony of Southern Rhodesia (1955); Colony of Sudan (1949); Colony of Uganda (1955); House of Commons (1939, 1942, 1951); Schwartzberg (1978); Union of South Africa (1956).

[a] The indirect rule variable for Malaysia combines the court cases of Malaya, Sarawak, and North Borneo. The indirect rule statistic of Tanzania combines the court cases of Tanganyika and Zanzibar.

Second, the customary court variable provides a negative measure of the size of the state and the intensity of colonial rule. When customary authorities were empowered to control local courts and other legal-administrative institutions, they organized their own administrations and police forces that were largely outside of the control of the central colonial state. Under direct rule, on the other hand, the state provided legal-administrative institutions throughout the country, thereby creating a state that was much larger in per capita terms. Demonstrating the greater intensity of direct rule, the customary court variable is strongly and negatively correlated with per capita colonial police officers (−0.72) (see table 3.1 for data on colonial police officers).

Finally, the form of colonialism affected the infrastructural power of the state. Because direct rule created a highly integrated and large legal-administrative structure that did not depend on local intermediaries, it had relatively high levels of territorial presence and could implement policy in all regions of the colony. By contrast, the use of local patrimonial elites in indirectly ruled colonies left large regions of the colony without a strong colonial presence.

Operationalizing Precolonial Conditions

In order to test the precolonial hypothesis, I include four variables measuring different factors that proponents of the precolonial hypothesis argue have long-term effects on development. First, several studies find that a country's latitude affects soil, disease environment, and even culture and that these characteristics, in turn, shape long-term development. I therefore include a variable measuring distance from the equator. The data come from LaPorta, Lopez-de-Silanes, Shleifer, and Vishny (1999) and range from 0 to 1, with 0 designating a country's position on the equator and 1 designating a country's position on either of the poles.

Next, the analysis includes three measures of precolonial development level. First, population density at the onset of formal overseas colonization is used as a general proxy for precolonial development. Most basically, high population densities require high levels of production to sustain the population and make possible specialization and a division of labor (Lenski 1970). Similarly, Diamond (1997) and Putterman (2000) contend that population density is a long-term proxy for "broad human capital" level. The data for the variable were gathered by the author from Kuczynski (1948, 1949, 1953), McEvedy and Jones (1978), *Annual Colonial Reports* (British Colonial Office 1947, 1951, 1953, 1955a,b, 1956, 1958), and other historical sources.

The second precolonial development variable measures the history of precolonial statehood. It is taken from Putterman's (2007b) State Antiquity Index and measures three factors: the existence of a government above the tribal level, the proportion of the territory of a present country that this government controlled, and whether or not this government was indigenous or colonial. The data are measured over fifty-year periods, and the scores range from 0 to 50, with 0 suggesting that there was no government above the tribal level in a given country during a given fifty-year period and 50 suggesting the existence of an autonomous state present throughout the country's present territory. For this analysis, I measure precolonial statehood by averaging the unweighted index scores over the 200-year period prior to the onset of overseas colonialism.[3]

The final control for precolonial development measures when settled agriculture began, a factor Diamond (1997) and Lenski (1970) argue is potentially the most important historical determinant of the world's modern developmental hierarchies. Specifically, Diamond and Lenski claim that settled agriculture is a precondition for technological advancement, a division of labor, and the development of a state. This variable is taken from Putterman's (2007a) Agricultural Transitions Dataset and measures the onset of settled agriculture by counting the number of years between the onset of settled agriculture and AD 2000.[4]

Additional Independent Variables

Along with the variables measuring either colonial or precolonial conditions, two additional independent variables are included that combine both colonial and precolonial components. Because of this combination, the variables are unable to shed light on whether colonialism or precolonial factors determine long-term development. They are included, however, to control for factors that potentially affect long-term development.

First, the analysis includes a control for the extent of ethnic fractionalization because other analyses find a significant relationship between ethnic diversity and both economic performance and the quality of government (Easterly and Levine 1997; LaPorta, Lopez-de-Silanes, Shleifer, and Vishny 1999). The fractionalization measure is derived from the confirmatory factor analysis of Fearon's (2003) ethnic fractionalization and cultural diversity scores. While this variable is influenced greatly by precolonial ethnic fractionalization, one must recognize that British colonialism often promoted fractionalization by strengthening ethnic divisions and introducing Africans, Asians, and Europeans into their colonies.

Related to this last point, the final independent variable measures the percentage of the total population at independence that was European settlers, which is the focal variable of Acemoglu, Johnson, and Robinson's (2001) acclaimed analysis of colonial legacies. Notably, this variable provides a partial measurement of the form and intensity of colonialism and might simply be viewed as an alternative indicator of the form of colonial rule. Yet the variable is only moderately related to the customary court variable. As a consequence, the inclusion of the European settler variable in the statistical models allows the analysis to investigate the effects of colonial rule on developmental processes that are *not* attributable to the presence of a large number of Europeans, thereby allowing the customary court variable to better capture institutional aspects of direct and indirect colonial rule. In addition, because European settlement occurred in places with relatively benign disease environments and with exploitable natural resources (Acemoglu, Johnson, and Robinson 2001), the variable helps control for these precolonial characteristics that potentially affected long-term development.[5]

Testing Postcolonial Factors

A number of postcolonial factors might account for the uneven development of former British colonies over the past half century. Examples include wars and ethnic violence, policy, leadership, and the AIDS epidemic. Many of these postcolonial characteristics are extremely difficult to operationalize, and the inclusion of several additional independent variables would further reduce the degrees of freedom needed for the statistical analysis. Unlike the colonial and precolonial hypotheses, I therefore do not include additional independent variables to measure postcolonial characteristics that potentially affect development. Instead, I employ a time-lag design, using development indicators from both 1970 and 2000 as dependent variables and testing whether the impact of precolonial and colonial factors changes over time. If the postcolonial hypothesis is correct, either the colonial and precolonial variables should be unrelated to postcolonial development at both time periods or the predictive power of the precolonial and the colonial variables should diminish markedly between 1970 and 2000. If, on the other hand, the colonial and precolonial variables have equal or greater predictive power in 2000 than in 1970 and account for much of the variation in postcolonial development level, the findings provide evidence against strong versions of the postcolonial hypothesis.[6]

Dependent Variables

To test the causes of uneven development among former British colonies, I employ different measures of economic, human, and political development as dependent variables. All of these variables measure level of development between 1970 and 2005. Whereas the variables for economic and human development measure level of development during given years, the variables measuring political development average available scores during the postcolonial period in order to create general indicators of postcolonial governance.

I use per capita GDP in both 1970 and 2000 (PPP in constant 1996 US dollars) to operationalize the level of economic development. Data are taken from the Penn World Tables (Heston, Summers, and Aten 2006).[7] Next, both educational attainment and infant mortality rate are used as separate indicators of human development. Education is operationalized by taking the adult population's average number of years of education and is taken from Barro and Lee (2000). Data from 2000 are not available, so I use data from 1970 and 1995. For both years, several former British colonies are excluded from the analysis because they lack educational scores.[8] Infant mortality rate is used as a proxy for average societal health, and I use data from both 1970 and 2000. The data are taken from the World Bank's World Development Indicators (2007a).[9]

In order to operationalize postcolonial political development, I use variables measuring the level of democracy and governance. The democracy variable combines the Freedom House indices of political rights and liberties, inverts the scores, and converts them to a ten-point scale. Thus, the democracy measurement is continuous and ranges from 1 (least democratic) to 10 (most democratic). Freedom House scores are available from 1972, and I average the yearly scores between 1972 and 2005. The variable therefore measures average level of democratization over a thirty-three-year period.[10]

The governance indicators are taken from the World Bank and measure four characteristics: (1) government effectiveness, which measures the quality of the public service provision and the bureaucracy; (2) state stability, which measures perceptions of the likelihood that the government in power will be destabilized or overthrown; (3) lack of state corruption, which measures the extent to which public power is not exercised for private gain; and (4) rule of law, which measures the incidence of crime, the effectiveness and predictability of the judiciary, and the enforceability of contracts (World Bank 2007b). Each governance variable is scored so that the global average is 0, with one standard deviation being equivalent to one point. Based on this scoring, nearly all countries in the world fall between −2.5 and 2.5. For this analysis, I combine all four indicators into one aggregate governance variable. Moreover, governance data are available between 1996 and 2005, and I average the aggregate score over this period. The variable employed is therefore both an aggregate of four governance indicators and an average of the governance scores over a ten-year period.

Cases

As described in Chapter 2, diverse peoples and lands were colonized by the British. While such variety allows one to analyze differences among former colonies, it also poses a problem of unit homogeneity: the comparison of analytically distinct units might cause inaccuracies. As shown in Table 3.2, I exclude several former colonies in an attempt to make the set more homogeneous. In addition, I use two different sets of cases to maximize the number of colonies and inter-case variation on the one hand and to minimize the potential for unit heterogeneity on the other hand.

Former colonies that had less than 100,000 inhabitants at independence, merged with non-British territories at independence, were internal colonies, or were British Mandates in the Middle East are all excluded from the statistical analysis (see Table 3.2). The first restriction excludes several tiny islands that were—and still are in some cases—little more than colonial outposts. These micro-island colonies were distinct from other British colonies in terms of size and population. Next, I exclude British Somaliland, British Cameroon, and Aden because they merged with larger non-British territories after independence and therefore experienced hybrid legacies. Third, I exclude Ireland, Wales, and Scotland because they were—and depending on one's perspective, might continue to be—internal colonies: the English conquered these adjacent lands and incorporated them directly into their territory (see Hechter 1975). Finally, I exclude Iraq, Transjordan, and Palestine because they were colonized for very short periods of time (ten years for Transjordan, thirteen years for Iraq, and thirty years for Palestine) and because the last of the three was a very unique British colony given its high levels of settlement during British rule.

With the remaining thirty-nine cases, I use two different sets to test the correlates of development among former British colonies (see Table 3.2). The more limited set excludes six former British colonies: Australia, Canada, Egypt, New Zealand, South Africa, and the United States. I remove these cases because particular characteristics and one common trait differentiate them from other British colonies. The commonality is that all six gained their independences well before World War II, the end of which initiated the main period of colonial independence. This difference is potentially important because British colonial policy transformed radically beginning in the 1930s. In addition, the British learned from earlier cases how to implement a smooth transition to independence, a factor that potentially affected postcolonial development (Smith 1978).

Table 3.2 Case selection among British colonies.

Excluded from Analysis	Excluded from Set 2	Included in Sets 1 and 2
Micro Colonies	Australia	Bahamas
Antigua & Barbuda	Canada	Bangladesh
Dominica	Egypt	Barbados
Falkland Islands	New Zealand	Belize
Grenada	South Africa	Botswana
Kuwait	United States	Brunei
Maldives		Cyprus
Malta		Fiji
St. Kitts & Nevis		Gambia
St. Lucia		Ghana
St. Vincent & Grenadines		Guyana
Seychelles		Hong Kong
Tonga		India
Tuvalu		Jamaica
		Kenya
Hybrids		Lesotho
Cameroon		Malawi
Somalia		Malaysia
Yemen		Mauritius
		Nigeria
Internal Colonies		Pakistan
Ireland		Sierra Leone
Scotland		Singapore
Wales		Solomon Islands
		Sri Lanka
Mandate Territories		Sudan
Iraq		Swaziland
Jordan		Tanzania
Israel/Palestine		Trinidad & Tobago
		Uganda
		Zambia
		Zimbabwe

Besides their dates of independence, other particular circumstances exist that might warrant separate analysis. The four large-scale settlement colonies, for example, were in some ways closer to extensions of Great Britain than overseas colonies. As a result, settlers were not prone to the same levels of exclusion and exploitation as other colonial peoples and

therefore experienced distinct and more benign forms of colonial domination. Next, South Africa was unified under British colonial rule for less
than a decade prior to the granting of self-rule within the Commonwealth
in 1910. Because of such a brief period of unified rule, South Africa combines the legacies of both Dutch (Boer) and British colonial rule. Finally,
although Egypt experienced nearly seven decades of British influence, it
was a formal colony for less than a decade, and all other colonies in this
data set were formally colonized for at least forty years.

Diagnostic Exams

Diagnostic exams have been performed to check for nonlinearity, multicollinearity, influential cases, and heteroskedasticity. In most cases, the
data are consistent with the assumptions of linear multivariate analysis.
Per capita GDP, precolonial population density, and the percentage of
total population composed of Europeans, however, have curvilinear relationships with independent variables due to high-end outliers. Because
the European population variable is a more powerful predictor when
unmodified, only the per capita GDP and the precolonial population density variables are logged. Checks on multicollinearity uncover only minor
relationships among the variables: the variance inflation factor scores
for all variables are below 3, suggesting that the relationships among
the independent variables are relatively weak and do not degrade the
precision of the statistical estimates. Using Cook's distance to calculate
case influence, four or fewer cases are highlighted as potentially influential in the different models. When these cases are omitted from the
set, however, the results remain largely unchanged.[11] Finally, tests find
that heteroskedasticity might affect the results of infant mortality rate in
2000, yet rerunning the models with robust standard errors produces
similar results.[12]

Findings I: Development Level in 1970

Table 3.3 gives the results of the OLS models using three different indicators of development level in 1970 as the dependent variables: per capita
GDP, average educational attainment, and infant mortality rate. For all
three dependent variables, model 1 uses the set of 39 former British colonies and includes only the customary court variable, model 2 uses the set
of 39 former British colonies and includes all independent variables, and
model 3 includes all independent variables but uses the more limited set

Table 3.3 OLS analysis of per capita GDP (1970), average educational attainment (1970), and infant mortality rate (1970)

Variables	Per capita GDP (log)			Average school attainment			Infant mortality rate		
	Model 1	Model 2	Model 3	Model 1	Model 2	Model 3	Model 1	Model 2	Model 3
Customary courts	−0.026**	−0.022**	−0.020**	−0.065**	−0.046**	−0.046**	1.181**	1.102**	1.016**
	(0.004)	(0.006)	(0.006)	(0.013)	(0.012)	(0.012)	(0.193)	(0.304)	(0.307)
Latitude		−0.535	−1.088		−1.461	0.593		60.187	69.407
		(1.224)	(1.457)		(2.376)	(2.746)		(63.382)	(73.955)
Precolonial population density (log)		−0.051	−0.035		0.232	0.309		2.35	3.194
		(0.080)	(0.085)		(0.165)	(0.165)		(4.145)	(4.302)
Precolonial state history		−0.002	0.005		−0.045*	−0.012		0.315	0.329
		(0.009)	(0.010)		(0.021)	(0.023)		(0.452)	(0.485)
Precolonial agriculture		−0.000	0.000		0.000	−0.000		−0.001	−0.005
		(0.000)	(0.000)		(0.000)	(0.000)		(0.004)	(0.004)
% European		1.219	15.605		6.003**	81.466*		−55.305	−299.701
		(0.647)	(7.720)		(1.278)	(29.396)		(33.511)	(391.821)
Ethnic fractionalization		0.126	0.075		−0.090	1.136		−17.749	0.273
		(0.570)	(0.688)		(1.227)	(1.382)		(29.529)	(34.914)
Constant	8.720**	8.724**	8.272**	5.684**	5.283**	2.850*	51.030**	51.502*	57.146*
	(0.174)	(0.402)	(0.539)	(0.553)	(0.813)	(1.213)	(8.488)	(20.793)	(27.367)
n	39	39	33	31	31	26	39	39	33
R^2	0.54	0.68	0.64	0.46	0.84	0.70	0.50	0.60	0.60

** $p < .01$; * $p < .05$.

of 33 former British colonies (excluding Australia, Canada, Egypt, New Zealand, South Africa, and the United States).

Looking at the results for economic development, the customary court variable is significantly and negatively related to GDP in model 1, and the variable independently accounts for over 50 percent of the variation in per capita GDP in 1970. When the controls are added in model 2 and when the more limited set is used in model 3, the customary court variable continues to be very strongly and significantly related to per capita GDP, suggesting that the form of colonialism potentially affected economic development. Specifically, the findings provide evidence that indirect rule had more negative effects on economic development than direct rule. No other independent variable is significantly related to GDP, and the models therefore strongly support the colonial hypothesis but provide little support for the precolonial hypothesis.

The results of the models using average school attainment in 1970 as the dependent variable are similar to those for per capita GDP. As shown in the table, the colonial variable is strongly, negatively, and significantly related to educational attainment in all models, and the colonial variable independently accounts for nearly half of the variation. The percentage of European population is the only other variable significantly related to educational attainment in 1970. The positive relationship suggests that European settlement affected educational development either through a higher proclivity of Europeans to invest in education, the disease environment in which Europeans settled (lower mortality rates potentially increase returns on investments in human capital and therefore promote education), or both.

Similar to the models on economic and educational development, the results for societal health in 1970 provide clear evidence in support of the colonial hypothesis. Indeed, the colonial variable is strongly and positively related to infant mortality in all models. Independently, the variable accounts for half of the variation in infant mortality rate, and its coefficients show that a one point increase in the percentage of total court cases heard in customary courts is associated with a one point increase in infant mortality rate. No other independent variable is significantly related to infant mortality.

Findings II: Development Level in 1995 or 2000

While Table 3.3 provides consistent evidence in favor of the colonial hypothesis and very little support for the precolonial hypothesis, it is unable to test whether postcolonial factors promoted uneven development. Table 3.4

Table 3.4 OLS analysis of per capita GDP (2000), average educational attainment (1995), and infant mortality rate (2000)

Variables	Per capita GDP (log)			Average school attainment			Infant mortality rate		
	Model 1	Model 2	Model 3	Model 1	Model 2	Model 3	Model 1	Model 2	Model 3
Customary courts	-0.033**	-0.028**	-0.027**	-0.072**	-0.069**	-0.067**	1.049**	1.010**	0.969**
	(0.004)	(0.006)	(0.006)	(0.013)	(0.015)	(0.016)	(0.120)	(0.204)	(0.232)
Latitude		0.914	0.818		1.088	1.806		35.644	48.362
		(1.219)	(1.522)		(2.934)	(3.612)		(42.624)	(55.902)
Precolonial population density (log)		-0.64	-0.062		0.288	0.342		0.794	1.103
		(0.080)	(0.089)		(0.204)	(0.217)		(2.787)	(3.251)
Precolonial state history		0.008	0.010		-0.028	0.003		0.022	0.030
		(0.009)	(0.010)		(0.026)	(0.030)		(0.304)	(0.366)
Precolonial agriculture		0	0.000		-0.000	-0.000		-0.001	-0.003
		(0.000)	(0.000)		(0.000)	(0.000)		(0.003)	(0.003)
% European		0.648	6.150		4.671**	68.973		-29.087	-85.925
		(0.644)	(8.066)		(1.578)	(38.674)		(22.536)	(296.172)
Ethnic fractionalization		-0.048	-0.215		1.947	2.564		-4.794	3.547
		(0.568)	(0.719)		(1.515)	(1.818)		(19.858)	(26.391)
Constant	9.472**	9.093**	8.913**	8.100**	6.970**	5.120**	17.242**	20.242	19.336
	(0.162)	(0.400)	(0.563)	(0.546)	(1.003)	(1.596)	(5.286)	(13.983)	(20.686)
n	39	39	33	31	31	26	39	39	33
R^2	0.68	0.75	0.71	0.52	0.78	0.64	0.67	0.70	0.66

$** p < .01; * p < .05.$

gives the OLS results using economic, educational, and health development in either 1995 or 2000 as the dependent variables. In combination
with the 1970 models, the table provides insight into whether or not the
effect of colonialism diminished over the twenty-five- to thirty-year period,
a situation that would support the hypothesis that postcolonial change
accounts for the uneven development of former British colonies. For all
three dependent variables shown in the table, model 1 includes the customary court variable using the full set of former British colonies, model 2
includes all independent variables using the full set, and model 3 includes
all independent variables using the more limited set of 33 colonies.

As in the models of development level in 1970, the customary court variable is consistently and significantly related to all three dependent variables.
In addition, the form of colonialism accounts for more variation at the dawn
of the third millennium than in 1970: the R^2-values of model 1 increased
from 0.54 to 0.68 for per capita GDP, from 0.46 to 0.52 for educational
attainment, and from 0.50 to 0.67 for infant mortality rate. The European
population variable is the only other independent variable with a significant
relationship in any of the models, and it is significantly related to educational attainment and infant mortality rate only in model 2 but loses its
significance once the European settler colonies are removed from the set in
model 3.[13] A comparison of the models therefore demonstrates that the predictive power of the form of colonial rule did not diminish even after several
decades of independence but actually increased. In so doing, the comparison provides evidence that postcolonial change is not the primary cause of
uneven development among former British colonies but that the form of
colonialism is an important determinant of long-term development.

The growing predictive power of the variable measuring the extent of
indirect rule is somewhat counterintuitive, as one would expect the impact
of colonialism to diminish as the time since independence increases. Yet
the finding coincides with path-dependent claims that institutions can
reinforce long-term processes and thereby cause growing developmental
inequality (North 1990). Indeed, because states are important determinants of development and because their basic structures remain relatively
unchanged over long periods of time, one might expect the developmental divide between countries with effective and defective states to widen.
If this is in fact the case, colonial states should have maintained their
general forms after independence and continued to affect developmental
processes throughout the postcolonial period, with the states of former
indirectly ruled colonies continuing to deter development and the states
of former directly ruled colonies continuing to promote it. This scenario

therefore suggests that former directly ruled colonies should presently
have more effective states than former indirectly ruled colonies, an issue
to which I now turn.

Findings III: Postcolonial Governance

Table 3.5 lists the OLS results for average levels of democracy and governance among former British colonies. For both dependent variables,
model 1 includes the customary court variable and the full set of British
colonies, model 2 includes all independent variables and the full set of
British colonies, and model 3 includes all independent variables but uses
the more limited set of 33 British colonies.

Looking at the results for democracy, the R^2-values are slightly less than
in the previous models but are nonetheless quite high, accounting for
between 33 and 57 percent of the variation in average level of democracy
between 1972 and 2005. Moreover, the customary court variable remains
the only variable that is significantly and consistently related to the dependent variable. The only other independent variable that is significant in
any of the models is state history, suggesting that precolonial state development might hinder postcolonial democratization.[14]

Turning to the aggregate governance indicator, a quick glance at the
results highlights the strength of one variable: the extent of indirect colonial rule. Indeed, it is negatively and extremely significantly related to the
average level of governance between 1996–2005 in all models, and model
1 shows that the variable independently accounts for half of the variation in
governance. No other variable has consistent and significant relationships.
And while the variable in Table 3.5 combines four different governance
indicators (government effectiveness, political stability, rule of law, and lack
of corruption), the colonial variable has negative and strongly significant
($p < 0.01$) relationships with each of the four when they are used individu-
ally as dependent variables (results not shown). Thus, the form of colonialism is strongly related to postcolonial governance, providing evidence that
colonial state legacies enforce path-dependent developmental processes.

Testing the Direction of Causation

Despite consistent evidence in support of the colonial hypothesis, statistical relationships are not always able to provide insight into the direction
of causation, and it remains possible that development shaped the form
of colonialism but not the reverse. Specifically, the level of precolonial

Table 3.5 OLS analysis of average level of democracy (1972–2005) and aggregate governance (1996–2005)

	Democracy			Governance		
Variables	Model 1	Model 2	Model 3	Model 1	Model 2	Model 3
Customary courts	−0.047**	−0.040*	−0.043*	−0.085**	−0.076**	−0.074**
	(0.011)	(0.017)	(0.018)	(0.014)	(0.021)	(0.023)
Latitude		1.809	3.831		1	1.44
		(3.269)	(4.073)		(4.286)	(5.617)
Precolonial population		0.104	0.157		−0.013	−0.003
density (log)		(0.235)	(0.262)		(0.280)	(0.327)
Precolonial state history		−0.052*	−0.047		0.032	0.04
		(0.024)	(0.027)		(0.031)	(0.037)
Precolonial agriculture		0	0		0	0
		(0.000)	(0.000)		(0.000)	(0.000)
% European		1.822	15.658		5.296*	24.531
		(1.706)	(21.257)		(2.266)	(29.762)
Ethnic fractionalization		0.299	0.871		1.145	1.446
		(1.526)	(1.930)		(1.997)	(2.652)
Constant	7.605**	7.743**	6.897**	2.730**	1.703	0.832
	(0.492)	(1.060)	(1.481)	(0.633)	(1.406)	(2.079)
n	38	38	32	39	39	33
R^2	0.33	0.57	0.48	0.49	0.67	0.50

** $p < .01$; * $p < .05$.

development might have determined the form of colonial rule, and the findings might simply show that precolonial development—as measured by the form of colonialism—is related to postcolonial development.

In order to look into this possibility, I regress the customary court variable on the three variables measuring precolonial development (population density, state history, and onset of settled agriculture) using both sets of former British colonies. As shown in Table 3.6, the three precolonial development variables account for 30 percent of the variation in the form of colonialism using the set of 39 former colonies and 23 percent using the more limited set of 33. Precolonial development is therefore moderately related to the form that colonialism took but hardly enough for the direction of causation in the models above to go from development to the form of colonialism, an interpretation that is also supported by low variance inflation factor scores (all of which are below three). Furthermore,

Table 3.6 OLS analysis of the extent of indirect rule

Variables	Full set	Limited set
Precolonial population	9.194**	8.490**
density (log)	(2.418)	(2.887)
Precolonial state history	−0.063	−0.126
	(0.326)	(0.360)
Precolonial agriculture	−0.005	−0.004
	(0.003)	(0.003)
Constant	40.321**	42.292**
	(8.629)	(10.234)
n	39	33
R^2	0.3	0.23

** $p < .01$; * $p < .05$.

precolonial population density is the only precolonial variable that is significantly related to the form of colonialism, and it is positively related to the extent of indirect rule using both sets of cases. Thus, the extent of indirect rule is negatively related to postcolonial development but positively related to precolonial development, a mismatch that is difficult to explain if endogeneity drives the relationship between the form of British colonialism and postcolonial development.

Notably, the positive and significant relationship between precolonial population density and indirect rule is contrary to the findings of Diamond (1997), Herbst (2000), and Lenski (1970), all of whom claim that high population density promotes state building and intensive rule. The positive relationship discovered in this analysis appears to be driven by the effects of indigenous populations on the cost of direct and indirect colonial rule, as the presence of a large population made possible greater resistance to intensive colonialism yet provided the colonizers with indigenous leaders and institutions that could be manipulated to construct a system of indirect rule. In this way, British colonialism appears to have been a critical event that ultimately advantaged backwardness: it created more effective states in regions that were less likely to develop them on their own but less effective states in regions with a greater likelihood of either possessing or building effective states. Similar to the findings of Acemoglu, Johnson, and Robinson (2002) and Mahoney (2003), these results therefore suggest that British colonialism caused a developmental reversal of fortune and provide strong evidence that endogeneity does not drive the statistical findings.

Case Conformity of Botswana, Guyana, Mauritius, and Sierra Leone

In addition to highlighting relationships, statistical methods allow researchers to see how individual cases conform to general trends. Table 3.7 shows the case conformity of Mauritius, Sierra Leone, Guyana, and Botswana by listing their residuals. The residuals measure the difference between the predicted value of development and the actual value, and the scores therefore show whether a country's development record is higher or lower than expected given the statistical findings. Here, the predicted value for each dependent value is based on the first model in all of the tables above.[15] Table 3.7 also includes the standard deviation of residuals for all former British colonies with available data in order to give a general reference against which to gauge individual residual scores.

The table shows that directly ruled Mauritius and indirectly ruled Sierra Leone generally conform to the statistical analysis. All of Mauritius' residuals except for average educational attainment are within one standard deviation, and the residual for education is only slightly greater than one standard deviation below the predicted value. The former directly ruled colony is thus, generally speaking, an on-line case. Likewise, four of Sierra Leone's five residuals are within one standard deviation, although infant mortality rate in 2000 is much higher than expected. The Sierra Leone case study therefore provides an opportunity to investigate the developmental trajectory of a relatively non-outlying case that was ruled indirectly.

While Mauritius and Sierra Leone generally conform to the statistical findings, directly ruled Guyana and indirectly ruled Botswana do not. Based on the table, Guyana's development record over the past forty years has been consistently and considerably lower than expected. Specifically, all residuals suggest lower levels of development than expected given Guyana's direct form of rule, only one predicted score (democracy) is within one standard deviation of the actual score, and three predicted scores (governance, GDP, and infant mortality rate) are approximately two standard deviations from the actual score. The analysis of Guyana therefore provides an opportunity to investigate factors that caused this former directly ruled colony's unexpectedly poor developmental record.

Finally, Botswana is a positive outlier in terms of economic and political development, as its residuals for democracy, governance, and GDP are all between one-and-a-half and two standard deviations above the predicted values. Taking a more historical view of economic development, Botswana's per capita GDP in 1970 was one standard deviation below the predicted value, suggesting a remarkable transformation over the thirty-year period.

Table 3.7 Residual scores of Botswana, Guyana, Mauritius, and Sierra Leone

	Democracy, 1972–2000	Governance, 1996–2005	GDP, 2000	Infant mortality, 2000	Education, 1995
Mauritius	1.01	−0.02	0.15	−1.44	−2.15
Sierra Leone	0.15	−0.54	−0.26	64.78	−0.65
Guyana	−1.22	−4.10	−1.25	34.76	−1.68
Botswana	2.57	3.90	0.84	11.65	−0.03
Standard deviation	1.62	2.15	0.56	16.54	1.66

In terms of human development, however, Botswana's residuals are only mediocre. Average societal education in 1995 is almost exactly what the model predicts, and infant mortality rate in 2000 is slightly higher than expected given Botswana's extent of indirect rule. Similar to the economic residuals, the country's residuals for human development hide longer-term change. In 1970, Botswana's average educational attainment was one standard deviation below the predicted value, showing considerable improvement between 1970 and 1995. In terms of health, Botswana's trajectory has followed a bumpy trajectory: its residual for infant mortality rate in 1970 was near zero, by 1990 health improvements allowed infant deaths to fall to one standard deviation below the predicted value, but the country's infant mortality rate rose to nearly 12 deaths per 1,000 infants higher than the predicted value by 2000. Notably, these figures highlight impressive health improvements that occurred during the first few decades of independence but that were largely negated since the mid-1980s by the HIV/AIDS epidemic. Indeed, life expectancy in Botswana in 2005 is estimated to be twenty-eight years lower than it would have been if the AIDS epidemic did not hit (Avert 2007).

Summary

While controlling for several variables and employing multiple models and different sets, the extent of indirect colonial rule is strongly and consistently related to a number of development indicators. Moreover, when the colonial variable is used as the only independent variable, the R^2-values of the different models show that the extent of indirect rule explains between 33 and 68 percent of the variation of economic, human, and political development. All aspects of the statistical analysis therefore provide consistent and powerful evidence in favor of the colonial hypothesis.

The findings lend little support to either the precolonial or the post-colonial hypothesis. Regarding the latter, the models including both colonial and precolonial variables account for between 60 and 82 percent of the variation in per capita GDP, school attainment, and infant mortality in 1970, leaving relatively little to possibly be explained by postcolonial factors. In addition, the variation explained by the customary court variable actually increases between 1970 and 2000, the reverse of what one would expect if postcolonial change was the main cause of uneven development among former British colonies.

As for the precolonial hypothesis, no variable measuring precolonial characteristics is consistently and significantly related to postcolonial development. In fact, the only variable other than the form of colonialism that is significantly related to development in more than one model is the percentage of the population of European origins. This variable, however, is not significantly related in all models and usually loses its significance when the smaller set of former British colonies is used, suggesting that the four large-scale settler colonies drive the relationships. Furthermore, the variable does not simply measure precolonial factors: along with precolonial disease environment and resources, it obviously measures colonially induced population transfers, which potentially shaped developmental processes. The findings therefore provide no concrete evidence that precolonial conditions have reinforced long-term development.

Finally, the statistical analysis tests the direction of causation by investigating the relationship between the form of colonialism and precolonial development. The results show that precolonial development explains relatively little of the variation in the form of colonialism and that precolonial development is positively related to the extent of indirect colonial rule, which in turn is negatively related to postcolonial development. The findings therefore provide evidence that the relationship flows from colonialism to development and support claims that colonialism was a dynamic historical event that transformed developmental trajectories.

All in all, the statistical analysis provides strong and consistent evidence that the different state institutional legacies of British colonialism account for much of the variation in postcolonial development. One cannot, however, view these results as conclusive for at least three reasons. First, cross-national analysis cannot possibly control for all relevant variables, and one therefore can never know if a relationship is spurious. Moreover, data for cross-national analysis—especially historical analyses—are often of questionable quality given high levels of aggregation and imprecise measurements of complex concepts. Finally, statistical analysis has difficulty highlighting causal mechanisms. As a consequence of these problems, more evidence is needed about the determinants of uneven development among former British colonies. Throughout the remainder of this book, I provide comparative-historical evidence as an additional basis of inference.

Mauritius

Direct Rule and Development

4

Mauritius is a tropical island the size of Rhode Island and is located in the Indian Ocean off the east coast of Madagascar. Of the country's 1.2 million inhabitants, 48 percent are Hindus of Indian origin, 27 percent are categorized as "Creoles" and claim African or mixed African descent, 17 percent are Muslims of Indian origin, 3 percent are ethnic Chinese, and 2 percent claim European heritage. None of these groups is indigenous, as the island was uninhabited until Dutch sailors founded a small settlement in 1598, which proved unproductive and was deserted by 1710. Five years later, the French claimed the island and established a more successful settlement in 1722. During French control of the island (1715–1810), hundreds of French men and women came to Mauritius (then known as Ile de France) and created a vibrant economy based on piracy, trade, and plantations, the last of which required the importation of Malagasy and African slaves. During the Napoleonic Wars, the British captured Mauritius and ruled it for the next 158 years (1810–1968). In 1835, much to the chagrin of the French plantation owners, the British Colonial Office outlawed slavery. Yet because labor was still needed for the sugar industry, and because the British colonial government depended on sugar for revenue, hundreds of thousands of indentured workers from

India and elsewhere were brought to the island. Thus, by independence in 1968, Mauritius had passed through the hands of three European powers and had been transformed from an uninhabited island to a land of 700,000 people who originated from three continents, spoke a variety of languages, and practiced four of the world's major religions.

Although recent analyses find that ethnic diversity impedes economic growth, limits democracy, and diminishes state effectiveness (Easterly and Levine 1997; LaPorta, Lopez-de-Silanes, Shleifer, and Vishny 1999), postcolonial Mauritius has experienced broad-based development despite having one of the world's most diverse populations. Indeed, its per capita economic growth rate has averaged 5 percent over the past three decades, average life expectancy has risen to over seventy-three years, literacy is nearly universal, and the country is one of the most democratic in the developing world. Given this developmental success, many refer to it as an "African tiger" or the "Mauritian Miracle" and claim that Mauritius is a remarkable example of third-world development. If one considers the country's direct form of British colonial rule, however, Mauritius' developmentalism is more typical than exceptional. Indeed, as described previously, the case strongly conforms to Chapter 3's statistical findings.

In this chapter, I analyze the determinants of Mauritian development in order to explore mechanisms linking direct colonial rule and development, thereby shedding light on whether or not the relationship between the two is causal. As depicted in Figure 4.1, I find that present Mauritian development levels are the continuation of a long-term trajectory resulting from a conjuncture—or intersection point—of two interrelated historical processes that were both shaped by Mauritius' direct form of colonial rule. The first causal chain involves the creation of an integrated state with a relatively high capacity to act corporately and implement policy throughout its territory. This was made possible by direct rule's dependence on both bureaucratic organization and infrastructural power. The second causal path concerns the development of a society with relatively dense associational ties. This path was set in motion by the colonial state's active regulation of societal relations, as legal and administrative support empowered societal actors to free themselves from dependent relations with the plantation elite and form relatively free villages of peasants throughout the island.

Although a colonial state with relatively high administrative and regulative capacities and a society with relatively dense associational ties were both crucial to Mauritian development, they were not by themselves sufficient for this outcome. Rather, it was also essential that both colonial

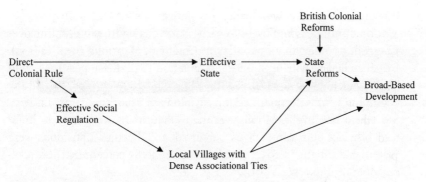

Figure 4.1 Colonial Roots of Mauritius' Developmental Trajectory

officials and societal actors chose to collaborate and pursue similar developmental objectives, which did not occur during the previous 130 years of colonial rule. Yet the combination of a prolonged period of labor unrest and mobilization in the 1930s and 1940s and the more interventionist policy of the British government after World War II transformed both colonial development policy and relations between Mauritian state and society and thereby sparked impressive developmental improvements that have continued over the past half century.

All in all, the case provides evidence that the Mauritian state's capacity to act collectively, penetrate society, and engage society in positive-sum relations helped drive the country's developmental success. The case also shows that relatively high levels of state bureaucratization, infrastructural power, and inclusiveness made possible these characteristics and, in turn, are legacies of direct colonial rule. The case study therefore strongly supports the theoretical framework presented in Chapter 2 and provides qualitative evidence that the statistical relationship between direct rule and development is causal.

The Pre–World War II Colonial Setting: State, Society, and Regime

The Colonial State

Although located off the coast of Africa, the Mauritian colonial state was different from other British colonies in Africa and much more similar to directly ruled colonial states in the Caribbean and Asia. Instead of having a minuscule administration dependent on indigenous strongmen for the control of rural populations, it had a relatively large legal-administrative apparatus with direct and formal control over the entire colony. Under this direct form of colonial rule, the Mauritian state was staffed by over 4,000 nonmilitary employees as early as 1900, a figure representing over 1 percent of the colony's population (Colony of Mauritius 1901: L1–L75). Britain relied heavily on the local population to fill these positions, with Mauritians holding approximately 93 percent of all state positions at the beginning of the twentieth century (Colony of Mauritius 1901: L1–L75). Most held low-level positions, yet many Mauritians were mid- to high-level officials: approximately 65 percent of all officer-level positions were held by Mauritians in 1932, a number rising to 85 percent by 1960 (Colony of Mauritius 1932, 1960).[1]

The colonial administration in Mauritius was centralized both organizationally and geographically. The colonial governor was the Crown's representative in the colony, had great administrative and legislative powers, and was able to dominate politics in colonial Mauritius. The colonial secretary, who served as the chief executive officer under the governor, was in charge of the Secretariat, which was "the central office of the Government and the clearing office for interdepartmental correspondence, the channel of communication between the Governor and the other departments or the general public" (Jeffries 1938: 128). In 1934, the Secretariat employed only twenty-five individuals while coordinating the activities of some twenty departments (Colony of Mauritius 1934). Because of their power, the quality of the colonial administration depended to a great extent on the quality of both the colonial governor and the Secretariat. In addition to being organizationally centralized, the administration was located almost exclusively in Port Louis, the capital city. As one British official complained,

> The administration of Mauritius is over centralized. There is no District Administration, no District Health Service. Generally speaking, magistrates, doctors, teachers, engineers and labour inspectors do not live among the people they administer. . . . The administration is consequently largely out of touch with the people. (British Colonial Office 1943)

Although interaction between rural Mauritians and most colonial departments was rare because of this administrative centralization, the official quoted above recognized that the colonial state's presence was felt by all Mauritians through its regulatory institutions. Indeed, Table 4.1 shows that the state in colonial Mauritius had a much greater capacity to regulate society than in other British colonial states in Africa. For example, the colonial state in Mauritius lacked customary courts and had

Table 4.1 Regulatory institutions: Mauritius, Singapore, and British Africa, 1955

Country	Per capita state revenue (£)	Police officers per 1,000 citizens	Administrative court cases per 1,000 citizens	Customary legal institutions
Mauritius	16.4	2.1	68.5	absent
Singapore	20.0	3.3	62.5	absent
British Africa[a]	4.3	0.7	7.8	present

Sources: Colony of Mauritius 1956; British Colonial Office 1953, 1955b.

[a] This group includes Botswana, Gambia, Ghana, Kenya, Lesotho, Malawi, Nigeria, Sierra Leone, Swaziland, Tanzania, Uganda, and Zambia.

four times the per capita state revenue, three times the police officers per capita, and ten times the administrative court cases per capita. As shown in the table, Mauritian legal-administrative institutions were far more similar to colonial Singapore, another former British colony that experienced direct rule.

During the French colonial period (1715–1810), formal legal and law enforcement institutions were established in Mauritius, both of which were reproduced during British rule (1810–1968). Despite the French legacy, several reforms rationalized the legal institutions during the nineteenth century. For example, while the British retained yet amended the preexisting 1808 French Civil Code, they promulgated the first Mauritian Penal Code in 1838 in order to provide a broad and formal legal framework governing social relations (DeBroglio and Neerunjun 1961: 2–4). Because most of Mauritian civil law continued to be based on preexisting French codes, British officials were often unable to serve as magistrates. Consequently, throughout the period of British colonialism, the Mauritian legal system was usually administered by Mauritians with some French legal training, a situation causing the legal system to be more autonomous from the colonial administration than elsewhere in British Africa, where courts were run by administrative officials (Hailey 1938; Gann and Duignan 1978: 236; Seidman 1978). Because nearly all magistrates were from the Franco-Mauritian community, the legal structure tended to be biased toward—although not dominated by—elite interests (Clifford 1938: 4; Hooper 1938b).

Considering the organization of law and law enforcement, the British centralized the legal structure in 1851 by creating a Supreme Court under the control of a British magistrate who oversaw ten district courts scattered throughout the colony (DeBroglio and Neerunjun 1961: 8). In order to enforce the law, Mauritian courts actively collaborated with the police department, which had approximately fifty stations located in all corners of the island. After the reorganization of the legal institutions in the 1850s, tension between judicial and law enforcement officials arose because of overlapping authority. By 1860, relations between the two were formalized, with the police in charge of their own discipline and administration yet required to follow and execute the legal orders given by magistrates (Paul 1997: 105). Around the same time, the colonial police force and the Port Louis municipal force were merged and placed under a single commissioner, creating a centralized, colony-wide police force for the first time (Paul 1997: 104). Although the head of police was initially a military position, officials decided to make it a civil position in 1889 in order to focus attention on domestic law enforcement and to improve relations between the police and the public (Paul 1997: 111). Finally, the duties and procedures of the police department were formalized in 1897 through the "General Codes and Standing Orders," creating rules that distinguished proper from improper conduct (Paul 1997: 118).

Thus, colony-wide legal and law enforcement institutions were present in Mauritius by the end of the nineteenth century, and both actively enforced the colony's laws as early as the mid-nineteenth century, thereby providing a rule-based framework to guide social relations. Indeed, in 1886, there were nearly 20,000 magistrate court cases (Colony of Mauritius 1887). In per capita terms, this represents 57 court cases per 1,000 Mauritians, a rate equivalent to that in the 1950s and 1960s, suggesting a high level of legal regulation for nearly a century before independence. Moreover, by the 1950s Mauritius had considerably more police officers per capita than Great Britain itself.[2]

The Colonial Society

Like the colonial state, Mauritian society was much more similar to those in the Caribbean than in sub-Saharan Africa. With the backing of the colonial state, Mauritian sugar estates imported and controlled African slaves and Indian workers through coercive power. As subordinate groups gained legal rights and economic resources, however, domination by the Franco-Mauritian plantation elite was curtailed, and Mauritius' formerly captive society was freed to develop more horizontal relations of interdependency.

Mauritian society was predominantly captive as late as the 1830s. Out of 92,000 inhabitants, 66,000 were African slaves, 18,000 were freed slaves of mixed descent, and 8,000 were white Franco-Mauritians

(Benedict 1965: 15). Throughout colonialism, these groups maintained a political and economic hierarchy despite being combined into a common census category ("General Population") after emancipation in 1835, with Franco-Mauritians on top, mixed Creoles emulating the Franco-Mauritian lifestyle in the middle, and the Creole masses at the bottom (Simmons 1976, 1982). After the British abolished slavery, many former slaves left the sugar estates, moving to Port Louis to find employment or establishing small fishing villages along the coast (Simmons 1976). To compensate for this lost labor, the colonial state coordinated the immigration of approximately 1,000 Chinese and 450,000 Indian indentured workers between 1835 and 1920, the overwhelming majority of whom arrived between 1843 and 1865.[3] These workers were initially required to work on sugar plantations for ten years and could then choose to return to their homelands or stay in Mauritius.

Although technically free, indentured workers were very poorly treated, were required by law to fulfill labor contracts signed with estates, and could be jailed if they were unable to prove employment (Carter 1995; Allen 1999). While not disregarding these hardships, the working conditions of Indians began to improve during the last quarter of the nineteenth century. By the late 1870s, nearly all labor contracts were for a year or less, showing that plantations had lost their ability to control workers, who now had the power to negotiate contracts (Allen 1999: 60). This change was influenced by a labor shortage, which strengthened the hand of workers vis-à-vis their employers. In addition, more active government monitoring of the living and working conditions of plantation laborers helped improve their livelihoods. For example, the government commissioned a report to investigate the treatment of Indian workers in 1872; the report prompted the government to permanently monitor the living and working conditions on the plantations (Carter 1995: 30). Legal support also helped improve working conditions. By the mid-nineteenth century, Indo-Mauritian laborers were able to access the legal system to protect their interests despite the political and economic clout of the Franco-Mauritian estates. Indeed, not only did over 10 percent of Indian workers file legal charges against their employers between 1860 and 1869, but nearly 71 percent of such cases resulted in successful convictions (Allen 1999: 69).

Notably, British plantation colonies in the Caribbean also had states that supported workers instead of simply pursuing the interests of the plantation elite. Mauritius is different from its Caribbean counterparts, however, in that colonial support occurred earlier. Stinchcombe (1995) finds that Britain's Caribbean colonies supported the plantation elite throughout the nineteenth century; and Rueschemeyer, Stephens, and Stephens (1992) claim that the British state supported workers in the Caribbean colonies only after World War II. One factor highlighted by Stinchcombe that helps account for earlier legal support in Mauritius is elite connections: unlike planters in the Caribbean, Mauritian planters were French instead of British and lacked strong political and economic ties to Great Britain. In addition, Mauritius' proximity to India and its large Indian population caused Gandhi and others to visit Mauritius and press colonial officials to protect Indian workers.

The growing strength of plantation workers promoted another dramatic transformation in Mauritian society: sugar estates sold off large parts of their land to Indo-Mauritians in a process known as *le grand morcellement*, or great division. Because of a global increase in sugar production in the mid-1800s, Mauritian sugar estates needed to cut costs and increase efficiency to remain profitable. Colonial support of worker rights obstructed initial attempts to maintain profits simply by squeezing labor. Consequently, the estates attempted to increase efficiency through the modernization of production, which in turn required large amounts of capital (Allen 1999). Because the Franco-Mauritian estate owners lacked access to capital in Europe or elsewhere, they were forced to finance modernization efforts locally through the sale of their least productive lands to local inhabitants (Allen 1999). Because the Indo-Mauritian population participated in the island's production of sugar, and because higher plantation wages allowed many frugal families to amass the capital needed to buy land, nearly all land sales involved Indo-Mauritians. Statistics collected by the colonial censuses capture this change in land distribution, with the number of acres of sugarcane controlled by Indo-Mauritians jumping from virtually nothing in the 1860s to 48,000 in 1910 and 86,000 in 1921 (Walter 1926). Thus, by the 1920s, there were approximately 15,000 Indian-owned farms, and these farms controlled 46 percent of the island's total area under sugarcane cultivation (Colony of Mauritius 1921).

With the sale of plantation land to former laborers, a redistribution of the rural population also occurred. Most notably, the number of workers living on the sugar estates decreased from 145,000 in 1881 to 73,000 in 1921, and hundreds of villages of small landowners emerged throughout the island (Walter 1926). Given the small size of their land, many Indo-Mauritian landholders continued to work for estates at least part-time.[4] Yet by living in communities outside the reach of the estates, the inhabitants of the villages were able to participate in active community life and organize many community associations.

Many of these associations were formed by Indian immigrants who had participated in similar associations back in India (Hollup 1994). One example was the *baitka*, a Hindu village organization adapted from caste-based associations that held community meetings, educational classes, religious ceremonies, and entertainment, "one, two, or even ten" of which were located in every rural village (Roy 1960: 353). Along with *baitkas*, hundreds of Indian cultural and mutual aid societies existed, nearly 300 of which were registered with the colonial government in 1961 as having corporately held and managed assets (Colony of Mauritius 1963). A notable example of these rural Indo-Mauritian associations was the Arya Samaj, an organization founded in India in 1875 that merged religious reform with social welfare activism. In 1952, the 116 Arya Samaj branches had 5,000 dues-paying members as well as 30,000 followers regularly attending meetings (Mayput 1993: 38; Mauritius Legislative Council 1956c: 5–7).

Cooperative credit societies were another type of local association commonly found in Mauritian villages. In 1913 the colonial state initiated cooperative credit societies to provide small farmers with low-interest loans needed to increase the productivity of their land. By the end of the year, fifteen societies were formed, and by 1958 there were nearly 350 cooperative societies organized throughout the island with 35,000 members (Hooper 1938a: 149; Colony of Mauritius 1959a).

In summary, although Mauritian society was among the most hierarchic and unequal in the world in the early 1800s, these conditions weakened over a short period of time because of growing colonial support of the working classes. Such support allowed subordinate actors to purchase land, form small villages of landowners, and organize multiple associations. The case therefore vividly demonstrates how state support allowed individuals to free themselves from hierarchic relations of dependency and pursue their individual well-being. Still, colonial Mauritius remained far from egalitarian, as the planters retained wealth and power and held a privileged position within the colonial regime.

The Colonial Regime

Although the colonial state provided resources protecting basic individual rights for all ethnic groups by the early twentieth century, such legal regulation was not perfect and did not empower individuals to influence state policy. And while staffed primarily by local Mauritians, the administration was personally ruled by the colonial governor, who possessed both executive and legislative authority. Indeed, as in nearly all British colonies, the colonial regime had only limited relations with the local population, and those that did exist were almost completely limited to the Franco-Mauritian elite.

In 1831, the British established their first quasi-constitutional regime on Mauritius, with a colonial governor and his executive council (which included the chief of justice, the commissary of justice, the chief secretary of government, and the collector of customs) controlling the executive branch of the island. While the governor received directives from London, such directives were few. Moreover, he and the executive council collaborated actively and together had considerable discretionary authority. The Council of Government was the official legislative branch of the colony and consisted of the governor, the executive council, and several members of the Franco-Mauritian community.[5] The council could propose laws, yet the governor had the final authority to pass them.

Local governance was no less restrictive. The island was divided up into districts that were eventually subject to three different forms of rule: Municipal Council rule in Port Louis (established in 1849), Town Council rule in the four townships (established between 1889 and 1895), and Branch Road Boards in rural areas (established in 1900). The Municipal Council consisted of eighteen members elected under the same terms as the Council of Government (i.e., high property and financial qualifications until reforms in 1956 granted universal suffrage), with the mayor and deputy mayor appointed by the governor (Nepal 1982: 2). Its duties included building and maintaining roads and bridges, disease prevention, establishing and regulating markets, relief of the poor, providing water, maintaining a police force (until 1860), and fire prevention (Dukhira 1994: 132; Nepal 1982: 5). Following an outbreak of malaria in Port Louis in the 1860s, many wealthy residents moved to the Plains Wilhems region because the malaria-carrying mosquitoes could not live in the higher elevations (Dukhira 1994: 133). As a result of this new population distribution, four Town Councils with duties similar to those of the Municipal Council were established by 1895, each of which consisted of six commissioners appointed by the governor.[6]

Despite the creation of Town and Municipal Councils, rural parts of the island had no local government whatsoever until Ordinance no. 9 of 1900 established district boards known as Branch Road Boards to build and maintain transportation routes. These boards consisted of elected members of the Council of Government, the director of public works, government medical officers from each district, and three to seven individuals nominated annually by the governor (Nepal 1982: 8). The boards had limited scope, proved ineffectual, and were eventually abandoned in 1939 (Nepal 1984: 170). Consequently, throughout most of the British colonial period, local government was almost completely absent in rural areas.

Given voting restrictions and their economic prowess, Franco-Mauritians and elite Creoles filled nearly all elected and appointed positions within the government prior to World War II, and they therefore had very advantaged positions to protect and pursue their interests. In addition, the Franco-Mauritian elite were able to shape state policy through active economic relations in the Chamber of Agriculture, which served as an unofficial government department until the Department of Agriculture was organized in 1913. Even after the organization of the Department of Agriculture, the chamber was able to shape colonial policy because of the state's dependence on sugar revenue. "The Chamber was in many ways," writes Storey (1995), "the shadow government of Mauritius, and it usually succeeded in badgering the colonial state into doing its bidding, except on several occasions when its plans encountered opposition from the Colonial Office in London" (166). Franco-Mauritians could therefore influence colonial policy, while subordinate groups—particularly in rural areas—were unable to press their interests upon the colonial administration.

Postwar State Reform and Development

Although never static, state, society, and regime all transformed rapidly after World War II. This section focuses on the state, which maintained its basic structure but transformed in important ways after the war: its size expanded dramatically, and it became more infrastructurally powerful and more inclusive. With these changes and a growing concern about the well-being of colonial subjects, impressive developmental improvements occurred during the waning years of British rule.

The Expansion and Transformation of the Colonial State

Subordinate groups in urban areas (primarily Creoles and mixed Creoles) began to challenge the Franco-Mauritian elite by demanding access to the state in the early 1900s and again in the mid-1930s. Although these political movements failed to achieve mass political incorporation, the mobilization of Indo-Mauritian agricultural laborers and small landholders in the 1930s and 1940s created a more popular labor movement that cooperated with and ultimately came to dominate the urban-based Mauritian Labour Party (MLP). Through a combination of petition drives, sit-ins, mass marches, strikes, attacks on property, and violence, the agricultural labor movements of 1937, 1938, and 1943 successfully pressured the colonial government to expand subordinate group access to the government.

The proximate causes of the agricultural labor unrest were economic hardship faced by sugar workers and small planters because of the global depression, a decrease in the price paid for low-grade sugarcane without the prior notification of small planters, and the inability of small planters to sell their cane directly to preferred mills (Hooper 1938a: 3–4; Moody 1945: 24–32; Allgoo 1985: 15; Storey 1995). The political exclusion of rural people was also an important determinant of the disturbances and magnified the impact of economic problems. As noted above, the colony's governmental structure effectively imposed barriers between the state and subordinate groups in rural areas. Consequently, small farmers and sugar workers were unable to access the government, and protest was the only available means for them to express their interests. The dense and active associational networks within Mauritian villages, in turn, provided them with the mobilizational capacity needed to do just that.

Nevertheless, the labor movement was not the sole determinant of the reforms, since it did not independently force the colonial state to commence sweeping changes. Although showing the limits of British colonial domination and detrimentally affecting state revenue by bringing sugar production to a halt, violence was only periodic, and the disturbances were not sustainable once the colonial state took coercive measures (Hooper 1938a; Moody 1945; Allgoo 1985). An additional and likely more important cause of colonial state reforms was a change in British colonial policy during the 1940s in favor of direct intervention and social welfare development (Goldsworthy 1971; Gupta 1975; Seidman 1978: 109; Howe 1993). With this change, colonial officials in Mauritius shifted their focus from the maintenance of law and order to human well-being and began to implement reforms preparing the colony for self-rule.

The resulting political reforms increased the size and composition of the Mauritian colonial state. Prior to World War II, Mauritius already had an enormous colonial state by African standards. Yet its administrative apparatus was largely limited to urban areas, leaving rural areas isolated and under the sole supervision of the police and courts. Following the war, the colonial state began to grow rapidly. Indeed, between 1947 and 1967 the number of nonmilitary state employees increased sevenfold from 4,000 to 28,000, the number of official-level positions increased nearly fivefold (from 300 in 1950 to 1,300 in 1967), and Mauritians increasingly held high-level positions within the colonial state (Colony of Mauritius

1948b, 1950b, 1967b, 1968a). This expansion, in turn, increased state infrastructural power and inclusiveness. In particular, the creation or restructuring of three main organizations increased the state's territorial presence and allowed societal actors to participate in policy making and implementation: district administration and local councils, the Legislative Assembly, and the Department of Labour.

The government established district administration and local councils throughout rural areas after 1947 in an attempt to expand the state's administrative presence in rural areas and develop "an active, democratically healthy citizenship at the base of the political and civic institutions of the island" (Mauritius Legislative Council 1956a: 2). Four district offices were founded after World War II, and each was headed by a civil commissioner, who acted as the "principle administrative and executive officer of Government in their districts" (Colony of Mauritius 1954c: 4). Besides overseeing the daily administrative duties within the district, the commissioner also supervised, guided, and collaborated with the newly created village and district councils to implement colonial policy locally, and by the early 1950s there were nearly 100 village councils (Nepal 1982: 29). Village councils were made up of elected local representatives and government officials and were empowered to establish and maintain collective and public goods needed for the well-being of the villagers.[7] District councils, in turn, were composed both of select members from village councils within the district and of government officials.

In addition to reforming government at the local level, colonial officials transformed and renamed the Council of Government in 1947. Twelve members were now appointed by the governor to the new Legislative Assembly, the number of elected representatives increased to nineteen, and property and income suffrage requirements were removed. In 1957, a ministerial system was established in which elected members served as the ministers of colonial departments. Since ministers now headed departments and had ties to one another as well as the colonial governor, the creation of ministries helped to decentralize authority within the state apparatus and thereby decreased the Secretariat's control of information flows. A year later, the government increased the number of elected representatives to forty and granted universal adult suffrage. The first Mauritian prime minister ascended to power in 1961, a full seven years before Mauritian independence (Dukhira 1994).

The creation of the Department of Labour was an additional institutional transformation that increased both state infrastructural power and inclusiveness. The government created the department after the

1937 disturbances to increase ties between the government and unions and engage the latter in state-led mediation with business. These efforts were unsuccessful, and the Moody Report (1945) noted that the failure of unions to organize and represent the interests of laborers and the inability of the industrial courts to adequately support the claims of workers were proximate causes of the 1938 and 1943 disturbances. Consequently, the colonial government expanded the Department of Labour, hired a British labor organizer to actively organize unions, and restructured the rules of the industrial courts to strengthen the position of labor (Allgoo 1985: 39; Oodiah 1988: 8; Bhagirutty 1988: 23).

These expansionary reforms were implemented with relative ease, and several factors promoted their success. First, although transforming the state, the reforms did not radically change the structure of state legal-administrative institutions. Instead, they built on and filled in the gaps of the preexisting state institutions and therefore did not require difficult structural reforms.

Similarly, the presence of a state with relatively high legal-administrative capacities facilitated the reforms. For example, state expansion obviously required increased state revenue, and the Mauritian state already had an efficient system of revenue extraction before the postwar reforms, collecting 17 percent of the colony's GNP in 1947 (Colony of Mauritius 1948b). By implementing corporate and personal income taxes in 1950, the state's revenue rose to over 25 percent of GNP by 1967 (Colony of Mauritius 1968b). In addition to increased revenue, state building required the capacity to organize a larger and more geographically dispersed state apparatus. As a colonial commissioner analyzing the organization of the state noted, the expansion of the colonial state caused considerable strain (Meacock 1955: 7). Colonial officials did not ignore these problems, however, and the colonial state demonstrated the capacity to successfully manage state expansion. For instance, between the end of World War II and Mauritian independence, six special colonial commissions monitored the progress of the postwar administrative expansion.[8] Furthermore, the permanent Public Service Commission was established in 1953 to hire, promote, discipline, and provide examinations for official-level government jobs in an attempt to institutionalize meritocratic practices (Weir 1955: 4).[9] Although the commission was an organization monitoring officials in all departments, some individual departments established their own internal bodies to improve bureaucratic practices among the rank and file. For example, the Department of the Police used meritocratic methods for hiring its employees and supervised its officers to maintain discipline;

1,600 police officers were disciplined between 1946 and 1952, an average of 30 percent of the police force per year (Colony of Mauritius 1947–53). Finally, the colonial state implemented a training program in order for the growing number of state officials to have the skills needed for high- and mid-level positions.[10]

Cooperative relations between the British officials and the Mauritian Labour Party (MLP) are a third factor that facilitated state building in late-colonial Mauritius. Prior to the post–World War II constitutional reforms, the Franco-Mauritians controlled nearly all of the civilian positions within the Council of Government, something they proudly expressed to both state officials and subordinate groups by referring to themselves as the "Oligarchs." With the expansion of suffrage, however, the MLP became the dominant political party, controlling thirteen of the nineteen elected seats to the council in 1948 while the Oligarchs possessed only one. Fearing any dramatic transfer of power and influence, all of the governor's appointees to the council were conservatives who openly protected the interests of the French and Creole elites. Because of the obvious bias, relations between the MLP and the colonial officials soured. As Simmons (1982) notes, "The nominations destroyed whatever goodwill had been built up during the constitutional negotiations. The elected members, convinced now that the government did not want to cooperate with them, began to oppose it at every turn" (110–11). Yet because of the prolabor and prorural policies of the state—both of which were key policy positions of the MLP—tension neither degenerated into open conflict nor proved an effective obstacle to the decentralizing and human welfare reforms.

With the arrival of a new governor in 1954 and the creation of a ministerial system of departmental administration in 1957, relations between MLP representatives and colonial officials improved markedly. The governor and his administration soon realized that the MLP—which was supported by small and mid-sized landowners—was the most moderate party in the colony. As a colonial official remarked, "we must recognise the need to play along with the moderate politicians, who at present have most of the political power, and who in spite of belonging to what is called the Labour Party are politically in the center, with an irresponsible opposition to the right and to the left" (Robertson 1959). In response to this change, the MLP soon warmed to colonial officials and began collaborating with them. Assisted by this more active collaboration between the state and the MLP, the governor noted that an "administrative revolution" occurred in which power was transferred to local politicians while politicians and state officials continued to respect one another's interests (Scott 1959: 1). He therefore claimed that "the path was cleared for an attack on the problems of Mauritius itself" (2).

Besides improved relations at the upper echelon of the state, state-society relations in the trenches expanded and also promoted successful reforms. With the extension of the state into all corners of the colony, the points of individual access to the state increased. Consequently, broad segments of society participated in and helped build local institutions. The creation of district and village councils in the late 1940s and early 1950s is a telling example of state-capacity building through positive-sum relations between state and society. Indeed, the state initiated the construction of village councils, provided limited revenue, and supervised their activities; but the village councils were built and run through local participation (Mauritius Legislative Council 1951a, 1951b). Without the financial support, technical guidance, and long-term coordination provided by the state, the day-to-day functioning of the village councils would have been impossible and the local population would have been excluded from local governance (Scott 1955). While recognizing the importance of the colonial administration, very few state officials participated in the actual management of village councils,[11] something that was performed by local actors and helped shape state policy to fit local circumstances. Preexisting associational structures facilitated local participation in village councils. For instance, local associations made villagers more amenable to participation within village councils. As one political historian notes, village councils "developed somewhat quickly through the tremendous spadework that has been done for decades by trade unions, cooperative societies, and the religious and cultural organizations" (Roy 1960: 352). In addition, *baitkas* and other village associations provided organizational resources that state officials harnessed to construct village councils with preexisting ties to local communities (Benedict 1965: 45–46).

Collaborative relations between state and societal actors also facilitated the state's effort to organize labor unions. As noted previously, the administration believed that the best way to prevent future disturbances was to organize labor and grant labor representatives access to state decision-making processes. Unions, however, were poorly organized and represented only a fraction of the laborers. To overcome this difficulty, the British sent a union organizer, Kenneth Baker, to Mauritius in 1946. With his assistance, the number of union members jumped from 13,500 in 1947 to 48,500 in 1968, and the percentage of agricultural laborers jumped from 30 percent to 70 percent of total union members over the same period (Colony of Mauritius 1947, 1964a, 1964b). Such rapid growth was possible because Baker interacted with and educated agricultural workers through local *baitkas*. "Rather than set up a separate organization to provide education," writes Simmons (1982), "Baker hoped to use the *baitkas*. . . . Baker had quickly recognized the importance of these institutions and the potential network they offered, and was the first colonial officer in Mauritius to try to work through rather than around them" (83). With the organization of labor, in turn, the colonial state was able to engage both labor and capital in state-led mediation to limit the number of strikes and to augment the effectiveness of the Labour Courts. Demonstrating this success, between 1947 and 1967 there were 5.5 strikes per year, while the yearly average of labor disputes settled through state institutional channels was nearly 3,000 (Colony of Mauritius 1948–59, 1962–68).

The State and Development during Late Colonialism

With the refocusing of political priorities on the well-being of Mauritians and the expansion of the state, state-led development was now possible. As shown in Table 4.2, impressive developmental improvements occurred during the final decades of colonial rule. Over a quarter century, the infant mortality rate fell by 59 percent, and the overall death rate declined by 67 percent, school attendance quadrupled, and the number of cases of poverty assistance grew by leaps and bounds. Notably, the state was the most important determinant of these improvements, both orchestrating development policy and engaging societal actors in order to implement policy throughout the colony.

With the postwar reforms, the administration expanded to cover the entire island. District administration was constructed, colonial departments were decentralized, local councils were created, and members of all of them interacted with one another. Each district's civil commissioner supervised and therefore interacted regularly with village council and district council members. Moreover, because several department officials either shared the district administration's office or had their own offices in close proximity, the district administration had contact with officials from other departments.[12] Thus, after the reforms, the local administration in colonial Mauritius consisted of dense interlocking networks of officials that stretched into all communities.

This growing administrative presence in rural areas, in turn, allowed state officials to direct colony-wide development campaigns. In order to

Table 4.2 Social welfare development in Mauritius, 1935–1967

Infant mortality rate (per 1,000)	Death rate (per 1,000)	School attendance	Social security cases assisted
1935–40: 153.3	1936–45: 28.3	1938: 42,000	1947: 7,284
1950–59: 75.4	1946–50: 20.8	1947: 51,000	1952: 22,082
1960–67: 63.3	1951–58: 14.0	1957: 115,000	1959: 48,815
	1960–67: 9.3	1967: 179,000	1967: 121,874

Sources: Colony of Mauritius 1939, 1951–68, 1955, 1959a, 1968a; Koenig 1931; Mauritius Economic Commission 1948; Mauritius Legislative Council 1956b; Titmuss 1968.

eradicate malaria, for example, the administration drained swamps, ran educational campaigns, and sprayed insecticides. These tasks needed to occur throughout the colony to be successful, and they succeeded because of the size and reach of the state. Similarly, the state expanded the colony's educational system by building and running schools in all corners of the colony, allowing the number of pupils to increase by 250 percent between 1947 and 1967.

Besides state administrative expansion, relations between state and societal actors also transformed through the establishment of multiple and active ties between local political institutions and broad segments of the population. Collaborative relations, in turn, made possible developmental improvements by expanding the organizational capacity of the state. Specifically, it made possible the simultaneous exploitation of the state's centralized coordination, resources, and technical skill and the adaptiveness, local knowledge, low cost, and active participation of local associations (Lange 2003a, 2005b).

Local communities, for instance, demanded and actively participated in the expansion of the island's educational system. Village councils opened and managed their own schools with assistance from government. In addition, Mauritian society was able to participate in educational expansion locally through nearly a hundred educational associations and nationally through ten educational committees that linked local associations to the state. While the associations helped build and staff schools, the committees represented the interests of voluntary groups and met regularly with the director of education and other top officials to advise and assist state educational policy (Government of Mauritius 1969: 2; Colony of Mauritius 1954a: 4).

Active collaboration also facilitated improvements in societal health. The colonial state opened thirty-two child and maternal welfare centers in rural areas between 1950 and 1967, and these centers were modeled after the seven urban welfare centers founded by the Maternity and Child Welfare Society in 1925 (Titmuss 1968: 166). Moreover, both publicly and privately run maternal welfare centers had active relations with several local associations that assisted their staffing, finance, and management (Colony of Mauritius 1955). Health improvements were also made possible by societal participation in state-led efforts to control infectious diseases. Village councils worked with the state to construct irrigation systems, canalize rivers, drain marshes, and apply insecticide to the internal surfaces of buildings in efforts to reduce water- and insect-borne diseases (Mauritius Legislative Council 1956b; Reddi 2005).[13] Through these programs and the expansion of medical facilities, the number of yearly deaths caused by malaria decreased from 3,534 in 1945—representing 23 percent of all deaths—to 0 by 1956, while the number of deaths ascribed to infectious and parasitic diseases decreased steadily from 4,052 in 1948 to only 187 by 1967 (Colony of Mauritius 1967a).

Mauritian agricultural cooperative credit societies provide a third example of development via state-society synergy. The colonial state initiated co-ops during the early twentieth century in order to increase the amount of capital available to small farmers. The legislation left farmers to organize and run societies locally but committed the state to assist co-op management and to provide an initial capital advance. With the assistance of co-ops, the percentage of sugarcane cultivated by small farmers increased by two-thirds between 1912 and 1959 (from 27 to 45 percent of the colony's total production), accounting for much of the 170 percent increase in sugar production during the same period (Colony of Mauritius 1912, 1959b). Moreover, the success of co-ops helped finance the Mauritian Cooperative Central Bank, which was founded by the colonial state in 1948 through the pooling of co-op profits. With capital reserves equivalent to over 3 percent of Mauritian GNP in 1966 (Colony of Mauritius 1967b), the bank provided a source of large loans at low interest rates, something further increasing the resources of Mauritian farmers. Thus, as one official analyzing small farmers in Mauritius remarked, co-ops helped create a vibrant credit market: "The system of taking credit permeates every sphere of activity within the sugar organisation in Mauritius and indeed most spheres of activity outside the industry. . . . Without credit all activities in the island would be frozen" (Ridley 1941: 6).

Finally, local associations collaborated with the state to provide welfare programs. For example, village council representatives sat on poor law boards and were in charge of distributing funds to needy village members

Table 4.3 Number and membership of Mauritian associations, 1950–1964

	Co-ops		Labor/employer's unions		State-registered associations		Total	
Year	Orgs.	Members	Orgs.	Members	Orgs.	Members	Orgs.	Members
1950	220	15,387	25	18,207	39	31,978	284	65,572
1954	290	26,421	32	16,342	262	45,461	584	88,224
1959	342	33,514	56	27,540	346	57,261	744	118,315
1964	322	33,070	80	47,304	569	78,535	971	158,909

Sources: Colony of Mauritius 1951, 1957, 1962, 1965.

(Yeldman 1948: 11). Moreover, as noted in *The Annual Report of the Ministry of Labour and Social Security* in 1964,

> Assistance Officers work in close collaboration with voluntary organisations
> such as the British Red Cross, Saint Vincent de Paul, the Maternity and Child
> Welfare Society, the Child Care Society, etc., which often recommend to them
> deserving cases which the members of these organisations come across in
> the course of their visits. The Assistance Officers in their turn refer to these
> voluntary organisations cases of deserving families needing some material
> comforts or medical assistance for which the Public Assistance scale does not
> provide. (Colony of Mauritius 1964a: 7)

Notably, the state assisted over 100,000 cases in 1964 despite the fact that
the Social Welfare Division of the Ministry of Labour and Social Security employed only ten administrative officers, suggesting that the state's
capacity to provide resources to the poor depended overwhelmingly on
the colony's 200 beneficent and mutual aid associations (Government of
Mauritius 1969: 2; Colony of Mauritius 1964a, 1967b).

These examples provide evidence that inclusiveness improved the
developmental capacity of the Mauritian state during late colonialism. At
the same time, societal associations also benefited from greater access to
state resources and the administration's superior ability to plan and implement colony-wide programs. As a consequence, there was a dramatic
increase in the number and membership of cooperative credit societies,
labor and employer's unions, and other associations with corporately held
assets between 1950 and 1964 (see Table 4.3).[14] In the case of Mauritius,
the expansion of the state did not cause the contraction of civil society but
instead strengthened it.

"The Mauritian Miracle": The Continuation of a Developmental Trajectory

Several analyses claim that postcolonial Mauritius has been a remarkable case of broad-based development and that this success was made possible by an effective postcolonial state (Brautigam 1997, 2004; Carroll and Carroll 1999; Dommen and Dommen 1997; Goldsmith 1999; Meisenhelder 1997; Nath 2001). Meisenhelder (1997), for example, finds that development in postcolonial Mauritius "depended on the decisions and resources of a capable and relatively autonomous state bureaucracy, a 'developmental state'" (288). Moreover, Brautigam (1997, 2004) and Carroll and Carroll (1999) acknowledge that the Mauritian developmental state benefited from high levels of state inclusiveness. The resemblance between recent descriptions of state-led development and state-led development during late colonialism is striking and does not appear to be coincidental. Indeed, postcolonial development clearly follows a trajectory begun during colonialism, and this trajectory was enforced by a relatively effective state that resembles and continues many of the policies of its colonial predecessor.

The Mauritian state's effective economic management provides an insightful example of state-led development during the postcolonial period and helps highlight how these activities began during late colonialism but continued after independence. In fact, it was the continuation of these activities over several decades during both the colonial and postcolonial periods that made possible Mauritius' economic expansion. Until World War II, colonial economic policy was focused squarely on sugar production, which accounted for 93 percent of all exports at independence. In 1961, Nobel laureate in economics J. E. Meade wrote a critical report claiming that an overreliance on sugar combined with rapid population growth placed Mauritius on the path for a fast-approaching Malthusian disaster (Meade 1961). Not a good outlook for a country about to gain its independence. Fortunately, his apocalyptic predictions were avoided by a reduction in fertility rates and rapid economic diversification and growth, and the state played an important role in both.

Efforts to lower fertility rates began even before the Meade Report, with the founding of the Mauritius Family Planning Association in 1957. The association was founded in response to unprecedented population growth caused by aforementioned health improvements. While the average annual population growth rate was quite low before World War II, it ballooned to 2.3 percent between 1944 and 1952 and 3.1 percent between 1953 and 1962 (Pochun 2001: 260). Because of strong government promotion of family planning, higher female educational attainment after World War II, and increased economic opportunities for women outside of the home during the 1970s and 1980s, marriage and total fertility rates declined dramatically: between 1952 and 1963, the marriage rate of Mauritian women aged fifteen to nineteen declined from 40 percent to 12 percent, and the total fertility declined from 5.9 to 3.4; this continued to fall to only 2.2 by 1983 (Pochun 2001: 261, 264, 265).

While government efforts to reduce fertility began in the 1950s and produced results after a decade or two, its attempts to diversify the economy began in the early 1960s and started paying off by the early 1980s. In his report, Meade (1961) recognized that the sugar industry could provide only a fraction of the jobs needed for the colony's growing population and that fluctuations in the price of sugar negatively affected all aspects of the economy. He therefore recommended both import-substitution industrialization (ISI) and export-oriented industrialization (EOI) strategies of economic development. Until 1970, government industrialization policy was very limited in size, focused on ISI, and experienced very limited success given the country's tiny domestic market. In that year, however, state bureaucrats designed and guided an effort to promote industrialization through exports.

Mauritian state attempts to increase local manufacturing copied export-oriented policy from East Asia through the Export Processing Zone Act (EPZ), which encouraged the manufacturing of goods for export through state subsidies and tax benefits. By 1977, nearly 100 firms employing a total of 20,000 people had been established under the auspices of the act, numbers that rose to 508 firms employing some 90,000 people by 1999 (Durbarry 2001: 110, 114). The initial success of EOI came from the advantages provided by the act as well as new legislation preventing Mauritian capital from being invested abroad. The high profits of the domestic sugar industry between 1970 and 1975 therefore provided a fortuitous initial impetus to local investment in manufacturing. By the 1980s and 1990s, foreigners began to invest in EPZ firms due to low risks to investment and Mauritius' advantaged access to Western markets, giving the Mauritian economy a mix of both foreign and domestic firms.

Although it is frequently praised as an economic success, Mauritius' path to economic expansion was not without difficulties. During the late 1970s and early 1980s, the Mauritian economy was still heavily dependent on sugar and suffered when its price fell precipitously, causing high levels of unemployment, inflation, government debt, and trade deficits. In order to adjust for these macroeconomic problems, the government turned to the IMF and World Bank, who recommended unpopular austerity measures. The structural adjustment programs (SAPs) ultimately succeeded, making Mauritius a poster child of the World Bank and IMF (Gulhati and Nallari 1990). Such success was not caused simply by the guidance of international financial institutions. Rather, it was made possible by a relatively effective state.

First, and most importantly, the Mauritian state effectively implemented the reforms over three successive governments (Gulhati and Nallari 1990). Second, the state-led EOI efforts had begun to materialize before the SAPs, which allowed the economy to take off once it had stabilized (Meisenhelder 1997: 291). Finally, the SAPs were unpopular, yet the government implemented them without violent opposition because the state continued to have institutionalized channels of consultation with a wide spectrum of economic and civil-societal associations. Specifically, inclusiveness helped legitimize the policies by allowing state officials to explain the purpose and necessity of the reforms (Brautigam 1997, 2004; Carroll and Carroll 1999, 2000). In addition, high levels of inclusiveness forced the government to respect social interests, causing it to successfully oppose several IMF and World Bank directives and insist that the reforms be based on Mauritius' particular needs (Gulhati and Nallari 1990: 39).

Since the late 1980s, the government has attempted to diversify the Mauritian economy even further. For one thing, it has pursued a strategy of making Mauritius a regional banking power, and finance grew by nearly 20 percent annually between 1988 and 1996 (Lamusse 2001: 33). Currently, the government is focusing its effort on making Mauritius a global IT hub by building a cyber city and implementing policy to attract foreign and local investment in the IT industry (Ackbarally 2002). In so doing, it is attempting to exploit the country's relatively high levels of human capital, stability, ties to India and China, and fluency in both French and English. Despite the initial success of the cyber city and its subsequent expansion, this attempt to promote IT development is a very risky move. Only the future can tell whether this new round of state-led economic expansion is as successful as the first. Given past success and the continued effectiveness of the Mauritian state, there are at least two reasons to be optimistic.

Conclusion

In this chapter, I provide evidence that the state has been an influential force behind Mauritius' impressive development. I describe how the state protected worker rights and thereby prevented the Franco-Mauritian elite from completely and arbitrarily dominating subordinate groups. The state also promoted development by providing clean water, schools, and other collective and public goods and successfully directing and diversifying the national economy. In addition, the state collaborated with societal actors in order to collectively promote national development. Finally, I show that relatively high levels of bureaucracy, infrastructural power, and inclusiveness made possible this developmental state. While bureaucracy and infrastructural power endowed the state with the capacity to act corporately and implement policy throughout the country, inclusiveness allowed the state to engage societal actors in positive-sum relations. Notably, I trace the origins of this developmental state and find that it is rooted in direct colonial rule. In this way, the qualitative analysis of Mauritius highlights mechanisms linking direct colonial rule to postcolonial development and provides evidence that the relationship between the two is causal.

The case does not show that the colonial state always promoted development, however. Instead, its overall developmental capacity was not exploited until after World War II, when societal pressure and a change in colonial policy forced the state to focus on improving the well-being of Mauritians. Mauritius therefore shows that broad-based development requires a developmental will—not just a developmental capacity—and that colonial officials often lacked such a will.

I also find that the developmental capacity of the Mauritian state was not constant over time. Throughout most of the colonial period, for instance, the infrastructural reach of the administration was largely confined to urban areas, and state inclusiveness was limited to relations between state officials and local elites. After World War II, however, major reforms were implemented that reinforced and intensified the state's direct form. Its larger size, growing presence at the grassroots level, and engagement of broader segments of society all proved vital to subsequent state-led development.

Sierra Leone

Indirect Rule and Despotism

5

After revolting, floating around the Atlantic for months on the brink of starvation, and winning a hard-fought battle in the United States Supreme Court, the slaves aboard the *Amistad* were brought to the Sierra Leone Colony in 1842 to begin new and free lives. Although the *Amistad* freedom fighters undoubtedly rejoiced upon their return to Africa, today Sierra Leone is not a country many people wish to visit, let alone live in. Throughout the 1990s, the country experienced a bloody and ruthless civil war. The war displaced over one-third of the population; killed tens of thousands of men, women, and children; and brutalized the population through systematic murder, mutilation, rape, and kidnapping. Although the war ended in 2001, the country is still suffering from wartime atrocities and remains a developmental basket case.

Not surprisingly, Sierra Leone has one of the lowest Human Development Index scores in the world today: according to the United Nations' *Human Development Report* (2003), Sierra Leone has the world's highest infant mortality rate, the world's shortest life expectancy, and the world's lowest per capita GDP. Table 5.1 shows that the country's social development was much lower than that of Mauritius and even other former British colonies in Africa before the conflict began. Moreover, as highlighted in Table 5.2,

Table 5.1 Development levels of Sierra Leone, Mauritius, and British Africa, 1990s

Country	Average annual per capita GDP growth, 1975–98 (%)	Life expectancy, 1987 (years)	Under-5 mortality, 1990 (deaths per 1,000)	Primary enrollment rate, 1990 (%)	Secondary enrollment rate, 1990 (%)
Sierra Leone	−3.2	37	189	50	17
Mauritius	4.3	69	20	109	53
Remainder of British Africa[a]	0.9	48	89	88	26

Source: World Bank 2002.

Table 5.2 Development levels of Sierra Leone, Mauritius, and British Africa, 1960s

Country	GNP per capita, 1960 (1995$)	Life expectancy, 1960 (years)	Infant mortality, 1962 (deaths per 1,000)	Primary enrollment, 1960 (%)	Secondary enrollment, 1960 (%)
Sierra Leone	264	31.6	215	23	2.0
Mauritius	1,140	59.4	61	98	24.0
Remainder of British Africa[a]	292	41.7	146	46	3.1

Source: World Bank 2002.

the country's development levels were lower than those of other British colonies in Africa in the 1960s. Therefore, although civil war has undoubtedly had a nefarious impact on development, the country's present development levels appear to be the continuation of a trajectory begun years ago.

In this chapter, I analyze the determinants of Sierra Leone's poor development record and find that it was set in motion by indirect colonial rule. As depicted in Figure 5.1, indirect rule institutionalized an ineffective and despotic state, which reinforced Sierra Leone's poor developmental trajectory both during and after colonialism. Specifically, colonial rule created a nonbureaucratic, infrastructurally weak, and noninclusive state that not only failed to promote development but actually actively obstructed it. The case therefore provides evidence that despotism and limited state capacity are legacies of indirect rule and, in turn, help drive the negative relationship between indirect colonial rule and postcolonial development.

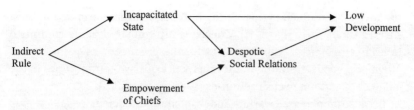

Figure 5.1 Colonial Roots of Sierra Leone's Developmental Trajectory

Precolonial Society

Prior to the fifteenth century, Sierra Leone was a sparsely populated land inhabited by peoples who combined hunter-gatherer lifestyles with horticultural production. Around 1400, however, four centuries of in-migration from Central West Africa dramatically reshaped the region's population composition. The first groups to enter the region fled the conquest empires spreading throughout West Africa and were subsequently followed by four distinct waves of invasion and conquest by various Mane armies between 1540 and 1725 (Wylie 1977: 15). Along with the in-migration of large numbers of people, the population movement also transformed the organization of social relations in Sierra Leone by introducing new military technologies, new forms of political organization, and crops that facilitated settled agriculture.

A century after these population movements began, a second source of externally induced transformation occurred through contact with European explorers and traders. This began with the Portuguese in the early sixteenth century and soon included the Dutch, English, and French. Europeans transformed local societies by introducing New World crops and by trading with the local population. Europeans established coastal trading posts for the acquisition of gold, ivory, slaves, timber, and palm oil, resulting in the emergence of trade networks linking the African interior to the coast (Wylie 1977).

Although conflict and conquest characterized Sierra Leone before the arrival of Europeans, their influence exacerbated local warfare in two ways. First, it caused the emergence of lucrative trade routes and sparked conflict over their control (Wylie 1977). Most importantly, contact with European traders increased local slave raiding (Wylie 1977: 56).[1] Because of the considerable revenue that could be earned by selling slaves to Europeans, slave raiding rapidly expanded and became a major cause of local warfare. Because of local labor scarcity and European demand for tropical products, it continued even after the European slave trade ended in West Africa (Abraham 1978: 10–11). Consequently, military leaders continued to lead campaigns to capture slaves for the production of palm oil and other local goods, resulting in the emergence of slave communities in the eighteenth and nineteenth centuries (Wylie 1977: 38, 77).

Because of increased warfare and instability, new defensive settlements were built throughout Sierra Leone. These new settlements encircled a stockaded town that was built to withstand prolonged military attack (Siddle 1968; Abraham 1978: 15–18). These towns, in turn, were surrounded by several satellite villages that provided the central town with food. Each of these settlements was ruled by a chief who served as the military leader and usually participated in collaborative relations with other settlements to create a larger political structure able to conquer or fend off adversaries (Abraham 1978: 30–41; Wylie 1977: 5). Although each chief had significant autonomy, one was selected to be the leader and exercised disproportionate influence over the other chiefs within the federated state.

Colonial Rule and Its Impact on Chiefly Powers

While power relations transformed since the 1400s as a result of immigrants, invaders, and traders, the declaration of a British protectorate over the Sierra Leone hinterlands initiated a period of even more punctuated social change (Abraham 1978; Bushe 1932; Clapham 1982; Dorjahn 1960; Finnegan and Murray 1970; Hailey 1951; Kilson 1966; Migdal 1988; Reno 1995; Wylie 1977). The Sierra Leone Crown Colony, a 280-square-mile coastal enclave in West Africa, was proclaimed by the British government in 1787 in an area that had previously been chartered by merchant companies involved primarily in the slave trade. The colony was ruled through a centralized administration and a legal system based on British law and became a vibrant port-community home to local Africans as well as freed slaves from Canada, the United States, Jamaica, and Africa. Through the influence of missionaries and repatriated slaves, a mixed Creole society valuing a bourgeois and Christian lifestyle emerged (Creoles were the former slaves and their descendants living in Freetown). By the mid-1840s, a higher percentage of children in Freetown attended primary school than in either England or France (Reno 1995: 41). With these educational credentials and a high European death rate, the colonial state willingly hired locals to work within the colonial administration, and by 1892 Creoles held 45 percent of all senior positions (Reno 1995: 41; Fyfe 1962: 615).

Influenced by constant local warfare and imperial competition with the French, the British declared the Sierra Leone Protectorate over the 27,000-square-mile region surrounding the Sierra Leone Colony in 1896. The general goal of the protectorate government was initially to employ educated Creoles from the colony within the protectorate's legal-administrative institutions. Yet the Hut Tax Rebellion of 1898—which was provoked by attempts to subjugate the protectorate's population; resulted in the killing of approximately 1,000 Creole administrators, traders, and missionaries; and was suppressed through equally brutal methods—showed just how difficult and expensive any direct form of colonial rule could be. Consequently, the British administration institutionalized a hands-off form of rule that empowered local elite to rule for the British through "traditional" means. The elite, who were given the title paramount chiefs, were generally selected according to their abilities to command authority locally and their willingness to collaborate with the British.

Although the Sierra Leone Colony and the Sierra Leone Protectorate remained separate administrative entities until 1951, the establishment of the protectorate caused the administration of the colony to become increasingly subordinate to protectorate interests because of the latter's large size and population. Moreover, the combination of racism and the belief that rule through chiefs and rule through Creoles were incompatible caused the colonial government to begin reserving high-level positions within the central administration for Europeans. As a consequence, the percentage of Creoles holding senior-level positions fell from 45 percent in 1892 to 16 percent in 1912 (Reno 1995). By 1945, only 7 percent of senior administrators were non-European (Government of Sierra Leone 1953: 78). Thus, although colonialism in Sierra Leone initially took a racially inclusive and direct form of rule, it eventually morphed into a relatively standard form of indirect rule, with a small British administration in the capital that ruled the indigenous periphery through collaborative relations with chiefs.

Central Legal-Administrative Institutions in Colonial Sierra Leone

Throughout the colonial period, the administration of the combined colony and protectorate was quite small. In 1919, over a century after the founding of the colony and two decades after British rule was firmly established in the protectorate, the colonial administration ruled approximately 1.5 million inhabitants with less than 1,800 employees. The size of the administration stayed relatively unchanged until post–World War II reforms expanded the administration to 6,500 in 1953 and 10,700 in 1959 (Government of Sierra Leone 1959: 3). Although the expansion was dramatic, the administration was still minuscule in comparison to those in other colonies. At the dawn of colonial independence, for example, less than 0.5 percent of the population was employed by the state in Sierra Leone, a figure one-eighth that of Mauritius.

Besides being small, the legal-administrative infrastructure was very unevenly dispersed throughout Sierra Leone, with nearly all of it concentrated in Freetown. The protectorate, on the other hand, was ruled by a tiny administration that consisted primarily of district commissioners and their assistants. Of the 1,757 state administrators in 1919, only 336 were in the provincial administration, with 271 of these being low-ranking policemen known as court messengers (Government of Sierra Leone 1920). The colonial state in Sierra Leone was therefore tiny, infrastructurally weak, and detached from the majority of the population (Phillips 1989). Consequently, colonial officials could not contemplate basic government functions outside of Freetown and focused almost exclusively on maintaining some semblance of law and order. For this, the minimalist colonial state was extremely dependent on chiefs.

Indirect Rule in the Protectorate

Because the British lacked the legal-administrative capacities to permanently control outlying regions of the Sierra Leone Protectorate, they had little choice but to copy indirect forms of rule that had been developing in other British colonies. As Robinson (1972) notes, indirect rule ultimately meant domination via collaboration. In Sierra Leone, this system of collaborative rule was based on a chain of administrative relationships that linked the central administration to the local population through two key intermediaries: district commissioners, who directed administrative affairs in one of ten districts, and paramount chiefs, who oversaw chiefdom politics.

As the key colonial officials within the peripheral regions, district commissioners (DCs) managed nearly all administrative tasks in the protectorate. In fact, after providing a seemingly endless list of duties, the *Colonial Annual Reports: Sierra Leone* concluded that the tasks of a DC "are multifarious and unending, and he is always on duty," later claiming that the DC "is the lynch-pin on which the success of the whole system of government depends" (Government of Sierra Leone 1947: 45). Among their numerous duties, DCs were most concerned with law and order, since its maintenance shaped their career advancement (Government of Sierra Leone 1954: 2; Abraham 1978). Until 1954, when the Department of the Police extended its jurisdiction to the protectorate, each DC personally directed a small force of messengers to enforce order and was given the authority to demand central reinforcements whenever necessary. In addition, each DC presided over a magistrate's court, which applied British law to local cases outside of the jurisdiction of customary courts.

The DCs, who were almost always European, oversaw a second level of administration and regulation led by indigenous paramount chiefs. The position of the chiefs was neither meritocratic nor completely hereditary. Instead, chiefs were selected by members of a local council called the tribal authority, which consisted of several dozen local elites, and were chosen from among the three or four royal families within the chiefdom. As the leader of the chiefdom, the chief was in charge of making local political decisions and collecting taxes. Yet, like the DCs, the maintenance of law and order was their most important function. As a result, chiefs were given the authority to oversee courts based on customary law and command chiefdom messengers to enforce law within the chiefdom. Customary courts had the jurisdiction to oversee cases that involved members of the chiefdom and administered all local civil cases and most criminal cases, with major criminal offences such as rape and murder heard in the DC's courts.

This collaborative form of rule empowered both DCs and paramount chiefs by enabling each to exploit their intermediary positions to control information and resource flows (see Lange 2003b). The DCs held key structural positions, what Burt (1992) calls structural holes, since each was an intermediary who supervised several chiefs who, in turn, had little or no contact with the colonial government or with one another. Despite their advantageous network positions, DCs rarely defied the central administration openly because they depended on their performance for promotion and could be promoted only to positions within the central colonial administration. While this dependence prevented blatant corruption and insubordination, the intermediary position of the DC provided them with the autonomy to disregard many of their duties without the fear of sanction, and the impossibility of actually performing all their duties gave DCs the incentive to do just that.

Paramount chiefs served as intermediaries linking the colonial administration to the local population and therefore were also positioned at structural holes that allowed them to control information and resource flows. As a colonial report on local government noted, administrators interacted almost exclusively with chiefs and subchiefs and met rarely if ever with subjects in the absence of chiefs (Colony of Sierra Leone 1955: 221). Even their interaction with chiefs was rare, thereby limiting the extent of colonial supervision. For example, colonial officials spent only 1,838 man-days inspecting chiefdoms in 1954, suggesting that only five officials per day inspected the 150 chiefdoms spread over 27,000 square miles (Government of Sierra Leone 1955a: 33). When combined with the ability of the DCs to shirk their duties due to their autonomy from the central administration, such supervision was likely extremely limited. This lack of regulation is also evident in colonial supervision of customary courts. In 1954, for example, only seven customary court cases per 1,000 were revised by DCs, and such revisions only modified the punishment, since the revisions were triggered by a maximum sanction mechanism: all legal decisions given by chiefs were recorded, and DCs modified the punishment of crimes that demanded sanctions higher than those allowed by the administrative courts (Colony of Sierra Leone 1955a: 10–11). This virtual absence of external review resulted from the lack of any formal appeals process for customary court cases (Hailey 1951: 313).

The supervision of the chiefs was also impaired by colonial dependence on chiefs for the maintenance of law and order. Indeed, one year before independence, the colonial governor of Sierra Leone proclaimed, "Maintenance of law and order throughout the country depends more upon the authority of the chief, of the chiefdom court and its committees than probably on any other single factor" (Dorman 1960). The small size and low infrastructural power of the provincial administration inhibited colonial state capacity to maintain law and order, and the district commissioners were therefore dependent on the paramount chiefs' intermediary position for the maintenance of orderly social relations throughout the protectorate. Consequently, open disregard of chiefly misrule became a common practice of the colonial government, effectively creating an extreme institutional bias in favor of chiefs that perpetuated their personal powers. For example, while discussing a certain chief who was faced with broad-societal opposition, the governor of Sierra Leone wrote, "Some allegations [against the chief] will no doubt be true, but we cannot worry about that. If this chief is not supported in these circumstances, none of them will dare to exercise any authority and our careful build up of security will collapse" (Dorman 1960). Nearly identical statements are found in most administrative documents discussing local opposition to chiefs (Bushe 1932; Government of Sierra Leone 1956a; Government of Sierra Leone 1957–59; Government of Sierra Leone 1960; Hall 1954).

Chiefs and the Transformation of Power Relations

With the establishment of legal-administrative institutions in 1896, imperial rule radically transformed power relations throughout the Sierra Leone Protectorate. Specifically, the form of imperial domination altered power relations through three processes: (1) the destruction of precolonial state systems, (2) the transformation of local authority, and (3) the provision of administrative and regulative powers to chiefs (Migdal 1988: 110). When combined with the ability of chiefs to control information and resource flows between the colonial administration and the local population and strong colonial backing, these factors significantly increased the personal power of the chiefs.

With the formation of the Sierra Leone Protectorate, the British dismantled the hierarchical structure of the indigenous federated states. In their place, they constructed new chiefdoms, the number of which fluctuated greatly throughout the colonial period and depended primarily on the whims and interests of the administration. This process, according to Abraham (1978), was begun by Governor Frederic Cardew after the Hut Tax Rebellion in 1898 "as a deliberate colonial strategy to destroy strong states and exploit local conflicts so as to maintain colonial dominance" (181). As a Sierra Leonean historian proclaims,

> [T]here were then no chiefdoms as they are now termed. Great warriors had ownership over extensive areas. But after the 1898 rebellion the British Government thought it best to split up these areas into chiefdoms, thus ultimately creating a lot of chiefs. This plan they thought would finally weaken the powers of any individual chief, as they indirectly planted disunity in the country. (Abraham 1978: 174)

Supporting this view, there were nine federated states in the Mane region of Sierra Leone in 1880, a number expanding abruptly to 27 chiefdoms in 1899, 82 chiefdoms in 1912, and 115 chiefdoms by 1924 (Abraham 1978: 175). By the 1920s, 216 chiefdoms existed throughout the whole protectorate, a number that proved unmanageable (even if successful at quelling opposition to colonial rule), causing the colonial administration to struggle to amalgamate chiefdoms. With limited success, the number was reduced to 146 by independence.

Besides breaking preexisting hierarchies and creating a large number of chiefs with equal rank, the colonial government transformed the basis of local authority. Before 1896, constant warfare required military might, which in turn necessitated a military leader who protected and directed a large number of subjects. Through the creation of formal chiefdoms ruled by paramount chiefs, however, the British colonial government demarcated chiefdom boundaries and declared that the individuals living within a territory were subjects of a specific chief. Thus, since the colonial government selected the paramount chiefs after 1898 and deposed chiefs who disregarded their colonial duties,[2] power now flowed from the colonial state (Dorjahn 1960; Abraham 1978). As Wylie (1977) writes, "Authority now rested solely with the British; theirs was the final and, as far as the law was concerned, the only sanction" (199).

Third, British colonialism transformed local power relations by giving paramount chiefs institutional resources to strengthen their authority in rural areas (Abraham 1978; Dorjahn 1960; Migdal 1988; Wylie 1977). As Finnegan and Murray (1970) write, "In contrast to the earlier situation, local rulers were now constitutionally recognized, their relations with each other and with their people laid down by law, and the officials around them defined. The chiefs and the 'new' chiefdoms in particular found that their positions were immensely stronger than those held by their earlier counterparts" (417; cited in Migdal 1988: 110). Along with formal recognition, chiefs were given the right to communal lands and labor and were empowered to run chiefdom courts, collect taxes, and direct chiefdom law enforcement officers, all of which left the chiefs with considerable institutional powers. Such powers, in turn, were augmented because they became the personal rights of chiefs and reduced chiefly dependence on subchiefs, who "were increasingly bypassed as unnecessary, even parasitic, vestiges" (Wylie 1977: 195).

Development during Late Colonialism

At the dawn of independence, Sierra Leone had the second lowest per capita GNP of all former British colonies despite having rich diamond reserves. Sierra Leone's human development was also abysmal, with the highest infant mortality rate of all former British colonies, the lowest life expectancy, the second lowest primary school enrollment rate, and the fourth lowest secondary school enrollment rate. In this section, I provide evidence that such low levels of development resulted in part from the indirect form of colonial rule. I describe how the minimal colonial state was incapable of implementing policy to promote social development. In addition, ineffective legal-administrative institutions empowered the chiefs and made possible despotic and predatory rule at the local level.

Colonial Development Projects

Paralleling Mauritius, the central administration in Sierra Leone recognized the need to begin basic development projects in the protectorate after World War II. Unlike Mauritius, however, colonial officials in Sierra Leone lacked the organizational capacity to actually implement development policy. As a result, the colonial government copied the development efforts of northern Nigeria and elsewhere in British Africa and placed chiefs in charge of building roads, schools, and clinics—something they were utterly unprepared to do (Visawasam 1973: 31).

To assist the chiefs with their development projects, the central government began to organize district councils. District councils were founded in 1946 and consisted of two representatives from each chiefdom, one of whom was the paramount chief, the other of whom was appointed by the chief. The district commissioners initially served as the presidents of the councils, yet in the early 1950s the members of each council chose their president. As a result of these conditions, chiefs soon controlled district councils, and—as a political intelligence report openly proclaimed in 1955—this control became a means for chiefs to divert resources from developmental activities:

> There can now be no doubt that the District Councils have been allowed to go too far, and too fast, in their present form and that, for the most part, they are completely out of touch with the rank and file of the population which sees little benefit accruing to them for their existence and which, on the contrary, sees their members apparently persistently using their position to enrich themselves. (Government of Sierra Leone 1955c: 14)

The Building Materials Scheme, which provided grants and loans for the construction of buildings, provides one example of chiefs lining their pockets and protecting their positions with funds earmarked for developmental activities. By 1961, the central government had provided £300,000 in grants and much more in loans through the scheme, money that was often used strictly for personal projects instead of community development (Kilson 1966: 208). Even when not directly employing the funds for their own benefit, the chiefs used them as a means of patronage, offering grants and loans to kin, subchiefs, and others as a means of maintaining their loyalty (Kilson 1966: 208).

While rampant rent seeking by chiefs drained development funds, an additional developmental dilemma facing colonial Sierra Leone was a dearth of revenue needed for the expansion of development projects. Although the economy of Sierra Leone was an important determinant of low revenue, chiefs limited state revenue even further because they were the principal agents used to collect taxes. As Dorjahn (1960) notes, chiefs collected and pocketed excessive rent from the local populations that did not end up in the books: "Thus in devious ways the chief was able to increase his income through autocratic action. The traditional emoluments proved insufficient to finance the chief in his new role, and with the power of Government apparently behind him and the breakdown of the traditional checks on autocracy, the chief could and did graft extensively" (135). Because of this rent-seeking, the 128 chiefdoms with treasury records officially collected only £134,302 in 1948. To make matters worse, only £28,085 of this was spent on agriculture, education, forestry, health care, and public works (Hailey 1951: 307–8). Alternatively, £83,870 was spent on chiefdom administration, funds that ultimately ended up in the hands of chiefs and their supporters.

In addition, chiefs in areas with diamond deposits were able to disrupt colonial efforts to increase revenue through the exploitation of diamond reserves. Rich diamond deposits were discovered in and around the Kono District of the Sierra Leone Protectorate in the late 1930s. Initially, the government gave the Sierra Leone Selections Trust (SLST) a monopoly over the mining of diamonds, yet the company turned to the chiefs for assistance once it proved unable to stop illegal mining. To resolve the problem, the colonial government increased its dependence on chiefs instead of internalizing production. "Africans would benefit from diamond resources," Reno (1995) writes, "but only under direct government control. But again, the remedy for 'bad' policies required greater reliance on chief cooperation" (63).

First, the government began paying chiefs in the diamond-rich chiefdoms extravagant amounts of money for following government directives. For example, in 1955 the Mineral Area Development Administration (MADA) was formed under the false pretenses of promoting local development in areas of diamond mining. Reno (1995) notes that the development funds were simply used as cash payments to chiefs in exchange for their enforcement of mining regulation through the customary courts, something the chiefs paid lip service to but disregarded given the bribes they received for overlooking illegal mining, the profits that could be made by employing their own illegal miners, and the inability and unwillingness of the administration to sanction chiefs (66). In addition, the government gave chiefs the right to assign private licenses for mining in certain regions of the chiefdoms, which simply increased the ability of the chief to rent-seek without guaranteeing any increase in diamond revenue (Cartwright 1970: 72; Reno 1995: 63). Thus, some chiefs and their collaborators became extremely wealthy through diamonds, while the colonial coffers remained empty.

[handwritten annotation: Chiefs profit greatly from Diamonds, state does not]

The Anti-Chief Revolt of 1955–56: Insight into Chiefly Despotism

As described above, chiefly abuses had very negative effects on the implementation of development policy in late-colonial Sierra Leone and, in turn, were the result of an incapacitated colonial state that empowered local elites in order to gain some semblance of control over the colony. Besides allowing chiefs to misuse development funds, the powers of chiefs limited social development in another way as well: it allowed the chiefs to exploit their subjects, preventing the latter from pursuing their personal well-being. People did not simply accept chiefly exploitation, however, and periodic revolts against chiefly misrule began to occur after World War I. These movements climaxed between November 1955 and March 1956, when tens of thousands of individuals living throughout the Sierra Leone Protectorate revolted against their chiefs in violent displays of defiance, prompting the colonial police and military to intervene on forty-six occasions and arrest nearly 1,500 individuals. Such was the violence and scale of the uprising that a commissioner investigating the incident described the series of events as a "civil war" between chiefs and subjects while the *1955 Report on the Administration of the Provinces* claimed that the uprising was a "Chiefdom Revolution" (Government of Sierra Leone 1955a, 1956b). Because of the breakdown of order throughout the protectorate and the centrality of the colonial government's law-and-order imperative, the Colonial Office in London commissioned multiple investigations into the causes of protectorate-wide revolt that today provide an unusually well-documented description of the extent of chiefly autocracy in the Sierra Leone Protectorate during late colonialism. In so doing, the commissions also provide insight into the structural causes of such widespread abuse of power.

In its summary, the Cox Report declared that chiefly despotism was the most proximate cause of the disturbances:

We have found, and therefore we have described, a degree of demoralisation among the people in their customary institutions and in their approach to the statutory duties with which they have been entrusted, which has shocked us. Dishonesty has become accepted as a normal ingredient of life to such an extent that no one has been concerned to fight it or even complain about it. The ordinary peasant or fisherman seems originally to have accepted a degree of corruption which was tolerable; at a later stage he has been cowed into accepting it; finally he rebelled. (Government of Sierra Leone 1956b: 9)

Elsewhere, an official listed common examples of chiefly misrule: "widespread use of forced labour on chiefs farms, unpaid and often unfed; levies not allowed in law . . . ; beating up and manhandling complainants; fining people out of court and retaining the fines; keeping back a substantial part of community development grants; and straightforward embezzlement" (Dorman 1957). Not surprisingly, the colonial administration in Sierra Leone completely supported the findings of the external commission, claiming that the "disturbances were led by ordinarily law-abiding people who were fed up with the extortions and tyranny practiced by Paramount Chiefs and their underlings" (Government of Sierra Leone 1955b). The Cox Report did not simply blame the chiefs for the disturbances, however. Instead, it described the administration as "execrated and partly disabled" and declared that "[g]overnment itself is to blame for permitting a condition of affairs wherein such disaffection could flourish" (Government of Sierra Leone 1956b: 221, 15).

Faulty colonial administration in the protectorate was caused primarily by its puny size and low levels of infrastructural power, which limited the capacity of administrators to supervise local affairs (Government of Sierra Leone 1956b: 221). Moreover, the intermediary position of district commissioners provided them with the autonomy to disregard their duties. Thus, as one high-ranking official at the Colonial Office in London claimed, "On the face of it, it looks like thoroughly bad district administration. . . . One wonders whether there is regular village to village visiting for instance" (Hudson 1956).

Besides simply failing to prevent chiefly abuses, the form of colonial rule in Sierra Leone actually promoted them in various ways. For example, the commissioned reports provide evidence that this lack of supervision was magnified by two institutional practices described above: the district administration interacted almost exclusively with the chiefs, and it supported the actions and interests of chiefs under all circumstances. Using hundreds of interviews with local inhabitants in the regions in which disturbances occurred as evidence, the Cox Report claimed that these two factors effectively imposed a barrier between district commissioners and local inhabitants and gave chiefs free rein over their subjects:

We have found that ready access to the Government by the disgruntled or oppressed through the District Commissioner has become thought of as unavailable. Either 'the D.C. sends us back to the Paramount Chief' or 'the D.C. cannot help us now we are in the hands of the Chiefs' or 'the Paramount Chief is now bigger than the D.C.' or some such words have been repeatedly used to us. (Government of Sierra Leone 1956b: 48–49)

Under these circumstances, the chiefs were able to simply deny charges of impropriety and to counter them with their own. As one informant stated, "If anyone complains against the Paramount Chief, the Section Chiefs are told by the Paramount Chief that they must not give evidence in favour of the man complaining against the chief, but, instead, to give evidence against him" (Government of Sierra Leone 1957–59: 44).

Colonial rule promoted chiefly abuses even more directly through its effects on local power relations. Although the lack of supervision allowed chiefs to maintain a high level of autonomy from the colonial government, these were not sufficient conditions for despotism since local constraints could limit the power of chiefs. Yet the imposition of colonial rule quite arbitrarily transformed the previous relations between rulers and subjects, freeing chiefs from previous forms of social constraint (Cartwright 1970: 28–30; Wylie 1977). In addition, the control of customary courts and chiefdom messengers by chiefs provided coercive resources that empowered them to rule their chiefdoms with little concern for the interests of local inhabitants.

The chiefdom messengers were agents employed by chiefs to enforce customary and colonial law. The messengers were chosen and paid by the chiefs, making them de facto enforcers of chiefly desires. Reviewing the evidence gathered by its inquiry, the Cox Report wrote, "[W]e find as a fact that the messengers, using or threatening to use their powers of arrest, have been the instruments of the Paramount Chiefs' will. . . . This duty far transcends that of preventing and detecting crime and even the duty of preserving the peace except to the extent that it is the Chiefs' 'peace' that is preserved" (Government of Sierra Leone 1956b: 196).

While the court messengers were a coercive resource empowering chiefs, customary courts allowed them to influence social relations. Chiefs were able to exploit their control of customary courts to support key allies, weaken opponents, and earn money through bribes (Hudson 1956). Because the colonial administration almost always supported chiefs, subjects had no alternative other than to accept chiefly rulings. As one informant stated matter-of-factly, "If you complain against the Paramount

Chief he sends you away from the country. One never appeals against the Chief's decision" (Government of Sierra Leone 1957–59: 17–18).

The position of chiefs as head of the customary court also allowed them to define custom, a power that gave chiefs control of land and labor. Others note that a biased understanding of precolonial land use caused British colonial officials to endow chiefs with great control over chiefdom lands (Chanock 1985; Mamdani 1996), and chiefs in Sierra Leone were given similar powers (Hailey 1951). Indeed, the lack of colonial involvement in land issues is highlighted by the fact that the primary authoritative document on land tenure at the end of colonialism consisted of "some notes compiled in 1912" (Dorman 1959). As a result of these powers and lack of colonial involvement, chiefs were able to control local land and parcel it out as they saw fit. Moreover, with the introduction of commercial agriculture, they were able to claim communal and unclaimed plots of land as their own.

The simple control of land is not economically advantageous unless someone's labor is employed to grow and collect crops. With large land holdings, chiefs lacked the capacity to utilize their lands for crop production through the use of their own labor. Their control of custom, however, made it possible for them to demand labor as tribute. As hundreds of informants testified after the riots, chiefs actively exploited their control over local labor by forcing men and women to cultivate their lands without any form of compensation (Government of Sierra Leone 1956b: 166). Indeed, it was only in the 1950s that the British administration forbade chiefs from using impoverished peasants as slaves (Hailey 1951).

The Maintenance of Decentralized Despotism

Despite the damning testimonies leveled against the chiefs after the riots, no major institutional reforms were made during the final years of colonial rule to weaken their positions. Why, then, did the colonial government continue to support a system of rule known to be defective and exploitative? One reason undoubtedly relates to extremely high levels of colonial dependence on chiefs, which made any administrative overhaul logistically difficult and extremely expensive. Equally importantly, Sierra Leonean politicians collaborated with the chiefs, and both fought to protect the positions of chiefs, causing the structure of local government and the organization of national power relations to remain relatively unchanged at independence and even decades later.

The first Legislative Council elections occurred in Sierra Leone in 1951 and sparked the rise of the Sierra Leone People's Party (SLPP). The SLPP was formed and led by Dr. Milton Margai, who was the son of a chief and began his political career organizing an informal council of chiefs. Given Margai's background and the power and influence of chiefs, the SLPP allied with the chiefs in an attempt to gain political power. In fact, the SLPP was connected so closely with the chiefs that the party did not even attempt to create any local organization, choosing instead to work directly through the chiefs. Consequently, a symbiotic relationship emerged in which chiefs made sure SLPP candidates were elected, while the SLPP protected the interests of chiefs (Cartwright 1970).

Several telling examples of the symbiotic relationship between the SLPP and the chiefs exist. For instance, the Legislative Council debated the right of the administration to depose chiefs, with SLPP members suggesting that "chiefs ought to be protected at almost any cost and paid reasonably" (Government of Sierra Leone 1956b: 149). As a result, an amendment in 1954 removed the right to depose chiefs from the administration and gave it to the SLPP ministers. A Sierra Leone Political Intelligence Report discussing the causes of the 1955–56 riots noted that this arrangement "encouraged" chiefs to partake in "rapacious" behavior by "white-washing one chief after another who had been deposed for extortion and oppression during the years prior to the introduction of the ministerial system, who in every case, and often on most unsuitable occasions, were held up as the injured innocents of administerial vindictiveness" (Government of Sierra Leone 1955c: 13). After the riots, several chiefs were investigated for misrule, and eight were eventually suspended or deposed because of colonial insistence that examples be made of corrupt officials. Within a few years, however, nearly all the chiefs were back in power thanks largely to ministerial pressure, and the ministers convinced the colonial government to pay nearly £400,000 to these and other chiefs for loss of property that occurred during the riots (Cartwright 1970: 84; Dorman 1957).

Ministers also made sure that chiefs remained powerful. As Cartwright (1970) claims, the willingness of SLPP officials "to allow local institutions to go on much as before even after the 1955–56 riots suggested how far they were committed to preserving the powers and privileges of the chiefs" (102). As a result, the chiefs maintained their powers throughout the independence process and even afterwards. In a damning analysis of local government in Sierra Leone written over a decade after independence, a United Nations Development Programme report claimed that the postcolonial administration left chiefs in charge of local government, resulting in the continuation of clientelist relations linking the administration, chiefs, and local population (Visawasam 1973). Similar to reports written decades earlier, the analysis claimed that "[r]eports of the Auditor General on the accounts of the Chiefdom Administrations are full of evidence of bad financial management, poor accounting, fraud, shortage and unauthorized expenditure. In fact these are so universal that it is almost true to say that if one has read a single report of the Auditor General one has read them all" (Visawasam 1973: 36–37). As a result, development projects were almost nonexistent and perceptible only because of the presence of paid employees (Visawasam 1973).

Beyond simply maintaining their positions, some chiefly powers even expanded after independence. In 1972, for instance, a new law suspended all democratic aspects of the district councils, allowing chiefs to rule them according to their personal wills (Fanthrope 2001: 381). The law also granted chiefs the authority to distinguish who was a "native" of their chiefdoms. As a consequence, chiefs were given the power to decide who could receive village land and who could not, and village land therefore became increasingly restricted to powerful families of chiefly supporters, leaving many rural inhabitants landless or without sufficient land.

Although the postcolonial state in Sierra Leone remained decentralized, despotic, and ineffective, it was not completely static after independence. After rapid and haphazard state expansion and localization, the colonial withdrawal resulted in an unstable legal-administrative apparatus that continued to be infrastructurally weak, poorly bureaucratized, and hardly inclusive. Postcolonial leaders therefore had little choice but to personalize and militarize the state by building up the military and using it as the primary means of maintaining their positions and regulating society. The leaders also began to distribute state resources through elaborate networks of patron-client relations in an attempt to maintain some form of support among influential social actors. In this way, independence brought personal and coercive rule to the upper echelon of the state, creating an overall system of domination that was "extractive, rapacious, and venal" (Hayward 1989: 177).

The initial transfer of power at independence in 1961 went quite smoothly. Dr. Milton Margai was elected to lead Sierra Leone into independence and used his broad-based support to maintain political stability. After his death in 1964, however, the weakness of the postcolonial state quickly became apparent. Milton's half brother, Albert, was his successor, and Albert began to protect his weak position by filling the cabinet with supporters and packing the military with soldiers from his home region. His military readjustments paid quick dividends when his electoral defeat by Siaka Stevens in 1967 was followed by a coup that reinstated Albert Margai. The military reforms were not sufficiently thorough, however, as a second coup less than a year later removed him from power and placed Stevens at the head of state.

Although Stevens came to power with considerable social support, his power was quite limited. Most importantly, the military was divided and full of his opponents, the state was fissiparous and incapable of performing basic functions, and most of the chiefs supported the opposition. He therefore began to purge the military and created his own presidential guard (Kandeh 2002: 191). He also removed several chiefs from their positions and convinced all others that the only way for them to maintain their positions was to support him (Allen 1978: 203; Hayward 1989: 167–68). Next, he took complete control of the civil service, hiring and firing based on personal allegiance (Kpundeh 1999: 212; Kandeh 2002: 181). As a final attempt to cement his personal power, Stevens changed the constitution to make Sierra Leone a one-party state.

All in all, Stevens' increased his personal control over legal-administrative institutions and the military and used the latter to maintain his position. His coercive power did not eliminate his dependence on others, however. Instead, he manipulated state resources to control social relations among government officials, chiefs, and diamond traders (Abraham 2001: 206; Allen 1978: 203; Fanthrope 2001; Kandeh 2002: 180; Reno 1995). These relations were mutually beneficial and resulted in a personalized system of rule similar to what Stinchcombe (1999) calls *caudillismo*:

> In *caudillo* governments, the ties between central and local powers are not built on social and moral materials about what the center should be and do. Instead, the relations between patron and client, hero and follower, are the cultural materials of government. Center and periphery are tied together by interpersonal loyalty and exchanges rather than by public services to be performed, responsibilities to localities to be discharged, or elections by localities on the basis of national programs to be recognized. (70)

Under this system of personalized patron-client relations, any bureaucratic aspect of the state was removed and state decay became "endemic" (Hayward 1989: 165).

The patrimonial state structure, in turn, made possible widespread state predation. According to Fanthrope (2001), "Stevens' fundamental

strategy was to convert the most productive sectors of the national economy (diamonds and foreign exchange) into patrimonial resources" (363),
while Kandeh (2002) claims that Stevens' "plundering logic of political
domination transformed Sierra Leone into one of the world's leading producers of human misery" (180). Indeed, at the same time resources were
stolen by venal officials and placed in foreign bank accounts, agricultural
production decreased, per capita GDP actually declined, and state investment in education and health care fell to abysmal levels.

After a decade and a half of destructive personal rule, signs of Stevens'
demise began to appear in the mid-1980s (Hayward 1989: 171, 175). In
an attempt to bypass a violent downfall, he resigned in 1985 and handed
power to Brigadier General Joseph Momoh. Momoh quickly showed his
autonomy from Stevens and began to assemble his own *caudillo*-based
state. Many of the problems that frightened Stevens from office remained,
however, and ultimately caused complete state collapse.

First and foremost, the nonbureaucratic and infrastructurally weak
state structure prevented corporate action. The inability to provide basic
developmental goods was a sign of this ineffectiveness and ultimately
led to an increasingly impoverished and desperate population (Kandeh
2002: 185). Legal-administrative ineffectiveness, in turn, caused Momoh
to mimic his predecessor and depend heavily on state coercion to both
stay in power and regulate social relations. Unfortunately for him, even
the police and military were poorly organized and undisciplined, causing
coups to be an ever-present danger.

A second problem that Stevens passed to Momoh was the state's dimin-
ishing resource base. State revenue from diamond mining, for instance,
declined after foreign mining companies closed operations in Sierra
Leone because of ineffective political regulation and instability. Moreover, the difficulties caused by extreme economic mismanagement and
predation forced Momoh to turn toward the IMF for assistance, which
reduced his autonomy to use state resources as desired (Hayward 1989:
174–76; Reno 1995; Kandeh 2002: 186). Finally, the end of the cold war
decreased foreign assistance needed so badly by Momoh's regime (Reno
1995). Because of these financial difficulties, Momoh's capacity to rein
in strongmen through mutually dependent relationships was greatly
reduced, leading to the fragmentation of his support network (Reno 1995:
113–45; Richards 1996: xviii).

With an ineffective state, widespread social discontent, and the breakdown of patron-client relations, Sierra Leone provided a fecund environment for violence and civil war. In addition, the presence of lootable

resources in the form of diamonds and competition over their control promoted just this (Collier 2000; Fearon and Laitin 2003; Snyder and Bhavnani 2005). The revolt began in 1991 after the arrival of some 100 rebels supported by both Liberia and Libya. The rebels killed, maimed, and raped civilians in a campaign of violence and intimidation (Abraham 2001: 207). While kidnapping and forced military service were one way the rebel forces grew, both the revolt's rapid proliferation despite the small number of rebels and its focused attacks on unpopular chiefs suggest that many local inhabitants were easily influenced to partake in the violence and looting (Richards 1996: 8). In addition, the lack of state presence in rural areas allowed the revolt to gain a firm footing before any military action occurred. When Momoh's military response finally did come, it was ineffective since his troops could not be controlled; they simply joined the pillage and violence, earning government soldiers the name "sobels": soldier by day, rebel by night.[3] Thus, marauding and indistinguishable bands of soldiers and rebels laid waste to the country and began a brutal and seemingly pointless civil war that brought predation to its summit and development to its nadir. Although this outcome was not the necessary result of indirect rule, the country's fragmented, ineffective, and infrastructurally weak *caudillo* state was a colonial legacy. Because these state characteristics were proximate causes of the civil war, colonialism must be implicated in this human catastrophe as well as the less dramatic yet equally devastating disaster that preceded it (i.e., state predation and low development).

Comparison with Mauritius

Comparison of Sierra Leone and Mauritius highlights interesting parallels as well as key differences that help pinpoint the mechanisms underlying their different developmental trajectories. One surprising similarity between the two is that neither had a strong administrative presence in the rural areas throughout the majority of the colonial period. Indeed, while the rural areas of Sierra Leone were ruled indirectly through chiefs, there was only limited administration in the rural areas of Mauritius until after the Second World War. Moreover, the rural Mauritians who lived on the plantations—especially the African slaves and later the first generation of Indian indentured workers—were subject to the domination of an elite who tried to rule their plantations as if they were beyond the reach of the colonial state. As a result, Mauritius could have ended up with its own form of decentralized despotism. That it did not helps to explain its different developmental outcome.

Comparison of the two cases provides evidence that three main factors prevented colonialism in Mauritius from becoming decentralized and despotic and therefore help to explain the positive relationship between the extent of direct rule and development. First, despite being largely absent in rural areas, the administration of Mauritius was larger, more bureaucratic, more effective, and more infrastructurally powerful than in Sierra Leone. As a result, the Mauritian state was better able to implement policy, especially policy affecting state building, democratization, and development during the independence period. In addition, the size, history, and indigenous staffing of the central state in colonial Mauritius promoted the institutionalization of bureaucratic organization and procedures and thereby impeded the personalization of the state after independence. In contrast, the central administration in Sierra Leone was minuscule, staffed largely by Europeans throughout the colonial period, and present only in Freetown. The abrupt expansion and localization that occurred during the independence period therefore failed to either institutionalize bureaucratic procedures or to create effective legal-administrative institutions and thereby made possible both the personal takeover of the state by postcolonial leaders and the expansion of predatory practices.

Second, although the administration had only a limited presence in the rural areas of Mauritius, the legal system reached into all corners of the colony. This relatively effective and autonomous legal framework strengthened subordinate groups at the expense of the plantation elite, thereby making possible the construction of villages of peasants that were free from plantation control and characterized by dense associational ties. In Sierra Leone, however, local chiefs controlled the law and were able to wield it to dominate their subjects and institutionalize vertical relations of dependence. Thus, differences in legal institutions and their effects on the overall structure of society promoted personal rule and decentralized despotism in Sierra Leone but helped to circumvent them in Mauritius.

A third key difference between colonial Mauritius and Sierra Leone concerns the formal use of intermediaries in Sierra Leone. As mentioned above, the rural villages in Mauritius were within the rubric of the colonial state's legal system yet lacked a system of formal administration until after World War II. As a consequence, the colonial state was forced to create local administration in order to implement the postwar reforms, and the construction of rural administration in Mauritius dramatically expanded the infrastructural power of the state and multiplied the points of interaction between local inhabitants and state officials. The interface between state and society therefore lacked structural holes and made possible a relatively free exchange of information and resources. In Sierra Leone, on the other hand, local chiefs controlled both law and administration, and the colonial state was therefore constrained by local chiefs who protected their interests at the expense of any centralized control. As a consequence, administrative reforms simply built upon the preexisting chiefly administration, the administrative capacity of the Sierra Leonean state remained extremely limited, and the protectorate's rural population continued to be cut off from the central administration.

Comparison of Mauritius and Sierra Leone therefore provides evidence that Britain created different legal-administrative institutions in directly and indirectly ruled colonies and that these institutions, in turn, are important determinants of long-term developmental trajectories. In Mauritius, relatively effective legal institutions empowered subordinate groups, allowing them to better pursue their well-being both independently and in collaboration with the state. In addition, the relatively infrastructurally powerful and bureaucratic organization of the Mauritian administration allowed it to act corporately and engage societal actors, both of which allowed it to successfully implement developmental policy once the Colonial Office became interested in promoting the well-being of its colonial subjects. Finally, independence reforms built on the preexisting state structures, thereby greatly expanding the developmental capacity of the Mauritian state. In contrast, the administration in Sierra Leone was minuscule and incapable of engaging rural actors because of its absence in rural areas and the extreme power of chiefs, who dominated local administrations and controlled customary law. Independence reforms simply built on and thereby strengthened the preexisting system of indirect rule and the continued ineffectiveness of the legal-administrative institutions promoted personal and coercive rule at all levels of the state.

A comparative-historical analysis of Mauritius and Sierra Leone therefore suggests that state institutional differences linked to the form of colonialism underlie the relationship between direct colonial rule and development and strongly supports the theoretical framework presented in Chapter 2. Given that Mauritius and Sierra Leone are only two of many former British colonies, however, the insight from these cases is not conclusive. Moreover, a few former British colonies do not conform to the statistical relationship. In the next two chapters, I investigate two such cases: Guyana and Botswana. As statistical outliers, both provide opportunities to check the accuracy of the institutional mechanisms highlighted in the Mauritian and Sierra Leonean case studies.

Guyana

6

A Case of Despotism Despite Direct Rule

Guyana is the only English-speaking country on the South American mainland. Geographically, it is the size of Great Britain and consists of a thin agricultural belt along the Caribbean coast followed by dense tropical forests, mountains, and savannahs that stretch deep into the South American interior. The country's social environment follows its geographical contours, with over 90 percent of the country's inhabitants living along the coast, leaving the remaining 96 percent of the country with only a smattering of people. While small, the country's population is diverse, consisting of indigenous Amerindians (7 percent of the population) as well as different groups that came to the country—either willingly or forcibly—for the production of sugar: South Asians (50 percent of the population), Africans (36 percent), Europeans (less than 1 percent), Chinese (1 percent), and various mixed peoples (5 percent).

Although located on opposite ends of the earth and having very different physical environments, the histories of Guyana and Mauritius are quite similar. Both were captured from other colonial powers during the Napoleonic Wars, were ruled through a centralized and direct form of British colonialism for the next 150 years, and had similar populations and plantation-based economies

Table 6.1 Human development in colonial Guyana and Mauritius, 1936–47

Country	Death rate, 1936–45 (per 1,000)	Infant mortality rate, 1935–40 (per 1,000)	School attendance, 1947 (% of total population)	Literacy, 1944–46 (% of total population)
Mauritius	28.3	153.3	11.9	24.1
Guyana	19.6	124.6	17.5	56.2

Sources: Mandle 1973: 81, 88, 96; Mauritius Economic Commission 1948; Colony of Mauritius 1947.

founded on the production of sugar. As a result of the plantation economies, both Guyana and Mauritius were rife with inequalities; had rigid
social hierarchies; and experienced racial conflict among the white elite,
former African slaves, and former South Asian indentured workers. As
shown in Table 6.1, both also had similar levels of development during the
1930s and 1940s, with Guyana—then known as British Guiana—having
slightly lower infant mortality and death rates, a slightly higher education
rate, and a much more literate population.

Despite these similarities, Guyana and Mauritius have experienced
very different developmental trajectories over the last half century. While
development improved markedly in Mauritius during late colonialism, no
developmental upshot occurred in Guyana, causing a growing developmental gap between the two. Mauritius' per capita GDP in 1970 was only
50 percent larger than Guyana's ($834 versus $569) but rose to over four
times that of Guyana by 2005 ($4,403 versus $980) (World Bank 2007a).
Similarly, whereas Mauritius had 17 fewer infant deaths per 1,000 in 1970
(64 versus 81), the gap grew to 34 in 2005 (13 versus 47) (World Bank
2007a). These developmental differences, in turn, are captured by Chapter 2's statistical findings, as Mauritius generally conforms to the statistical relationships but Guyana is a negative outlier.

In this chapter, I analyze Guyana in order to explore the causes of its
unexpectedly low development levels and to check the accuracy of the
mechanisms highlighted in the Mauritian case study. Ultimately, the
chapter provides evidence that Guyana is a statistical outlier because the
state institutional legacy of British colonialism did not follow the normal
pattern during the independence process. Unlike Mauritius, the state
transformations in late-colonial Guyana neither strengthened preexisting state structures, increased inclusiveness, nor began state-led development efforts. Instead, the state became personalized and militarized,

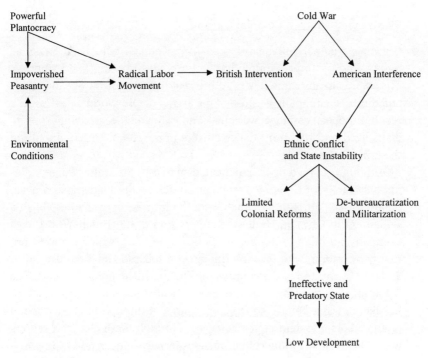

Figure 6.1 Colonial Roots of Guyana's Developmental Trajectory

and its legal-administrative capacities diminished, all of which promoted developmentally destructive state action. In this way, detailed analysis of the outlier provides a corrective to perceptions that colonial legacies are unchanging but helps confirm the mechanisms highlighted in the previous chapters by showing that nonbureaucratic, noninclusive, and militarized states deter development.

My overall argument suggests that the independence period was a critical-juncture period during which the intersection of class inequality and cold war politics readjusted the country's developmental trajectory. As depicted in Figure 6.1, the most proximate causes of Guyana's ineffective and despotic state were ethnic conflict and the colonial government's failure to implement state reforms and development programs during the 1950s and 1960s. These, in turn, were caused by the extreme power of the plantation elite—which led to a more radical labor movement and conflict between local politicians and the colonial administration during the late colonial period—and American cold war policy bent on destabilizing leftist regimes.

Plantation Society in Colonial Guyana

Guyana's original inhabitants were Amerindians who lived in small groups and combined simple horticulture with hunting and gathering. They were already quite few in number at the time of European contact and diminished rapidly because of the arrival of Old World diseases. As a result, European conquest was quick and easy, and the surviving Amerindians lived removed from the colonizers in the remote interior south of the thin coastal plain.

Although claimed by the Spanish, explored by Sir Walter Raleigh during his search for El Dorado, and considered by the Pilgrims as a destination for settlement, the Dutch were the first Europeans to establish a settlement in Guyana. Under the supervision of the Dutch West Indies Company, an inland settlement was begun in 1623, which survived primarily by trading with the Amerindians for tobacco and a red dye called annatto. By the end of the century, the Dutch settled along the coast. The coastal region and its rich soil had been a tidal plain under as much as five feet of water before the Dutch reclaimed it through the construction of an elaborate system of sea defenses. Through these changes, settlers were able to grow cotton, coffee, and—especially—sugar, and by the mid-eighteenth century Guyana had transformed into a plantation colony.

Plantation agriculture received a boost in 1745 with the breakup of the Dutch West Indies' monopoly, and Guyana was soon opened to settlement, sparking the arrival of many British planters who had abandoned their lands on various Caribbean islands because of soil depletion. With their arrival, the production of sugar increased, and the Dutch colony's economy became increasingly dominated by British plantations. After the British captured Guyana during the Napoleonic Wars, it gained a matching British administration and remained a British colony until its independence in 1966.

Life in colonial Guyana revolved around plantations. At the abolition of slavery in 1838, some 308 plantations existed, a number that began to decline quite rapidly because of economic hardship and modernization efforts that consolidated sugar estates into larger entities (Adamson 1972: 160). Thus, there were only 173 plantations in 1853, a number that continued to decline to 46 in 1904 (Adamson 1972: 160, 211). At independence, one company—Bookers' Sugar Estates Limited, a subsidiary of Booker Brothers, McConnell and Company, which sponsors the Booker Prize for Fiction—produced 90 percent of the colony's sugar, causing some to claim that the "B.G." for British Guiana actually stood for "Booker's Guiana" (Ince 1974: 37; Hollet 1999: 248–75).

As elsewhere, plantation agriculture depended on the construction of exploitative institutions based on white management of African labor—"Strange that an article like sugar so sweet and necessary for human existence should have occasioned such crimes and bloodshed" (Eric Williams, quoted in Jagan 1997: 69). Twenty-five years after Great Britain captured Guyana from the Dutch, however, it abolished slavery throughout its colonies. Because most former slaves left the plantations, the sugar estates in Guyana faced a labor crisis, which caused them to import indentured workers from Madeira, Sierra Leone, China, and elsewhere in the Caribbean. When these efforts failed, the colonial government and sugar planters followed the Mauritian example and began to import South Asian indentured workers in the 1840s. The South Asian workers generally came to Guyana having already signed an agreement to work on a plantation for a period of five years. If they continued to work on a plantation for an additional five years, they received a free return trip to India. By 1917, some 230,000 South Asians had arrived, and the overwhelming majority of them stayed.

The plantation owners in Guyana were stronger than those in colonial Mauritius, and the Guyanese peasants were weaker. Similarly, state inclusiveness was very low in colonial Guyana, as the peasants were almost completely excluded from relations with the state while a minuscule group of planters exerted considerable influence over legal-administrative institutions. Under these circumstances, sugar was king, while those who labored to produce it were marginalized and faced extremely hash living conditions.

Although the production of sugar is always labor intensive, that in Guyana was an extreme case. Rodney (1981) describes the reclamation of land as "the humanization of the Guyanese coastal landscape" (xviii). "Humanization" is an appropriate term not only because inhospitable mangrove swamps were transformed into neatly planned fields but because of the enormous amount of human labor that was necessary for the great transformation. According to a colonial commission in 1948, besides clearing the land and constructing a sea defense, each square mile of cane cultivation required the construction of forty-nine miles of drainage canals and ditches and sixteen miles of higher-level waterways for transportation and irrigation. This infrastructure, in turn, required the removal of 100 million tons of water-logged sludge and clay (Rodney 1981: xviii). Once constructed, this tropical Netherlands required high levels of maintenance given the constant tidal bombardment and the blockage of canals and waterways with sludge and tropical vegetation (Adamson 1972: 168).

The extraordinary costs and amount of labor necessary for the maintenance of the irrigation/polder infrastructure was often beyond the means
of land-owning peasants and was an important cause of their economic
plight. Moreover, because the drainage infrastructure on the lands of
small farmers was first constructed for large plantations, any peasant who
was able to buy estate land depended on the irrigation and polder system
of the entire plantation. The result was a complex collective action problem, which, according to a government official inspecting villages in 1881,
caused a no-win situation for peasant farmers: "The industrious man who
works his bed of land and keeps his draining trench . . . clean of grass
suffers materially because his neighbor . . . will not dig or clean the small
drains attached to his lot; . . . the industrious man's ground becomes a
swamp and his labour lost" (Adamson 1970: 392). Thus, with only limited
means of upkeep and dependent on other poor peasants for the maintenance of adjacent lands, peasant production was marginal and rarely
resulted in surpluses (Despres 1967: 49–50).

Besides the difficulties caused by the physical environment, the peasants faced an additional impediment in the form of a powerful plantocracy. Although the plantocracy's relative power vis-à-vis the peasants was
quite high because of the production constraints faced by the peasants,
their absolute power was also greater than that of the Mauritian planters due to their economic and political ties to London. In the 1870s, for
example, some twenty-five British parliamentarians had ties to the West
Indies, and there were powerful lobbying groups pressing their interests
in London (Rodney 1981: 122). In Guyana, such personalities as Jon Gladstone—father of Prime Minister William Gladstone—owned several plantations and used his political weight to convince the British government
to allow and financially assist the importation of South Asian indentured
workers after emancipation (Hollet 1999: 47–55). In fact, Glasgow (1970)
claims that the Guyanese planters were the most powerful group in the
Caribbean. He notes that they received £52 per slave as compensation
for emancipation and that the planters in Barbados and Jamaica received
only £21 and £20 respectively, writing that this "was eloquent testimony
to the superior position enjoyed by the Guianese planters" (60). Similar
to Barbados and Jamaica, Mauritian planters received £27 per slave (£2.1
million for 77,000 slaves), suggesting that they were weaker than their
Guyanese counterparts.

As a consequence of their power, the planters were able to exert great
influence over the colonial administration in Guyana. As one official in
the Colonial Office noted in the 1870s, Guyana was "a merchants' and

planters' oligarchy not much tempered, perhaps, by any apprehension that the Crown will really exert the latent power it claims of supreme and absolute legislation" (Adamson 1972: 79). Planter control of state budgets provided one important means of undermining colonial state autonomy. During Dutch rule, planters were able to formalize their financial powers through their control of the Combined Court, which was a representative assembly dominated by planters that had the power to approve or reject colonial budgets. After the British took Guyana from the Dutch, they retained the structure of the Combined Court, allowing the plantocracy to occupy "an interventionist position from which it controlled, almost completely, the economic structure of the colony" (Despres 1967: 37). For example, when a doctor submitted a report to the Colonial Office describing the miserable working conditions on the estates, his salary was reduced to one cent and the Combined Court threatened to cut all funding for medical supplies (Adamson 1972: 151–52).[1]

Besides influencing the budget, planter legislative powers made possible greater control of labor. The planters were able to pressure the administration to implement legislation restraining peasants—almost exclusively African at this time—from either buying or successfully managing their lands in the mid-1800s. This "legislative encirclement of the peasant" was accomplished through a series of ordinances that (1) prevented the joint purchase of land by more than twenty people, (2) doubled the price of Crown Land, (3) set the minimum size of Crown Lands that could be purchased at 100 acres, and (4) forbade the immigration of peasants to Surinam (Adamson 1970: 386–87, 398). As Adamson (1970) notes, the "economic intent of these measures was to drive ex-slaves back to the estates" (387).

The sugar estates also used their legislative powers to hinder the successful management of peasant lands. The planters, for example, prevented the central government from using state resources to maintain local roads and irrigation infrastructure outside of the plantations, which was the only possible means for peasants to overcome the collective action problem and thereby maintain the productivity of their small plots of lands (Adamson 1970: 401). The planters, on the other hand, used their control of a variety of statutory boards—the Drainage Board, the Central Board of Health, the Transport and Harbours Board, and the Local Government Board—to direct public investment into projects affecting their private plantations (Jagan 1997: 72–73).

Along with their executive and legislative powers, the planters also used the courts to control labor. As a former magistrate in colonial Guyana proclaimed in 1903,

[T]he law has been so framed and its net, covering all possible offences, was
woven so closely, that not even the smallest peccadilloes could escape its
meshes; so that, in fact, the manager, whenever a laborer annoyed him, had
almost always in reserve some trifling neglect or other legally defined offense
on which he could bring a complaint involving fine or imprisonment with
hard labour, or both. (Mandle 1973: 64)

Numbers support this claim. Between 1876 and 1896, planters made 300
charges against their workers for every one charge filed against planters
by workers (Ireland 1897: 23; Despres 1967: 57–58). This discrepancy is
even more telling in comparison with Mauritius. In the late nineteenth
century, Mauritian laborers brought nearly 40 times as many cases to
court against planters as their Guyanese counterparts (Ireland 1897: 23;
Despres 1967: 57–58; Allen 1999: 68).[2] Moreover, whereas 20 percent of
all indentured laborers were convicted by the colonial courts in Guyana in
1907 for breaking labor laws,[3] the figure for Mauritius was only 3 percent
(Rodney 1981: 41). Thus, whereas Mauritius' legal system was relatively
independent of planters, Guyanese planters controlled the legal system
and used it to exploit labor.

Because of these environmental and social impediments, both African
and South Asian peasants in Guyana faced great difficulties expanding
beyond subsistence agriculture and therefore remained quite dependent
on plantations (Adamson 1972: 85; Despres 1967: 49–50; Young 1958:
24–88). The free African villages that were formed and flourished during
the 1840s, for example, soon stagnated and declined, causing peasants
either to return to work on the estates or move to Georgetown, the economic and political capital of the colony. South Asians were more successful at establishing and maintaining villages given a more favorable
political environment at the time they acquired lands, their acquisition of
better lands, and their cultivation of rice, but their communities were a far
cry from the more vibrant communities in Mauritius (Silverman 1980).

Although lower-class Guyanese were more marginalized and exploited
than lower-class Mauritians, their overall well-being appears to have been
superior to the Mauritians' in at least two categories: health and education. Smith (1962) and Mandle (1973) find that human development in
Guyana began to improve after World War I through the public provisioning of schools, health care, water supplies, and sanitation. For example,
the expansion of health care facilities allowed 181,000 people to receive
medical care in 1934, a relatively high figure given a population of only
325,000 (Colony of British Guiana 1936: 157). Health improvements began

to show up in the death and infant mortality rates by the 1930s, and Smith (1962) finds that life expectancy rose from thirty-five in the early 1920s to fifty-five in the early 1950s (8). With lower death rates, the Guyanese population—which did not grow at all between 1910 and 1920—began to increase quickly, expanding by 41 percent between 1921 and 1948. In contrast, the Mauritian population increased by only 14 percent during the same time period due primarily to higher death rates.

Yet because agricultural production and employment opportunities did not increase during the population boom, lower-class Guyanese experienced increased poverty despite advances in human capital. Between 1938 and 1952, for example, both the total calories and grams of protein consumed by Guyanese workers decreased (Mandle 1973: 100). Moreover, the labor force grew by 100,000 between 1946 and 1960, yet the number of jobs increased by only 10,000 (Mandle 1973: 130). Thus, the health improvements allowed more Guyanese to live longer yet more impoverished lives, and most Guyanese were unable to exploit their improved education for economic gain.

Post–World War II Political Crisis: Ethnicization and Destabilization

Without any formal means of shaping legislation, under the oppressive control of the planter's law, and dependent on plantations for miserable wages, lower-class Guyanese were very marginalized and impoverished and could do little about their condition. Strikes, however, were one means through which they could attempt to improve their lives. The first strike occurred only four years after emancipation when planters unsuccessfully attempted to collude and lower wages. By the late nineteenth century, strikes had become a regular feature of estate life. During the thirteen years between 1886 and 1903 for which data are available, there were on average over sixteen strikes per year (Adamson 1972: 155). Violence was quite common during the strikes, and deaths occurred frequently. The labor disturbances continued well into the twentieth century because of continued poor wages and working conditions. Indeed, there were over 250 strikes between 1900 and 1950, resulting in the deaths of forty-seven workers (Sallahuddin 1994: 27). The most intense period of strife occurred in 1938, during which colony-wide disturbances brought the economy to a standstill for nearly nine months.

Like Guyana, Mauritius and several other British plantation colonies experienced violent labor disputes in 1938 and 1939, and the Colonial Office therefore commissioned a general inquiry—the Moyne Report—

into the determinants of labor problems. It recognized and strongly criticized the inequality and exploitation caused by plantation production and prompted social reforms in the plantation colonies and, in fact, throughout the entire British Empire (Lee 1967: 45). As in Mauritius, the normal result of these reforms in directly ruled colonies was the expansion of the state, increased inclusiveness and democratization, and a state-led effort to promote human development. In Guyana, however, none of these occurred. Instead, local radicalism and cold war politics combined to disrupt the movement toward self-rule. Specifically, in order to remove obstinate Marxist politicians from the government, the British suspended the constitution in 1953, tolerated politically and ethnically motivated strikes and riots as a means of destabilizing the colony, and manipulated elections and electoral rules until their man finally won.

The Rise and Fall of the People's Progressive Party

With the winds of change acknowledged, the British began to prepare Guyana for self-rule after World War II. The 1953 constitution was a political landmark because it dramatically expanded suffrage (which rose from 15 percent in 1947 to 45 percent in 1953) and established a ministerial system of government run by local politicians (Sallahuddin 1994: 29–30). As the only well-organized party pursuing the interests of the newly enfranchised working class, the People's Progressive Party (PPP) was able to win eighteen of the twenty legislative seats in the 1953 elections. The PPP was founded in 1950 by Dr. Cheddi Jagan, a dentist of South Asian descent, and his American wife, Janet. It organized the laboring classes using Marxist and anticolonial platforms. In an effort to grow and maintain their position as the only leftist party, the PPP recruited Forbes Burnham—a young Afro-Guyanese law student recently returned from London—who served as the PPP's first chairman.

Unlike most politicians in other British colonies who were elected on anticolonial and leftist platforms, the PPP showed contempt for their colonizers and refused to collaborate with them after their electoral victory. Although supporting the principle of democracy, the British expected politicians to cooperate with the administration and follow the guidance of the British. The result was political deadlock and open confrontation between colonial officials and indigenous politicians. After five months of squabbling between the PPP and colonial officials, the British suspended the constitution, sent in troops, and forcefully removed the PPP from power. In a statement explaining these extreme measures, the chief secretary of

British Guiana claimed that they were necessary in order to prevent communist subversion and revolution (Burrowes 1984: 55). These claims were unfounded, and the removal of a democratically elected regime was quite unheard of within the British Empire. Not only was the PPP forced to relinquish its control of the government, but the British forbade PPP members from holding political meetings, limited their right to travel freely throughout the country, and imprisoned several of the party's leaders, including committing Cheddi Jagan to six months at hard labor for talking with supporters on his way out of court (considered an illegal political meeting).

The personal characteristics of the politicians and officials undoubtedly promoted conflict between British officials and PPP politicians, yet structural factors were also influential. The abject living conditions of the ever-growing laboring classes and the colonial state's historic support of opulent and powerful planters caused large segments of the population to resent colonial rule and to demand a policy that would promote the well-being of the working class. The incessant strikes and riots between 1850 and 1950 attest to their desire for change, and these groups gave their full support to the PPP. In contrast, the Mauritian Labour Party was also left-leaning yet was constrained by a much larger and more powerful land-owning middle class that mitigated any of the party's radical inclinations. On the British side of the equation, the considerable influence of the sugar elite and, especially, American concern over the spread of communism in the Western Hemisphere caused the administration to be less tolerant of left-leaning politicians in Guyana.

The Rise of Ethnic Mobilization and Violence

With the suspension of the 1953 constitution, the British propped up an interim moderate government that remained in power for nearly five years. Despite this attempt to legitimize politicians who had submitted to colonial guidance, the PPP remained a popular force and won twelve of the fourteen seats when elections were finally reinstated in 1957. By this time, however, the PPP had split into two factions—one led by Jagan, the other by Burnham—with the Jagan faction winning nine seats and the Burnham group winning three. Because the British realized that their desired candidates had little public support and saw Burnham and his new People's National Congress (PNC) as more moderate and manipulable, they supported Burnham through both action and inaction. In doing so, they began a vicious cycle of ethnic mobilization and conflict that was reinforced through a series of elections, strikes, and riots.

A common criticism of the British is that they used a divide-and-rule policy that promoted the ethnicization of politics in Guyana. Such claims usually suggest that officials encouraged Burnham to split from the Jagan faction, which for all intents and purposes was the advent of ethnic politics in Guyana given that Burnham was African and Jagan was South Asian. Although official documents have surfaced showing that the British greatly preferred Burnham over Jagan (at least initially), and although the preferential treatment given to Burnham and his rapid shift toward the center suggest that some agreement might have occurred (Mars 2001: 359), both the tension between Jagan and Burnham and strong ethnic cleavages in Guyana predated the suspension of the 1953 constitution.

First, Burnham and the founding members of the PPP had personal disagreements early on. After joining the PPP, Burnham's oratorical skills gained him a large following. Disagreements immediately arose between him and the party founders because Burnham refused to work for the party, choosing instead to focus his attention on his law practice as well as his own position within the party. Tension between Burnham and the party founders heightened in 1953 after Burnham sparked "crisis week" by trying to wrestle control of the party from Jagan. Party members prevented Burnham from becoming head of the PPP while preserving some semblance of party unity. In the end, however, party cohesion was very tenuous.

Moreover, ethnic animosity existed long before conflict between Jagan and Burnham. Tension between Africans and South Asians began as soon as the latter arrived in Guyana; the Afro-Guyanese saw the South Asians as the new slaves, while the South Asians were proud of their culture and felt they were more advanced than the Africans (Glasgow 1970: 95–97). Aggravating the cleavage, Africans and South Asians often lived in separate communities, tended to hold different positions on the estates, and were used as scabs whenever the other group refused to work. Thus, as a West Indian Commission in 1897 states, Africans and South Asians "do not intermix and that, of course, is one of our great safeties in the colony when there has been any rioting. If our Negroes were troublesome every coolie on the estate would stand by one. If the coolie attacked me I could with confidence trust my Negro friends for keeping me from injury" (Latin American Bureau 1984: 17).

The cleavages that already existed within the PPP and Guyanese society do not absolve the British, however. Indeed, colonial officials promoted the ethnicization of politics through their support of Burnham and his PNC. One example of the effects of British policy on ethnic animosity is the holding of multiple elections, which ignited ethnic tension on three occasions, two of which would have been avoided if the British colonial office had simply accepted the outcome of the 1957 election. As Premdas (1995) notes, each subsequent election caused ethnic tension and competition to increase further and further via electoral mobilization, creating a vicious cycle of antagonism that exacerbated sectionalism (46).

During the 1957 elections, ethnic tensions ran high despite the fact that neither politician overtly played the ethnic card. Although the 1957 elections could have led the government into independence, and although Jagan pushed for it, Britain refused to consider this option. During the next elections in 1961, politicians mobilized their ethnic constituencies, and ethnic conflict occurred. Again, Britain refused to begin the independence process because of the PPP victory, forcing Jagan to unsuccessfully bring his case for independence before the UN (Ince 1974). Thus, a third and final election was held before independence. While the election itself would have provoked ethnic conflict, the conflict was exacerbated by the ethnic preferences embedded within the new constitution: PPP demands for lowering the voting age to eighteen were denied (South Asians had a much younger population), and a system of proportional representation was introduced (which benefited Burnham and his PNC).

In addition to increasing ethnic tension by demanding several elections and showing a preference toward one party/ethnic group, the British government refused to take positive steps to quell ethnic violence during three politically motivated strikes and riots. In doing so, it legitimized PNC violence and allowed ethnic tension to rise to such an extent that it verged on civil war.

The 1962 riots. The 1962 riots were a politically charged series of demonstrations that began in early February, sparked widespread arson and looting, and caused five deaths and eighty injuries. The demonstrations began in opposition to an austerity budget planned by renowned Cambridge economist Nicholas Kaldor and were fueled by numerous strikes that included unions representing government workers. The commission of inquiry into the disturbances found that the budget was sound—having been praised by both the *New York Times* and the *London Times* as courageous and necessary—and concluded that the riots were opportunistic and political, blaming the disturbances on Burnham, his union supporters, and the leader of the conservative party.

The 1963 strikes. The Labour Relations Bill of 1963 was introduced by the PPP as a means to get the most popular sugar workers union recognized, since the official union served the sugar industry better than the workers.[4] To do so, the PPP copied American labor law and proposed that unions be recognized through a secret ballot of workers. The bill provoked an eighty-day strike that crippled the government and economy and resulted in many deaths and injuries, bombings, arson, and looting. Once again, the cause of the strike was political. As Robert Willis, the strike mediator sent from London and "a man not noted for his mercy in bargaining for newspaper management," noted, "It was rapidly clear to me that the strike was wholly political. Jagan was giving in to everything the strikers wanted but as soon as he did they erected new demands" (Latin American Bureau 1984: 42).

Although no evidence exists that directly implicates the British officials in the 1963 strikes and riots, they indirectly promoted the riots by turning a blind eye on the events. First, despite the discovery of arms and explosives at PNC headquarters and a police report describing a PNC organization as terroristic, no legal action against the PNC was taken by the colonial authorities, providing evidence that British officials supported the violence by refusing to counter it (Latin American Bureau 1984: 43; Jagan 1997: 233). In addition, the British colonial officials did not force the striking government workers to return to work even though they performed vital functions, resulting in the virtual absence of all government and public services for nearly three months. Moreover, the administrative officials within the Civil Service Association had no legitimate reason to strike in 1963—other than that they were overwhelmingly black and supporters of the PNC—yet the British still did not force them to return to work and even refused to take "disciplinary action against civil servants who were reported to have attacked and intimidated some of their colleagues who remained on duty" (Jagan 1997: 262). Similarly, British officials refused to do anything to avert crises caused by the strikes, which prevented ships from being unloaded and air traffic to and from Guyana (Hintzen and Premdas 1982: 8). After repeatedly asking the British for assistance, Jagan was forced to turn to Cuba for oil in order to avoid a complete power outage. Finally, throughout the crisis British troops were never deployed to restore order.

The 1963–64 riots. Claiming that the 1962 and 1963 disturbances had demonstrated how ineffective the Jagan government was, the British called a constitutional conference in October 1963, the outcome of which were British demands for a new election under a system of proportional representation. News of this imposed constitution caused great dissatisfaction among the Indo-Guyanese community and sparked strikes and riots that included ethnic-based murder, rape, beating, and looting.

When the rioting finally ended in July 1964, some 150 people had been killed, 800 injured, and over 13,000 forcibly dislocated (Rolison 1974: 284). Remarkably, it was only after half a year of ethnic violence that the British sent in troops to impose a peace that was necessary for the upcoming elections that brought Burnham and his PNC into power (Rolison 1974: 285). The belated entry of British troops is surprising given that PPP officials declared early on that they had completely lost control of the African-dominated police. As one commentator writes, "[T]he events clearly demonstrated that the colonial government was prepared to allow the PNC to use the largely Afro-Guyanese security forces while PNC thugs terrorized the South Asian population. The PPP was therefore faced not only with political opposition but with hostile security forces which were only nominally under the control of the PPP Minister of Home Affairs" (Latin American Bureau 1984: 44). Showing the police bias, some thirty PPP members and only two PNC members were arrested during the riots (Latin American Bureau 1984: 44).

The Ugly Americans

British complacency about the PNC-led opposition to the PPP helped transform popular resentment against economic and political inequities into ethnic animosity and undoubtedly led to an escalation of ethnic politics and violence. They were not the only external power destabilizing Guyana, however. In fact, British policy towards the PPP and PNC was greatly influenced by American pressure,[5] and the US government was directly involved in the 1962 and 1963 riots (Rabe 2005). Thus, cold war politics were an important cause of political instability and ethnic conflict in colonial Guyana.

In its attempt to curb the spread of communism, the American Government's involvement in Third World politics expanded dramatically after World War II. In Central America and the Caribbean, American interests were greater than elsewhere due to geographical proximity. Thus, American interference began in Guatemala in 1954, spread to the Dominican Republic in order to prop up a ruthless dictator, and attempted to remove Castro from power in Cuba. In view of this activity, American intervention in colonial Guyana is no surprise.

The US became concerned with the Marxist rhetoric of the PPP after it came to power in 1953 and fully endorsed the British decision to suspend the constitution (Jagan 1997: 138; Rabe 2005: 45; Rose 2002). After the Bay of Pigs fiasco in 1961, American interest in Guyana increased further, with the Kennedy administration believing that "an independent British Guiana under Burnham would cause us many fewer problems than an independent British Guiana under Jagan" (Rolison 1974: 155). In that year, they pressed Great Britain to suspend the constitution once again, but the British refused (Rolison 1974: 157). Taking matters into their own hands, the American government influenced Guyana's union movement through numerous US-dominated organizations: the International Confederation of Free Trade Unions (ICFTU), the Inter-American Regional Organization (ORIT), the Public Service International (PSI), and the Institute of Free Labor Development (IFLD). Guyana had the highest proportion of IFLD-trained organizers in Latin America; the IFLD taught unionists "how to fight communism and ways and means of organizing opposition to the government" (Rolison 1974: 161–62). Through the other organizations, the US gained influence over most of Guyana's recognized unions, which were dominated by Afro-Guyanese. In particular, the CIA helped instigate the 1962 and 1963 strikes/riots through its control of the PSI (Ince 1974; Rabe 2005). According to one investigative reporter for the *New York Times*, CIA operatives "gave advice to local union leaders on how to organize and sustain a strike and provided funds, food, and medical supplies. At one point, one of the agents even served as a member of a bargaining committee that was negotiating with Jagan" (Rolison 1974: 165). Furthermore, President Kennedy, who saw the riots as a means to remove Jagan from power, chastised the British when they eventually stepped in to control the violence (Rabe 2005: 93).

Finally, the US used its influence to persuade Great Britain to change the constitution and hold new elections to benefit the PNC (Rabe 2005). As one of Kennedy's advisors noted in his memoirs, the administration held lengthy meetings with the British government in order to convince it that a proportional representation system would solve all its problems in Guyana (Schlesinger 1965: 779). Through the manipulation of the constitution, the Anglo-American conspiracy finally succeeded at getting their man in power. The price paid for this by the American government was quite low compared to that paid in Guatemala, Vietnam, and the Dominican Republic; as described in the next section, foreign interference cost the Guyanese dearly.

State Building and Development in Guyana, 1953–85

The conflict-ridden 1950s and 1960s ultimately had three interrelated and detrimental effects on Guyanese development. First, very little state-led development actually occurred during the last two decades of colonial rule. Second, state reforms were very minimal during the period despite preparation for independence. Finally, the domination of the civil service by PNC supporters and strong American backing allowed Burnham to co-opt the state's legal-administrative institutions as soon as he came to power in 1964 and build a personal and militarized system of rule characterized by state-led plunder and predation. Together, these three factors left a relatively ineffective and despotic state and severely limited developmental improvements.

State Decline and Underdevelopment during Late Colonialism

A comparison of Guyana and Mauritius during the late-colonial period highlights several factors that help to explain their different developmental outcomes. Ineffective local government, low levels of inclusiveness, and a defective and politicized state, for example, all afflicted Guyana but not Mauritius. Collaborative political relations in Mauritius and conflictual political relations in Guyana, in turn, underlie these differences and thereby go a long way in explaining their divergent developmental trajectories.

As described in Chapter 4, the Mauritian Labour Party, colonial officials, and indigenous administrators all actively collaborated to expand the state, construct local government, and implement development policy during the final years of colonialism. The situation in Guyana was quite different, as perpetual conflict between the PPP, colonial officials, and indigenous administrators prevented Jagan's government from implementing any such policy. As noted previously, colonial opposition to the PPP was caused by the party's radicalism and American pressure, whereas the PPP refused to collaborate with the British because the PPP viewed them as exploitative imperialists and stooges of the plantations. Besides destabilizing Guyana and promoting ethnic violence, this conflict caused a political deadlock, which limited both state-building and developmental reforms during late colonialism. As Sallahuddin (1994) claims, "If [the colonial officials] couldn't beat Jagan at the polls, then defeat him by frustrating his development plan" (189).

At this, colonial officials were aided by indigenous administrators, who were overwhelmingly Afro-Guyanese and therefore supported Burnham.[6] Because of the open resentment between the civil servants and the PPP, channels of communication and coordination closed, creating an effective barrier between PPP ministers and the administration (Lutchman 1970). Relations between the administration and the PPP were openly confrontational and even violent (Lutchman 1970: 28). Most importantly, administrators used their union—the British Guiana Civil Service Association (CSA)—to organize themselves in an attempt to weaken the government. During both the 1962 and 1963 strikes, the CSA struck against the government, in what one expert describes as open warfare with the government: "Their [CSA] role in the strike was far from passive; they not only were on strike but were very active in the organization of the strike and were in open opposition to the Government" (Lutchman 1970: 24). Notably, conflict between the CSA and the Jagan government further impeded the latter's ability to implement needed political and developmental reforms. It also impeded state building by eliminating any political will among the PPP to strengthen the administration. As Lutchman (1970) writes,

> The lack of confidence between the Government and the civil services manifested itself in the usual way. In many cases, there was a marked reluctance on the part of ministers to delegate authority to their civil servants irrespective of the pressure under which they found themselves. They also tended to ignore senior advisors altogether and consult with junior officers in whom they had greater confidence. (27)

Local government provides a clear example of the institutional stagnation caused by intrastate conflict in Guyana. Whereas local government flourished in Mauritius beginning in the late 1940s and helped provide needed developmental goods, similar reforms never occurred in Guyana, and the state remained largely absent at the local level. In both 1954 and 1955, separate commissions found that local government was completely unable to promote development in Guyana and that the local population lacked ties to the colonial state (Marshall 1955: 9). This developmental impotence and lack of inclusiveness was caused by the marginalization of the peasants and the fact that local authorities continued to be "bands of owners of property anxious to provide themselves with drainage and roads, rather than public authorities whose aim it should be to use the power of taxation to provide services which the individual alone cannot provide" (Seawar 1957). Despite these findings, local government and administration were still unchanged a decade and a half later: "It is generally agreed that the present system of local government in Guyana is unsuited to the tasks of thinking required of a developing country but, although the system has been under review since the early 1950s, with a view to effecting much needed reform, progress in this direction has been remarkably slow" (Lutchman 1971b: 95).

Beyond institutional stagnation at the local level, intrastate conflict also caused the degeneration of state structures at the center. With open conflict within the state, bureaucratic basics such as following organizational rules, a set organizational hierarchy, and meritocracy began to break down; the state's organizational capacity declined accordingly. An administrative commission in 1966, for example, claimed the state was experiencing crisis and decline. It found that the state was divided, that the civil service had a very low morale, that all esprit de corps had been destroyed over the past decade, and that politics—not merit—was seen as the only means of advancement within the administration (Burgess and Hunn 1966: 35). Three years later, a new report was full of old and new administrative problems: brain drain and the departure of civil servants to the private sector, constant political interference within the administration, low meritocracy, a lack of esprit de corps, dissatisfaction over low pay and decreasing status, and atrocious working conditions (Collins 1969: 5–6).

Burnham's Personalization of Power and Developmental Decline

Forbes Burnham finally vanquished Cheddi Jagan from power in 1964 and thereby became Guyana's first independent head of state. His rule lasted until his death in 1985 and was characterized by fraudulent elections, the misuse of state funds, violent coercion, and the complete takeover of the state and economy by Burnham and his PNC elite. While the legal-administrative institutions that Burnham usurped had only limited capacities to promote development because of their growing ineffectiveness during the late colonial period, his personal and militarized rule caused rampant state-led predation and therefore not only failed to promote development but actually impeded it.

Burnham's capture of the state's legal-administrative institutions occurred fairly rapidly after his election in 1964 and was made possible by the decrepit state of the administration, the civil service's strong support for the PNC, the state's very low levels of inclusiveness, and American and British complacency. With the administration under his thumb, he had considerable freedom and began to shape the state to suit his personal interests. One of his first moves was to take personal control over the Public Service Commission, which empowered him to hire and discipline legal-administrative officials at will. In doing so, he "established the controversial principle that any state employee could be dismissed at the pleasure of the Prime Minister without explanation and without the aggrieved party having recourse for redress" (Brotherson 1988: 64).

After this inauspicious beginning, Burnham proclaimed a "cooperative" republic in 1970 and began to increase state control over the economy. Within five years, he had nationalized several industries and controlled almost the entire economy. Despite Burnham's claims, the state was neither cooperative nor socialist. Instead, the relations of production remained unchanged, the only difference being the beneficiaries: Burnham and his PNC affiliates (Tennassee 1986: 29; Latin American Bureau 1984: 49–50; Rose 2002: 179). In all, thirty-two companies were nationalized, including the sugar and bauxite industries, and seventeen government enterprises were formed between 1971 and 1976, all of which were chaired by Burnham (Latin American Bureau 1984: 51).

Along with nationalization, Burnham also increased his control over imports and exports by creating the External Trade Bureau in 1970, which acted as a "mechanism for dispensing import licenses to favored businessmen" (Latin American Bureau 1984: 29). Its primary effects were the enrichment of a select few PNC officials and increasing popular dependence on the state for jobs. Recognizing the state's firm control over both production and international trade, Hintzen and Premdas (1982) remark that "[i]n a few short years most of the population, with the possible exception of a few professionals, had become economically dependent upon the Black-dominated state" (112).

Unfortunately for the Guyanese population, state control of the economy stimulated neither production nor consumption. Between 1970 and 1980, for instance, the production of bauxite and aluminum declined by nearly 40 percent annually while sugar production fell by nearly 10 percent (Tennassee 1986: 35; Latin American Bureau 1984: 31). In fact, although over 300,000 tons of aluminum were produced in 1970, the total steadily declined until aluminum production halted completely in 1983 (Rose 2002: 204). Overall, per capita GDP declined by over 20 percent between 1970 and 1990 (World Bank 2007a).

Consumption also suffered because of falling incomes and new import-export controls, the latter of which never functioned properly and simply caused an ever-increasing shortage of goods (Latin American Bureau 1984: 51). By 1982, only 3 of the 271 products on the price control list in 1978—sugar, rice, and chicken—were still available in stores, prompting the government to start a publicity campaign promoting rice instead of flour under the slogan that rice was the food of revolutionaries while bread was an imperialist food (Latin American Bureau 1984: 85). One result of the food shortage was increased malnutrition, which affected between 49 and 62 percent of all children under the age of five in 1983 (Rose 2002: 205).

These economic hardships were primarily caused by inappropriate policy and, especially, mismanagement. Corrupt practices by the PNC elite were the norm and simultaneously prevented developmental goods and promoted developmental bads. According to one source:

> The PNC strata embarked on various strategies [to abuse their positions for personal gain]. This was achieved by legislation and "accountancy robbery." One case in point was the disappearance of over one million dollars at the Ministry of Works and Hydraulics which could not be accounted for. . . . Another was through "protection money" from the business community, and "raids" on the rice industry. In a Mafian style, checks with sums written were sent to the business community for their signatures. Promises were made that the large contributors' names would be brought to the attention of the comrade leader [Burnham]. The "income tax" department was used as a threat to those who were not generous enough. Inflated tax sums were issued against unfriendly businessmen. (Tennassee 1986: 22)

When combined with incompetence, state corruption caused abysmally poor management of macro-economic indicators that was characterized by erratic policy without any sort of long-term strategy (Latin American Bureau 1984: 67). Total government deficits between 1977 and 1985, for instance, were nearly three times as large as the GDP (World Bank 2007a). In addition, the state began to expand the monetary supply, causing the consumer price index to increase by 212 percent between 1975 and 1983 (Latin American Bureau 1984: 63; Rose 2002: 209). Mismanagement also affected utilities, infrastructure, and services, all of which suffered after independence (Latin American Bureau 1984: 67; Rose 2002: 201; Singh 1988: 96). Poor pay, low investment, the lack of public spirit, and the personalization of state resources all combined to promote their decline.

While Guyanese development suffered, the personal power of Burnham continued to grow. In December 1974, Burnham initiated a policy of "Party Paramountcy," which effectively merged the PNC and the state, giving the PNC formal control of law and administration as well as direct access to state revenue (Lutchman 1979: 22; Rose 2002: 195). Because of this, state funds were used by the party with no strings attached. Thus, less than 3 percent of all funds received by PNC officials between 1975 and 1980 can be accounted for (Rose 2002: 195).

Burnham used extreme coercion to maintain his economic and political dominance. After coming to power, he dramatically expanded the country's security forces, which came to include the Guyanan Defense Force, the police, the Guyana National Service, and the People's Militia. Through rapid expansion, the number of security personnel grew from 2,000 in 1964 to 22,000 in 1977; the latter represented one in every thirty-five Guyanese citizens (Danns 1978: 16; Sallahuddin 1994: 308–9). Furthermore, the national defense budget increased from only 2 percent to over 14 percent (Danns 1978: 18). Danns (1978) notes that all segments of the security force were composed overwhelmingly of Africans (approximately 90 percent) and were simply appendages of the PNC and thus Burnham himself, the minister of defense.

With this military buildup, state coercion was rampant and became the basis of Burnham's rule. Indeed, legal-administrative institutions— although already co-opted by Burnham—became even more marginal and subordinate to the state's coercive apparatus. As a result, the state was quite effective at bullying its population but had great difficulty implementing any sort of policy that depended on legal-administrative institutions. Indeed, the state's provisioning of developmental goods was out of the question, and the militarized and personalized state preyed on society. For example, Burnham relied on murder and intimidation to stifle dissent. When poor urban blacks—traditionally Burnham's strongest supporters—started to protest against his misrule in 1979, Burnham oversaw strategic attacks and multiple political assassinations, including the murder of the outspoken and acclaimed academic Walter Rodney (Tennassee 1986: 309; Morrison 1998: 130–70). Burnham also orchestrated brutal and frequent attacks on the South Asian community in order to force its submission (Singh 1988: 86–88). All in all, with his control of the party, state, and economy and his personal and militarized rule, the "B.G." of British Guiana for all intents and purposes now stood for "Burnham's Guyana," and Burnham's despotic state had very negative effects on the ability of most Guyanese to pursue their well-being.

After Burnham's death in 1985, Desmond Hoyte—a leading member of the Burnham government—ascended to the presidency, and the Guyanese state remained militarized and coercive. Under increasing domestic and international pressure and facing severe economic conditions, Hoyte relinquished power and called elections in 1992, and Cheddi Jagan and his PPP regained control of the government after a thirty-year respite. Since then, the state's large coercive force has been dismantled, Guyana has continued to be a democracy, and the country's economy and human development have improved because of a dramatic decrease in state predation. Unfortunately, the political and developmental effects of years of conflict and despotic rule were great, and to this day the state remains largely ineffective in its struggle to provide developmental goods, leaving Guyana one of the poorest and most underdeveloped countries in the Western Hemisphere.

Comparisons with Mauritius and Sierra Leone

A comparison of Mauritius and Guyana provides evidence that different colonial transitions caused their developmental trajectories to split rapidly and markedly. In colonial Guyana, a conflictual and violent transition prevented developmental policy from being implemented, impeded state building reforms, limited inclusiveness, and promoted the personalization and militarization of the Guyanese state. During the final decades of colonialism in Mauritius, on the other hand, broad-based development policy was implemented, reforms strengthened legal-administrative institutions, and state inclusiveness increased markedly.

Given the important developmental effects of their different colonial transitions, one must ask why they occurred. Comparison of the two cases highlights class conflict, relations between colonial officials and domestic actors, and the cold war as interrelated causes. First, the Guyanese planters were stronger and the peasants weaker than their Mauritian counterparts, and the planters completely dominated relations between the colonial state and society. The power of the Guyanese planters was caused by their much stronger political and economic ties back to London, which was largely absent in Mauritius because the planters were of French origin. The peasants in Guyana were poorer than their Mauritian counterparts because they either did not own land or owned unproductive lands, thereby preventing them from forming vibrant rural villages as in Mauritius and engaging the state in active relations.

Class power differentials and low levels of inclusiveness, in turn, affected the extent to which the colonial transitions were either collaborative or confrontational. The independence process was much more confrontational in Guyana because lower-class Guyanese resented the power of the plantations, believed the colonial state unilaterally supported the interests of sugar, lacked institutional ties to the state, and were not constrained by a large land-owning middle class. Thus, while the Mauritian Labour Party actively collaborated with colonial officials during the last two decades of colonialism, the People's Progressive Party in Guyana badgered and attacked them.

And because of the more collaborative relations in Mauritius and the more confrontational transition in Guyana, colonial officials addressed problems of domestic violence and development in different ways. In Mauritius, ethnic tension existed and became conflictual during the independence process, but British officials immediately sent in troops and quelled the disturbances. On the other hand, British and American officials were concerned about the spread of communism and actually promoted violence and instability in Guyana in an attempt to remove Jagan and his PPP from power. In terms of development, broad-based and collaborative relations between Mauritian state and society facilitated the expansion of state infrastructural power, local political development and participation, and state-society synergy. Violence and confrontational politics in Guyana, however, prevented the implementation of political and developmental reforms.

Because of these characteristics, the state in Guyana lacked the capacity to provide developmental goods and actually promoted developmental bads through its heavy reliance on coercion, two factors that set the country on a different trajectory from Mauritius. In this, Guyana is similar to Sierra Leone in important ways. As in Sierra Leone under Siaka Stevens, the state in postcolonial Guyana became the personal domain of one man, Forbes Burnham. Both men reorganized the state in order to suit their needs, used it to usurp resources for personal use, created a military force in order to suppress opposition, and subordinated legal-administrative institutions to the military. The end result in both cases was a violent and predatory state with ineffective legal-administrative institutions.

Overall, the comparison of Guyana, Mauritius, and Sierra Leone provides evidence that state transformations during the independence process caused Guyana to be a statistical outlier. These changes prevented political and developmental reforms from being implemented, reduced the effectiveness of the legal-administrative institutions, and promoted a coercive and militarized state. In this way, Guyana departed from the normal trajectory of direct rule, and the Guyanese state gained many of the characteristics of more indirectly ruled former colonies despite the absence of chiefly collaborators. The case is therefore an exception that helps prove one rule—bureaucratization and inclusiveness positively affect development, and de-bureaucratization and exclusiveness negatively affect it—but forces the reevaluation of another—the legacies of British colonial rule sometimes transformed during the independence process.

Botswana

A Case of Development Despite Indirect Rule

7

Botswana is an arid, land-locked, and sparsely populated country located north of South Africa. Of all countries in the world, it experienced the greatest increase in the Human Development Index between 1975 and 1990, suggesting phenomenal improvements in the ability of the people of Botswana, known collectively as Batswana, to pursue their well-being. High rates of development, however, were unexpected at the time of the country's independence in 1966 because Botswana (formerly the Bechuanaland Protectorate) had one of the world's lowest per capita GDPs, lacked basic infrastructure, experienced recurrent droughts, and was surrounded by white-dominated states antagonistic to black rule.

The discovery of rich diamond deposits in the 1960s and 1970s provided resources necessary for rapid developmental improvements in Botswana. While Botswana has thrived, other African countries such as Sierra Leone, Angola, Nigeria, and the Democratic Republic of Congo have been unable to promote development through the exploitation of rich natural resources. One factor that might account for Botswana's success is the state's capacity to promote development. As several works recognize, the states in Nigeria, Sierra Leone, and Congo are patrimonial and fissiparous, and these characteristics cripple state effectiveness and free actors

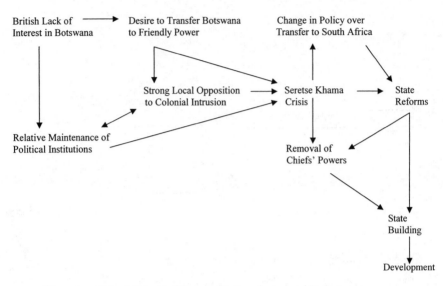

Figure 7.1 Colonial Roots of Botswana's Developmental Trajectory

to fight over the control of rich national resources (see Chapter 5 as well as Callaghy 1984; Evans 1995; Kohli 2004; Migdal 1988; Reno 1995). In contrast, a number of scholars find that the Botswanan state is bureaucratically organized, effectively regulates social relations, and has been able to exploit the country's rich diamond deposits in order to promote broad-based development (Edge 1998; Goldsmith 1999; Leftwich 2000; Lewis 1993; Samatar 1999).

While the presence of an effective state in Botswana helps answer one question, it raises another equally perplexing one: Where did Botswana's developmental state come from? Indeed, most of Botswana's population lived in indirectly ruled regions during the British colonial period, and it had one of the smallest colonial states. The case is therefore at odds with the findings of the previous chapters and forces one to reconsider the developmental legacy of indirect colonial rule.

In this chapter, I explore the causes of Botswana's surprisingly successful state building and development. As shown in Figure 7.1, I find that a chain of events—including the British Government's lack of interest in colonial Botswana and its subsequent efforts to give Botswana to South Africa—led to a succession crisis in Botswana's largest and most powerful chiefdom between 1948 and 1956. The crisis, in turn, caused the breakdown of previous forms of colonial rule in large parts of the protectorate and created incentives for the construction of a larger and more centralized state. As a consequence, extensive state reforms began in the late 1950s, continued over the next two decades, and increased the state's legal-administrative effectiveness by institutionalizing a more direct form of rule.

Similar to the Guyanese case study, the history of state building and development in Botswana demonstrates that independence was an important period during which critical institutional reforms could and did occur. It also parallels Guyana in that the institutional changes readjusted the country's developmental trajectory in ways predicted by the mechanisms highlighted in the Mauritian and Sierra Leonean case studies. In particular, Botswana's move away from indirect rule enhanced the state's legal-administrative capacities and thereby promoted broad-based development. Thus, despite being an outlier case that does not conform to the relationship between the form of colonialism and development, Botswana provides additional and strong evidence in support of the institutional mechanisms highlighted in the Mauritian and Sierra Leonean case studies.

Precolonial Botswana

The first inhabitants of Botswana were the San (also known as the Basarwa, Bushmen, or Khoisan), a diverse group of peoples romanticized as one of the last groups of hunter-gatherers in the world and known for their unique linguistic clicks. They lived throughout Botswana for several thousand years until Bantus began to settle in the region around AD 200, after which the new arrivals gradually pushed the San further and further into the Kalahari. The Bantus continued to arrive in waves over the next 1,700 years and brought with them new crops, livestock, and iron-age technologies. By the twelfth century, large-scale Bantu settlements emerged. The largest of these was founded in northeastern Botswana during the fifteenth century and was part of the Butwa Kingdom, which was inhabited by the ancestors of present-day Bakalanga and remained a powerful state for nearly 400 years by controlling the trade route between Botswana and the Indian Ocean. Between the sixteenth and twentieth centuries, new groups of Bantus (the Bayei, Bahambukushu, Bekulane, and Ovahero) arrived from the north and settled in northern Botswana around the Okavango Delta.

Along with these immigrants, several groups of Bantus from the Sotho linguistic group began to arrive in Botswana around AD 200, and a large in-migration of Sotho from the Tswana branch began approximately 400 years ago. The first of these Tswana tribes was the Bakwena. In the mid-eighteenth century, the Bakwena split into two additional tribes, the Bangwaketse and the Bangwato. The Batawana, in turn, broke away from the

Bangwato in 1795. In the 1870s, the last of the five major Tswana groups in modern Botswana—the Bakgatla—entered Botswana from the Transvaal. Although the five main Tswana communities have probably never made up more than half of the population of Botswana, their arrival had great repercussions on the other groups because they conquered and controlled most of present-day Botswana by the mid-1800s, thus integrating the diverse peoples of Botswana to various extents into Tswana social institutions.

Tswana social relations were based on agriculture and cattle and organized around a centralized chiefdom, or *morafe*. The *morafe* had a tripartite structure both geographically and socially. Geographically, each chiefdom had a capital village that served as the administrative center and occasionally had populations exceeding 25,000 inhabitants. The central village, in turn, was surrounded by two concentric circles that people migrated to and from depending on the season. The inner circle was an area of agricultural cultivation, and the outer circle was used for cattle posts and grazing lands. Other smaller outlying villages had similar organizational structures. They were ruled by subchiefs who paid allegiance to the chief, creating relatively large patrimonial chiefdoms.

Socially, all chiefdom inhabitants fell into one of three status groups. The highest consisted of the Tswana agnates who traced their heritage back to the original chiefdom founders. Chiefs and subchiefs generally claimed membership in this group. The middle group included low-status Tswana and non-Tswana who had integrated into the chiefdom. Finally, recently conquered peoples were forced to serve the Tswana elite, usually caring for their cattle in patron-client relations. While people within this group were usually able to advance beyond positions of semi-serfdom with time, conquered San had difficulty integrating into the tribe because of racial and cultural differences, creating a situation of perpetual dependence and marginalization that continues to this day.

The two key institutions of the Tswana *morafe* were the *kgosi* (chieftaincy) and *kgotla* (public assembly). The chieftaincy was a powerful position, having executive, judicial, and legislative power as well as a high level of discretion over chiefdom lands and cattle. Chiefs resided in the central villages and relied on subchiefs and headmen to administer the *morafe* population residing outside the capital. Despite the high concentration of power, the chief's position depended upon an exchange relationship, as the chief was given support in exchange for providing for the well-being of his chiefdom and its members through adept leadership and the use of his cattle wealth (Wylie 1990: 31).

In addition to the requirement of providing for one's peoples, the chief's decision-making ability was limited by the tribal assembly, or *kgotla*. Each chiefdom had regular meetings that were led by the chief and attended by adult men of all statuses. During these assemblies, the chiefs led discussions on matters pertaining to administrative, legislative, and judicial issues. After all desiring to speak had finished, the chief summarized the discussion and decided upon the chiefdom's line of action. The chief was free to decide against the general opinion of the assembly, but his power depended upon public support, especially the backing of the subchiefs. Consequently, if the chief chose to disregard the public consensus derived at the assemblies, his legitimacy was weakened and his position became vulnerable. Murder and desertion were common sanctions against chiefly misrule.

The Creation of the Bechuanaland Protectorate

The Boers began their Great Trek into the lands north of the Cape Colony in 1832. This movement of some 12,000 Boers dramatically affected the subsequent history of South Africa through war, conquest, enslavement, the dispossession of land, and the construction of racially segregated social institutions. Although most Africans outside of the future South Africa avoided the changes introduced by the Boers, the Great Trek did not leave all unscathed. In present-day Botswana, the Tswana chiefdoms were attacked by Mzilikazi—a renegade general of Shaka Zulu who controlled a large Ndebele army—after the Boers forced his warriors to flee to the north. Shortly after Mzilikazi's warriors left present-day Botswana and settled in Zimbabwe, the Boers began to enter Tswana territory.

Upon their arrival, the Boers demanded capitulation as well as land and labor. Describing Boer treatment of the Batswana in 1847, David Livingston, who founded his first mission in precolonial Botswana, wrote,

> In speaking of the relations between Dutch and native . . . [the Dutch] have taken possession of nearly all the fountains, and the natives live in the country only by sufferance. Each chief when called upon is obliged to furnish the emigrants with as many men as any piece of work may require, and except in the case of shepherds no wages are paid for labour. Labour is exacted as an equivalent for being allowed to live in the land of their forefathers. (Gunderson 1970: 109)

In response to these demands, several Tswana chiefs, led by Sechele I of the Bakwena, joined forces and began the Batswana-Boer War of 1852–53, which the Tswana won.[1] Despite their defeat, the Boers continued to press into Tswana territory over the next two decades. In a letter to the British queen's representative in 1876, Chief Khama of the Bangwato saw the presence of the Boers as such a problem that he asked for British protection against their incursions: "I write to you, Sir Henry, in order that your Queen may preserve for me my country, and put it under her protection. The Boers are coming into it and I don't like them. Their actions are cruel among us black people. They sell us and our children. I ask Her Majesty to defend me as she defends all her people" (Gunderson 1970: 121).

Several years after this request, the British sent a military expedition north and proclaimed a protectorate over Botswana in 1885. Despite past requests by chiefs and missionaries for protection, the primary motivations for colonial rule were geopolitical and economic. Most basically, the British created the protectorate in order to prevent the separation of the Cape Colony from other British colonies in Central and East Africa. This objective became a priority because an important road passed through Botswana, and this route became increasingly vital for trade and security after the discovery of gold and diamonds in the Transvaal. Thus, the British high commissioner wrote in 1885, "We have no intention in the country north of the Molopo [Botswana] except as a road into the interior; we might therefore confine ourselves for the present to preventing that part of the Protectorate being occupied by either filibusters or foreign powers, doing as little by way of administration or settlement as possible" (Hermans 1974: 90–91). As the subsequently history of Botswana suggests, the British largely succeeded in these minimalist goals.

Limited Colonial Influence in Botswana, 1885–1948

As elsewhere, colonialism in Botswana transformed social structures in different ways. The most important changes were the arrival of a few hundred white settlers and the beginning of widespread labor migration of Batswana males to South African mines. At the same time, the colonial presence in Botswana was considerably less intrusive than in other British colonies, causing local government to differ from those in other indirectly ruled colonies in two ways. First, the precolonial sociopolitical institutions of the Tswana chiefdoms were maintained to a greater extent than in Sierra Leone and other indirectly ruled colonies. Second, the "native" institutions retained a greater degree of autonomy from the colonial administration throughout the colonial period. As a consequence of the latter, colonial rule in Botswana was more parallel than in other indirectly ruled colonies.

This nonintrusive and parallel structure of rule limited British influence, provoking a former resident commissioner to complain that the tribal territories were "a sort of human Whipsnade"—in reference to a free-range wildlife park in Great Britain—in which the Africans were left to live as they did before British colonialism (Gunderson 1970: 179).

Limited Colonial Administration

After ten years of nominal control, the first permanent administration in Botswana was formed following the writing of the 1895 Agreement, which served as the ad hoc constitution of the Bechuanaland Protectorate until 1959 (Otlhogile 1975: 4). It set aside Tribal Territories for the five Tswana chiefdoms (eventually eight after the recognition of three minor chiefdoms in southern Botswana) and maintained the precolonial sociopolitical institutions by stating that the chiefs were to "rule their own people much as at present" (Gunderson 1970: 130–31). The chiefs agreed to collect revenue to pay for the British administration, to cede to the colonial government all lands not under their direct control, and to relinquish a strip of land along the eastern border of the protectorate. The Crown appointed a resident commissioner responsible to the high commissioner of the Cape Colony and in charge of the day-to-day administration of the protectorate.

Along with the Tribal Territories, the 1895 Agreement separated the protectorate's land into two additional administrative categories. First, the strip of land in southeastern Botswana ceded to the British, a concession of land granted to a South African company in northeastern Botswana (Tati), and a settlement in the middle of the Kalahari (Ghanzi) were all ruled directly because of the presence of European settlers and businesses. At their peak, only 3,000 Europeans lived in the protectorate, and the directly ruled region made up only a small portion of the protectorate's territory, albeit much of the best agricultural land.[2]

Outside of the chiefdoms and the directly ruled regions of European settlement, the remainder of the protectorate was categorized as Crown Land. This vast land in the north and west of the protectorate lacked white settlers, was very sparsely populated, and was not organized into chiefdoms. In much of these lands, the colonial administration established an indirect system of rule by recognizing individuals as subchiefs or headmen and empowering them to manage local affairs along supposedly traditional lines. In other parts, the Crown Lands were so sparsely populated and isolated that they were without any real system of colonial rule, and extensive regions of the Crown Lands were eventually recognized as game reserves and national parks.

Even after the 1895 Agreement, the British administration had only a weak presence in the eight chiefdoms and the Crown Lands, although the arrival of settlers caused growing European interference in the more directly ruled regions of the protectorate. For example, in 1915, thirty years after the proclamation of the protectorate, the colonial state in Botswana had only 277 staff, representing one administrator per 1,000 square miles (Hermans 1974: 102). And nine out of ten personnel were guards and policemen who patrolled the borders, demonstrating the colonial focus on the prevention of foreign occupation and the administrative disregard for domestic affairs (Hermans 1974: 102). By the mid-1930s, just thirty years before independence, Botswana had only twenty-two nonpolice officials stationed within the protectorate (Picard 1984: 88).

While limited British interest in the protectorate was an important determinant of the lax form of colonial domination, several additional factors restrained colonial interference. One reason for the extremely small number of British administrators in Botswana was the location of the administrative capital, Mafeking, which is located sixteen miles south of the border in South Africa. Indeed, as late as 1952, 42 percent of the senior and mid-level officers employed by the Bechuanaland Protectorate were still permanently stationed in South Africa, not Botswana. This unusual situation arose because of colonial economizing, as there were fully functional yet unused administrative buildings in Mafeking, preventing the budget-minded administration from building any in Botswana until 1965, the year before colonial independence.

A second factor that limited the colonial presence was the British intention to transfer Botswana to either the British South Africa Company or the Union of South Africa. The protectorate was almost given to Cecil Rhodes' British South Africa Company in the 1890s, prompting three Tswana chiefs and some supportive missionaries to travel to London to urge Secretary of State Joseph Chamberlain to keep the protectorate under the control of Her Majesty's Government (Parsons 1998). Although the trip ultimately succeeded in its goal, the respite was only temporary since the British began to consider the transfer of the protectorate to South Africa shortly thereafter.[3] In fact, between 1910 and the early 1950s, the transfer of Botswana to South African hands appeared almost certain. As late as 1953, for example, the British high commissioner to South Africa stated that the "only future [of the Bechuanaland Protectorate] is with the Union of South Africa" (Picard 1984: 86), and it was only a decade before independence that the issue of transfer was finally dropped. Throughout this period of uncertainty, colonial rule in Botswana was characterized by a "wait and see" attitude that deterred administrative reforms and infrastructural investment within the protectorate (Gunderson 1970: 159; Picard 1987: 41–42).

Tswana acceptance of and loyalty to British rule was a fourth factor limiting the extent of colonial domination because it allowed colonial officials to leave administrative duties in the hands of local elite. Given the external threat posed by the Boers, the protectorate actually offered some sort of *kind of* protection, and it was therefore in the interests of the chiefs to collaborate *loyal to GB* with the British. In addition to this more benign form of protection, acceptance of British rule offered protection from the British themselves. As Ramsay (1998b) notes, the Tswana chiefs collected the first Protectorate *accept* Hut Tax in 1899 without any complaints despite a devastating drought and *GB* famine between 1896 and 1899. This surprising lack of resistance likely *rule* occurred because the Batlhaping, a group of Tswana living over the border in South Africa, rebelled and refused to pay their hut tax in 1897, provoking the colonial administration to kill approximately 1,500 Batlhaping and capture 4,000 others who were subsequently sent to the Western Cape as forced labor (80). This British threat, however, was well known even before the slaughter of neighboring Tswana. When asked if he would oppose the British in 1868, Chief Sechele I of the Bakwena replied, "How could I? The great English would eat me up in one day" (Ramsay 1998b: 67).

Although the Tswana chiefdoms openly accepted British rule throughout the colonial period, they opposed increased colonial control of domestic affairs; this also helped to further limit the colonial presence. For example, attempts to make the parallel form of administration closer to the ideal of indirect rule between 1926 and 1936 failed because of local opposition *fight against* (Robertson 1979: 167). Throughout the period, the Tswana chiefs waged a *domestic interference* bitter struggle over the meaning of "protectorate" in an attempt to retain domestic autonomy, something they thought was necessary to prevent being handed over to South Africa. As Regent Chief Tshekedi Khama wrote in his legal case filed against the British government over the Native Administration and Native Tribunal Proclamations of 1934,

> We find that a Protectorate in Bechuanaland means: A territory, the soil of which does not belong to Great Britain but to its native inhabitants; the internal administration of which is in the hands of the natives, while the British Crown exercises protection of the lands and peoples' interests and exclusive guardianship over such administration. It is also a protection of the land and

its inhabitants against the neighboring Governments' and their peoples' interference. (Gunderson 1970: 126)

Although Tshekedi lost his legal case, he ultimately won the larger battle, as the British failed to implement political reforms that would have
brought the colony's system of indirect rule more in line with other British colonies on the continent (Picard 1987: 52–59).

Finally, missionaries helped restrain the colonial presence in two ways.
First, they encouraged the Tswana to ask for British protection during the
1870s, to accept it after it was unilaterally imposed on them in 1885, and
to insist on its continuation throughout the period of potential transfer.
As a result, local acceptance of British rule reduced the need for British
interference (Parsons 1998; Dachs 1998). And by encouraging chiefs to
accept British rule and supporting their interests, the missionaries helped
the Tswana gain a reputation as one of the most loyal peoples to the Crown
as well as the backing of influential religious and humanitarian groups in
Great Britain, both of which allowed the chiefs to oppose further colonial
intrusion without serious repercussions.

Second, the missionaries limited greater colonial influence by collaborating with the Tswana in opposition to colonial interference in the 1930s.
The missionaries believed that change would interfere with their work by
undermining the authority of chiefs who supported their missions and
by introducing new vices into the Tribal Territories. Thus, Resident Commissioner Rey, who was in charge of implementing the failed administrative reforms during the 1930s, continually fought with the missionaries,
referring to them as his "mortal foes," "intriguer[s]", and "useless, lying
idle, hypocritical, canting swine" (Rey 1988: 19, 132, 174). Elsewhere, he
claimed that the Catholics were the only good missionaries because they
taught respect for authority and did not "interfere with the Government"
yet later wished death upon all missionaries after they opposed his attempts
to diminish the economic autonomy of the Tswana chiefdoms: "I'd like to
stick my missionary crowd down a mine onto a stick of dynamite and blow
the whole damned lot to the heaven they're always bleating about" (39, 51).

The Maintenance of Precolonial Sociopolitical Institutions

The limited colonial presence in the Botswana chiefdoms, in turn, made
possible the maintenance of precolonial sociopolitical institutions to a
much greater extent than in most British colonies. As a consequence,
institutional constraints to local authority were not destroyed (although

[handwritten: chiefs weren't dramatically increased or decreased]

they were weakened), indirect rule did not increase the institutional powers of Tswana chiefs as much as elsewhere, and both of these limited
the extent to which colonial rule constructed a system of local despotism.
Thus, Robertson (1979) claims that "[a]mong the Tswana the traditional
way of life remained the norm although some adjustment had been made
to accommodate the demands of the new situation" (17–18), while Inger
(1985) suggests that "despite elements of a feudal class system of subser-
vience, there was also some evidence of a significant degree of democracy
and a responsiveness of most chiefs to public opinion" (31).

That colonial domination caused widespread transformation of indigenous social structures everywhere in which it occurred is beyond dis-
pute. As described in Chapter 2 and the Sierra Leone case study, one
major source of change in indirectly ruled colonies was the creation or
strengthening of chiefs. The expansion of chiefly powers also occurred in
Botswana because the colonial powers limited the two most common precolonial sanctions against chiefs—murder and desertion—and because
the colonial authorities began to actively support chiefs during local conflicts (Gunderson 1970: 135, 181; Picard 1987: 39; Robertson 1979: 21;
Schapera 1962: 80–81; Wylie 1990). Despite these changes, the power
of chiefs continued to be constrained by local institutions. Unlike chiefs
in Sierra Leone, Tswana chiefs in the eight chiefdoms were not colonial
constructs.[4] Instead, the British recognized the chiefs of the preexisting
chiefdoms as local authorities and did not attempt to use a divide-and-rule
strategy to obstruct local resistance to colonial domination. As a result of
this and the limited colonial presence, the tribal assembly continued to
be the institutional means through which the legislative, executive, and
judicial functions of the tribe were exercised. *[handwritten: tribal assembly]*

Several examples provide evidence that the power of the Tswana chiefs
continued to be limited by preexisting sociopolitical institutions after the
founding of the protectorate. First, in the few instances in which the British attempted to remove Tswana chiefs, there was strong local opposition
to the interference, and the two chiefs who were actually deposed continued to receive strong local support throughout their lives (Robertson
1979: 500). Indeed, according to Crowder, Parson, and Parsons (1990),

> Recalcitrant chiefs in colonial Botswana could not be removed easily to
> suit colonial officers of the day. Candidates for chief favored by the colonial
> administration could not be installed at will. As a result, chiefly non-compli-
> ance or a lack of enthusiasm could undermine colonial policy to a degree rare
> elsewhere in colonial Africa. (3)

In contrast, the few Tswana chiefs that did not ascend to the positions through traditional means had very weak authority. Describing a colonially imposed chief nearly a decade after he assumed power, a district commissioner wrote:

> He has no personal prestige and very little authority. His tribe do not regard him as the rightful chief but knowing he has the backing of the Government they do not openly defy him. They show their lack of respect through passive resistance, e.g. by failing to satisfy his judgments. (Ramsay 1998a: 109–10)

Similarly, the subchiefs and headmen appointed by the administration in the Crown Lands due to the absence of precolonial chiefs were very ineffective because they lacked legitimacy and were very dependent on coercion and colonial support (Government of the Bechuanaland Protectorate 1934; 1941). Thus, it is telling that the strongest claims of chiefly despotism in colonial Botswana are made by an administrator who worked as a district officer in the Crown Lands (Gillet 1973).

Sociolinguistic data also provide evidence that the overall impact of colonial rule on Tswana society was limited. Janson and Tsonope (1991) suggest that language is an active tool that enables individuals to function in society and that languages must therefore transform in accordance with social changes. They analyze historical transformations in Setswana, the first language of approximately 80 percent of all the Batswana, as a proxy for overall social transformation in Botswana. Very few changes in linguistic capacity occurred from the onset of interaction with Europeans until 1946, with an average of one new word per year between 1800 and 1895 and only 0.5 per year between 1896 and 1946. During this period, the spread of new technologies—largely through the expansion of trade networks, white settlement, and growing labor migration to South African mines—and the arrival of Christianity accounted for most of the new words. The authors therefore conclude that "[s]peakers of Setswana lived in a comparatively static society, and the language changed little, as did other institutions of that society" (128). During the final two decades of colonialism, however, new loan words increased by a factor of seven and exploded another sevenfold during the postcolonial period. There were over twenty-three new words per year on average between 1967 and 1985, a rate that is some fifty times that of the first fifty years of colonial rule. The largest category of new words in the postcolonial period was far and away "society," and close inspection of the words suggests this concentration "is clearly associated with a completely new distribution of power"

(125). As described below, this new distribution of power coincides with radical political reforms and was sparked by a chiefdom succession crisis in Botswana's largest and most powerful chiefdom.

The Seretse Khama Crisis and State Reform

In 1948, a succession crisis with racial intrigue occurred in the Bangwato chiefdom over the marriage of the future chief, Seretse Khama, to a white woman while he was studying law in London.[5] The marriage immediately caused strife between Seretse and his uncle, the Regent Chief Tshekedi. Moreover, given Botswana's uncertain political relations with South Africa and the latter's increasingly racist regime, the marriage caused considerable consternation among the administration. The crisis eventually led to Seretse's exile for six years, caused the breakdown of "native" administration in the Bangwato Territory, and ultimately transformed the chiefdom administration throughout the protectorate. "In the context of the Southern African social fabric," writes Robertson (1979), "the marriage set off a chain of events which plunged Bechuanaland into an era of unprecedented confrontation with the British and fomented dramatic political reorganization among the Ngwato and subsequently among the other chieftaincies" (283). Indeed, Picard (1984) recognizes that it "effectively terminated the indirect rule experiment in the Bechuanaland Protectorate" (90).

News of Seretse's marriage to a white woman infuriated Tshekedi, who viewed Seretse's failure to ask for tribal consent as a grave sign of disrespect and feared that a racially mixed heir to the chieftaincy would likely destroy the institution. After Seretse returned to the Bangwato Territory and was scolded by the tribe at two *kgotla* meetings, the tribe decided that Tshekedi was using the marriage as an excuse to usurp the chieftaincy from Seretse, the rightful heir, and overwhelmingly supported Seretse at the third meeting. Before Seretse could be sworn in as chief, however, a British commission decided that the marriage would harm British relations with South Africa and might provoke South African economic sanctions that would cripple Botswana's economy (Harrigan 1949). Consequently, the British government banished Seretse and Tshekedi from Botswana in 1950.

Seretse's exile had devastating effects within the Bangwato Territory and beyond. The tribe refused to collaborate with the colonial administration, and the chieftaincy was left vacant, requiring the improvisation of a more direct form of administration dependent on British officers and unpopular collaborators. The six-year period resulted in noncooperation and even overt conflict resulting in violence and deaths. Finally, in September 1956, the British ended the exiles of both Seretse and Tshekedi on the condition that both renounce the chieftaincy for themselves as well as for their children. The crisis ended with great jubilation as Seretse returned home, yet the "native" administration was irreparably damaged since the legitimate heir was forbidden from holding the position.

In order to create an alternative, the administration collaborated with Tshekedi and Seretse, who had reconciled by 1951, to build a tribal council to act as the new local government in the Bangwato Territory. The tribal council system consisted of smaller councils throughout the Bangwato Territory that served as tributaries for a central council, and the members were selected through the tribal assemblies. The Bangwato Tribal Council opened in November 1957 and proved so successful that others were organized in four other districts by 1959 (Robertson 1979: 425). Thus, the construction of a council system throughout the protectorate began to shift authority from the chief to a council (Picard 1984: 93).

While the construction of tribal councils throughout the protectorate was an important first step to the transformation of the system of administration, it proved to be only the beginning of a twenty-five-year period of intensive political restructuring. The reforms occurred in two key areas—democratization and state building—and completely overhauled the protectorate's version of indirect rule only a few years before independence, the extent of which was quite unparalleled in other indirectly ruled colonies. To pay for the reforms, the British government provided Botswana with 44 million Rand in budgetary grants-in-aid, a total nearly equal to the domestic revenue during the same period (48 million Rand) and twenty-two times as great as the total aid received by the protectorate during the previous fifty-eight years of British colonialism (Hermans 1974: 113). In addition, Great Britain subsidized the salaries of incoming British officers after 1961, which was necessary since the complete lack of any secondary education in Botswana until 1944 meant that "Africans were not prepared either by numbers or quality to participate in colonial or western institutions" (Government of the Bechuanaland Protectorate 1965: 26; Gunderson 1970: 256).[6]

Through diverse democratizing reforms, legislative and executive functions gradually passed from colonial officials to elected Batswana. After the return of Seretse, a Joint Advisory Council was created, which allowed both Batswana and European settlers to participate in the colonial government. The first elected Legislative Council in Botswana was created in 1961, and four Batswana were placed on the Executive Council and began to serve as ministers in training. Four years later, a new constitution was written that implemented universal adult suffrage and organized a ministerial system led by elected Batswana.

Increased democratization also occurred at the local level. In 1965 the tribal councils were renamed district councils and were now composed of and chaired by elected officials. Moreover, the duties of the councils expanded to include primary education, health and sanitation, public water supplies, and the construction and maintenance of public roads. Thus, unlike those in Sierra Leone, the district councils in Botswana usurped nearly all the executive and legislative responsibilities that the chiefs had previously held yet were not dominated by the chiefs.

Besides democratization, state expansion and bureaucratization also occurred during this period. After twenty years of colonial rule, the administration of Botswana was extremely small, with only 197 staff in 1905 (Government of the Bechuanaland Protectorate 1905). Over the next fifty years, it expanded slowly to reach over 1,000 personnel in 1957, with an average increase of eighteen new staff members per year (Government of the Bechuanaland Protectorate 1957a, 1957b, 1957c). After 1957, however, there was a rapid increase in both relative and absolute terms: the total establishment grew at an average yearly rate of 19 percent—an absolute increase of some 2,450 staff—between 1957 and 1968 (Republic of Botswana 1968). After independence, the administration continued to expand at a rate of nearly 20 percent per year, reaching nearly 10,000 staff members by 1975 (Republic of Botswana 1976b).

The expansion in personnel coincided with a restructuring of departmental organization. In 1945, there were thirteen departments in charge of only a few general activities, and the resident commissioner and secretariat formed the administrative core of the state apparatus (Government of the Bechuanaland Protectorate 1945). By the mid-1960s, a ministerial system with an elected president had been introduced, and the number of government departments jumped to over forty (Republic of Botswana 1968). The new departmental organization, in turn, coincided with the expansion of state activities and services that increasingly affected the lives of all Batswana.

Although the construction and bureaucratization of central state departments and ministries was the focus of administrative expansion during this period, local government and the ties linking district councils and the central administration were also increasingly bureaucratized. This began after the central administration became dissatisfied with their ability to work through the district councils to direct local development efforts. Consequently, the government increased central representation on the councils. In addition, the government expanded and formalized the ties among central and local government actors through "the bureaucratization of village-district communications," thereby increasing information and resource flows between the central administration and local districts and villages and decreasing the possibility of rent-seeking by intermediary brokers (Macartney 1978: 319–20).[7] In the process, however, local participation in administration was severely limited, and a top-down system of regional administration was constructed (Gunderson 1970; Macartney 1978; Picard 1987; Rankopo 2004; Robertson 1979). Local democratization and bureaucratization in Botswana were therefore less compatible than in late-colonial Mauritius, with bureaucratization taking priority.

Explaining State Building in Botswana

Although the crisis in the Bangwato Territory sparked the administrative transformation described above, it cannot explain the extent and form of the changes. As others note, good leadership by colonial officials and Batswana politicians was vital to successful state building in Botswana (Fawcus and Tilbury 2000; Harvey and Lewis 1990; Lewis 1993). Yet structural conditions facilitate some policies and provide severe constraints to others, requiring that one investigate the diverse factors that made possible purposive state building in Botswana.

Factors Promoting State Building in Botswana

One obvious requirement for the successful state reforms between 1957 and the early 1970s was a change in British policy concerning the possibility of transfer to South Africa. With the rise of apartheid and growing popular pressure in both Great Britain and Botswana, transfer was ruled out. As a result, investment in state legal-administrative institutions was necessary to make up for the past seventy-five years of neglect. Moreover, the crisis in the Bangwato Territory convinced the administration that rule through chiefs was unviable, and Great Britain therefore put forth a concerted effort to increase state centralization, infrastructural power, and bureaucratization between 1957 and 1966. In addition, because South Africa wanted to take over Botswana and use it as a Bantustan (African reserve), which would have required an indirect system of rule through chiefs, radical state reforms were a sign that Botswana would not and could not be transferred to South Africa (Anonymous 1956a: 4; Anonymous 1956b; Commonwealth Relations Office 1956: 2; Wray 1956).

Close, collaborative relations between the British administration and the local politicians associated with the Bechuanaland Democratic Party (BDP), which was founded by Seretse Khama in 1962, were another factor promoting rapid state building (Picard 1987: 139). Although the British administration was worried about his potential militancy upon his return to Botswana from exile, Seretse proved to be an important advocate of political reforms through his participation in both local and national councils. With the help of other moderate politicians opposed to both the maintenance of traditional institutions and nationalist radicalism in the Nkrumah fashion, he organized a party of moderate "new men" that established mutually supportive relations with the British administration based on their similar interests in democratization, state reform, and free markets (Fawcus and Tilbury 2000; Gunderson 1970; Parsons, Henderson, and Tlou 1995). Consequently, the BDP—and especially Seretse Khama and Quett Masire, Botswana's first president and vice president—was active in the development of the administration. Indeed, when an unpopular resident commissioner succeeded then–resident commissioner Peter Fawcus (who formed very close relations with Seretse and other BDP officials during his tenure) in 1963, the expatriate administration largely refused to work with him and displayed overwhelming support and loyalty to Seretse Khama and Quett Masire, allowing the reforms to continue (Parsons, Henderson, and Tlou 1995: 234). This loyalty, in turn, was earned by the BDP's refusal to bow to pressure to localize the administration rapidly. Although they felt localization was necessary, administrative efficiency took center stage, and Seretse dogmatically emphasized that efficiency would never be jeopardized by localization (Parsons, Henderson, and Tlou 1995: 232).[8]

Next, the maintenance of precolonial sociopolitical institutions promoted state building since they helped disseminate information on political reforms, engage local populations, and transfer legitimacy. First, and most basically, the *kgotla* provided the administration with the capacity to reach rural inhabitants and explain the changes that were occurring in local and national government. Obviously, the construction of a new administration does not occur in a vacuum, requiring that people understand how the new structures work and that they participate within them. Consequently, government officials frequented the tribal assemblies, using them as "the platform for announcements, financial statements, progress reports and the discussion of future and ongoing projects" (Macartney

1978: 282). With over 90 percent of respondents to a rural survey in 1981 claiming to have attended a *kgotla* meeting at least once and nearly 70 percent claiming to do so frequently, the tribal assembly provided a powerful tool for the dissemination of information (Odell 1985: 67).

The administration was also preoccupied with blending the new forms of administration with the old in order to transfer legitimacy and facilitate local participation, and the government therefore created administrative units that coincided with traditional boundaries (Macartney 1978: 341; Odell 1985; Peters 1994; Proctor 1968: 65). Chiefs were given ex officio positions within the local councils and administration, and village development committees used *kgotla* meetings as a forum to elect their members and recruit locals to help implement their programs (Macartney 1978: 259, 282). This interaction of the new Botswana state institutions with the traditional, in effect, imparted some of the deep-rooted legitimacy of the chieftaincy and the tribal assembly to the modern institutions:

> The main importance of the *Kgotla* lies in the fact that it represents the point of interaction of the traditional political system and the organizations of the central government and the district councils. It acts as the means of offering traditional legitimacy to the introduction of new ideas, ways of doing things and regulations issued by the new elites at the central and district level. (Odell 1985: 70)

Peters (1994) adds that "the most important point about the persisting legitimacy of the *kgotla* and of certain aspects of chiefly authority is that in combination with the new forums of councils, boards, committees, and parties they provide a rich, multiplex texture for political life" (223).

Although the maintenance of precolonial institutions proved fortuitous to state reforms during late colonialism, the construction of a bureaucratic structure linking local and central institutions actually required that the legislative and executive powers of chiefs be removed and their judicial functions more closely regulated. Consequently, the weakening of the chiefs is a fourth factor that contributed to successful state building during late colonialism and early independence. Between 1961 and 1970, the powers of the chiefs were systematically reduced until they were left with running customary courts, performing traditional ceremonies, and acting as the spokesmen for the tribes. Indeed, the power to appoint and remove chiefs was given to the government; and the chiefs lost the right to control mineral resources on tribal lands, collect stray cattle, control the allocation of tribal land, and collect taxes (Gillet 1973; Gunderson 1970: 286–

87; Macartney 1978: 35–40; Proctor 1968; Robertson 1979: 471; Temane 1977: 3). Moreover, the central government regulated customary courts more strictly and forced them to conform to the codes of the magistrates' courts (Brewer 1974).

The Lack of Impediments to State Building in Botswana

While the above circumstances were enabling factors, successful state building in Botswana was also made possible by the absence of factors that could have obstructed political reforms. In particular, the case studies of Sierra Leone and Guyana highlight four factors that could have hindered the success of state reforms but were largely absent in Botswana: strong opposition by chiefs, military intervention, geopolitical interference, and ethnic competition.

Given the previous strength of Tswana chiefs and their continued power elsewhere in Africa, their successful weakening must be seen as a gigantic political coup, requiring the consideration of factors that made possible a smooth transfer of power. The succession crisis and the chiefs' poor collective organization are two related determinants. As noted previously, the Bangwato chiefdom was the largest and most powerful in the protectorate. Because the "native" system of administration was destroyed during Seretse Khama's exile and because Seretse and his children were forbidden from becoming chiefs as a condition of his return, a federated system of rule based on autonomous traditional institutions was hardly feasible. In addition, the Bangwato chiefs had been the informal leaders of the Tswana chiefdoms throughout the colonial period because of their power, status, and a remarkable line of intelligent and active chiefs. After the demise of the Bangwato chieftaincy, therefore, the former leader among the chiefs was absent, decreasing the chiefs' capacity to organize an effective opposition.

To make matters even more difficult for the chiefs, the chieftaincy in the most senior Tswana tribe, the Bakwena, was also severely weakened. In 1931 the British removed the chief of the Bakwena because of supposed ineptitude and imposed their own chief, Kgari. Upon Kgari's death in 1962, a succession crisis emerged over past colonial interference, and the British imposed an illegitimate compromise candidate as chief, effectively reducing the Kwena chieftaincy to "political irrelevance" at a time in which the powers of chiefs were about to be reduced (Maundeni 1998: 130). Thus, at the time of political reform, the chieftaincy in the two dominant Tswana tribes was effectively destroyed, leaving the remaining chiefs weakened and disorganized.

In addition to their weak position, the chiefs were unable to stop reforms because there were no effective political parties opposed to extensive political reforms. Instead, the opposition parties self-destructed and split into several weak parties. In contrast, the BDP was extremely well organized and had close, collaborative relations with the administration, making any battle between traditionalists and reformers very unequal.

The chiefs also failed to put up timely opposition to the restructuring because they misunderstood the reforms. During the constitutional talks in 1963, the administration debated the position of the chiefs and decided that the best option was a House of Chiefs that would review legislation affecting the chiefdoms yet lack executive or legislative powers. Although the resident commissioner claims he attempted to clarify the chiefs' position in the new House, their informal leader, Chief Bathoen of the Ngwaketse, incorrectly saw the house as similar to the British House of Lords, was "mesmerized" by the thought of such a position, and therefore fully supported this option (Parsons, Henderson, and Tlou 1995: 211). Two years later, as the constitution was being finalized, the chiefs finally realized that they were losing significant power. By this time, however, significant changes to the constitution were not feasible, and the chiefs—already weakened—were forced to accept their lot.

The lack of a military legacy in Botswana also promoted political stability and thereby enhanced state-building efforts. While military intervention was a common impediment to state building throughout Africa, Botswana lacked a military at independence and did not organize one until 1977, a situation that freed the country from one of the most destabilizing forces in the postcolonial period. By the time the Botswanan government organized a military, a relatively effective state was present, and that state proved capable of training the soldiers and establishing civilian control over the military (N'Diaye 2004: 82–92).

The lack of destabilizing geopolitical interference also made possible rapid state building in Botswana. Whereas the Marxist rhetoric of the PPP provoked British and American interference that destabilized politics in Guyana, the BDP embraced liberal ideals and therefore received support from both the British and American governments. Moreover, unlike postcolonial Mozambique and Angola, which were controlled by groups that were antagonistic to apartheid South Africa, Botswana realized that poor relations with South Africa would be detrimental to the country's survival and therefore passively collaborated with the apartheid regime (Parsons, Henderson, and Tlou 1995). Consequently, whereas South Africa helped organize and equip military opposition in Mozambique and Angola, it never attempted a policy of destabilization in Botswana (Imrie and Young 1990).

Finally, state building in Botswana was not hampered by ethnic conflict as in Guyana and several other former British colonies. Although some suggest that Botswana has been blessed with a homogeneous population (Herbst 2000), the country's inhabitants are in fact quite diverse. First, the different Tswana tribes in the country form groups with separate identities and distinct dialects, and most waged wars against one another as late as the 1870s and competed with one another during both colonial and postcolonial periods. In addition to intra-Tswana divisions, there are a number of non-Tswana groups, with approximately twenty distinct indigenous languages spoken in the country (Anderson and Janson 1997: 7). Indeed, Schapera (1952: 126) categorizes the Batswana into ninety-seven ethnic and sub-ethnic groups, only forty-two of which are Tswana, and the 1946 census—the only census ever taken in Botswana with statistics on ethnic identity—shows that the largest ethnic community in Botswana is not one of the Tswana groups but the Bakalanga, a Shona-speaking group (Sillery 1952: 218). The census also found that 53 percent of the Africans in Botswana were non-Tswana, and Schapera (1952) notes that the census undercounted subordinate ethnic groups in the Tswana territories, suggesting that non-Tswana are a substantial majority.[9]

Despite this heterogeneity, ethnic conflict has not plagued social relations in Botswana largely because ethnic cleavages have not been employed for political mobilization. The BDP's firm nonethnic and nontribal position undoubtedly deterred ethnic conflict. Where ethnic cleavages do occur, nonethnic policy has often become ethnicized as soon as minority leaders played the ethnic card. In Botswana, a combination of several factors appear to have prevented this: (1) a limited number of "new men" competing for power at independence; (2) Seretse Khama's acknowledged and unrivaled position as the future independent president; (3) colonial and postcolonial policy that fought to minimize ethnic identities in an effort to maintain the precolonial Tswana hegemony; and (4) and the ability of precolonial, colonial, and postcolonial institutions to incorporate non-Tswana into the Tswana-dominated chiefdoms.

State-Led Development in Postcolonial Botswana

With the construction of an effective state in Botswana, state-led development was possible. The first objective of the government was simply fiscal solvency, a lofty goal given that foreign countries provided all of Botswana's nonrecurrent development budget and 40 percent of its recurrent budget at independence (Egner 1979: 24). Beginning in the late 1960s and early 1970s, the state began to invest heavily in large-scale diamond, copper, and nickel mining, the first of which was by far the most important, as Botswana quickly became one of the top diamond producers in the world. By 1976, over 13 percent of Botswana's GDP was derived from diamond mining, a percentage that rose steadily to 32 percent in 1982 and peaked at 51 percent in 1988 (Jeffries 1998: 303).

Despite the inherent difficulties of a mineral-based economy, the Botswanan government astutely managed the economy to make possible one of the fastest rates of economic growth in the world. First, in order to maximize its revenue, the government successfully renegotiated an agreement with De Beers in 1974, and Botswana received one of the most lucrative contracts ever awarded, with 75 percent of the profits going to the Botswanan government despite the fact that DeBeers provided nearly all of the capital investment (Jeffries 1998: 304). Next, the government used permanent revenue sources to fund recurrent expenditures but employed diamond revenue to invest in infrastructure and other exceptional expenditures in order to control the inflationary pressure caused by rapid increases in rentier revenue. Finally, noting that developmental gains through the exploitation of mineral resources are often more than offset by downswings in commodity revenue, the government accumulated reserves equivalent to several times the annual budget in order to protect against prolonged declines in either diamond prices or production (Jeffries 1998: 314).

Diamond revenue allowed dramatic increases in both nonrecurrent development expenditure and recurrent government expenditure, which, in turn, made possible the expansion of infrastructure and personnel needed for the provisioning of developmental goods (see Table 7.1). In January 1974, the government began the Accelerated Rural Development Programme (ARDP), and in one year 489 classrooms, 42 health posts, 21 health clinics, 8 maternity wards, 31 village water systems, 190 wells, 30 dams, 210 kilometers of road, and some 700 government buildings were constructed (Temane 1977: 5). Despite difficulties, the state proved quite capable of implementing a massive, centrally directed, local development program. Indeed, the ARDP "revealed and developed greater implementation capacity in the Districts than was expected," with both district development committees and district councils being active in the planning and implementation of the program (Temane 1977: 5).

After 1975, rural development remained the focus of the National Development Plan, and large-scale infrastructural investment increased.

Table 7.1 Nonrecurrent development expenditure and recurrent government expenditure in Botswana, 1931–86

Years	Nonrecurrent Development Expenditure		Recurrent Government Expenditure	
	Yearly average (1,000 pula)	% GDP	Yearly average (1,000 pula)	% GDP
1932–37	27.2	—	377.2	—
1938–42	73.7	—	459.0	—
1943–47	93.8	—	766.8	—
1948–52	188.1	—	1,150.8	—
1953–57	506.3	—	1,876.8	—
1958–62	1,224.2	—	4,028.2	—
1963–67	3,637.0	—	8,766.4	—
1968–72	6,563.2	—	16,099.0	—
1973–77	32,996.0	13.9	59,044.5	27.4
1978–82	100,378.2	16.2	246,124.4	39.7
1983–86	187,888.4	12.6	527,950.0	34.8

Sources: Hermans 1974; Republic of Botswana 1973a, 1974, 1975a, 1975b, 1976a, 1977a, 1978, 1979, 1980, 1981a, 1982a, 1982b, 1983, 1984a, 1985b, 1985c, 1986a, 1986b.

As shown in Table 7.2, both primary and secondary education began to expand in the late 1950s and accelerated in the 1970s and 1980s, with the number of primary students increasing elevenfold between 1960 and 1984 and the number of secondary students—as a result of the abysmally low number of students during colonialism—jumping an incredible 150-fold. The percentage of children attending school increased from only 21 percent in 1960 to 80 percent in 1978, and Botswana went from having one of the lowest education rates in British Africa to having one of the highest in a matter of years (Government of the Bechuanaland Protectorate 1964; Enger 1979: 14). Most impressively, the student-teacher ratio actually declined during this rapid educational expansion (see Table 7.2).

Besides increasing education, the infrastructural investments in the 1970s and 1980s also expanded the provision of health care in Botswana, which is clearly operationalized by the number of health care facilities, the number of medical visits, and the number of health care personnel (see Table 7.3). By 1984, between 85 and 90 percent of all Batswana lived within fifteen kilometers of a medical facility, allowing the number of births in clinics to jump from only 595 in 1950 to 20,560 in 1979 (Government of the Bechuanaland Protectorate 1963; Republic of Botswana 1984c: 25; Republic of Botswana 1981b: 91). Health improvements were

Table 7.2 Education in Botswana, 1950–84

	Primary education			Secondary education		
Year	Schools	Students	Student/Teacher Ratio	Schools	Students	Student/Teacher Ratio
1950	149	16,715	—	3	188	—
1955	166	21,015	—	4	242	—
1962	235	46,536	36:1	6	762	25:1
1967	252	71,577	42:1	9	1,854	16:1
1973	308	95,511	35:1	26	8,763	21:1
1979	394	156,664	32:1	36	16,716	22:1
1984	512	209,772	31:1	59	27,364	22:1

Sources: Government of the Bechuanaland Protectorate 1951b, 1956; Republic of Botswana 1985a; Kann and Taylor 1989.

also made possible by vaccination campaigns and the Village Water Supply Programme, which was begun in 1972 with Swedish assistance and provided 254 rural villages with clean water systems by 1985, with an additional 35 to 45 villages being provided water every year (Land 1987: 132). Through these infrastructural investments, 100 percent of urban Batswana and 91 percent of rural Batswana had access to improved drinking water sources in 2000 despite the country's arid environment (World Health Organization 2006).

Finally, the Botswana state also established a safety net to protect the poor. To this day, most of the rural population in Botswana subsists as small-scale farmers, with a plot of land and a small number of livestock. This sector is quite vulnerable to droughts, which occur every eight to eleven years because of the El Niño ocean current phenomenon. For example, Botswana experienced an eight-year drought in the 1980s. Small farms were particularly hard hit, with 54 percent of all cattle in herds of ten or less dying in 1983 alone and only 34 percent of households that planted crops being able to harvest anything between 1982 and 1984. In reaction, the government supplied 375,000 people, 59 percent of the total population, with food rations by the end of 1984 (Republic of Botswana 1985d: 4, 50). Due largely to these efforts, the malnutrition rate increased by only 5 percent, and only 1 percent of children were severely malnourished during the drought (Republic of Botswana 1985d: 5–6).

In addition to the food distribution program, the government organized the Department of Food Resources to plan for and coordinate relief programs and implement a six-point Agriculture Relief Programme to assist

Table 7.3 Health care in Botswana, 1930–84

Year	Clinics/ Hospitals	Medical Posts/ Stations	Medical Visits	Doctors	Nurses
1930	10	0	29,774	9	10
1950	12	9	98,877	10	56
1963	18	75	235,484	14	168
1973	66	148	420,000	41	443
1979	114	384	1,119,444	100	1,172
1984	143	626	1,740,831	142	2,743

Sources: Government of the Bechuanaland Protectorate 1931, 1951a, 1963; Republic of Botswana 1973b, 1981b, 1984b; Skogland 1977.

resource-poor farmers. Specifically, the Agriculture Relief Programme vaccinated cattle, subsidized feed, funded small water projects, marketed cattle in poor condition immediately, distributed seed for planting after drought years, and paid 85 percent of the cost of hiring plowing equipment (Republic of Botswana 1985d: 33). Thus, unlike most governments in Africa, Botswana uses the modern economic sector to subsidize small-scale, rural agriculture, not the reverse, which is evident in the BDP's strong rural support base.

Because of successful state-led development during the postcolonial period, Botswana is oftentimes presented as a poster child for development (Leftwich 2000; Samatar 1999; Stiglitz 2002). In spite of its many achievements, the country is hardly a case of unequivocal success. Rapid economic growth has not expanded production in rural areas and disproportionately benefits a small group of political and economic elite, resulting in ever-growing inequalities (Good 1993; Picard 1987: 263). In addition, economic diversification remains a distant goal, as the country's economy is still dependent on diamond mining (Good 2005; Good and Hughes 2002). And while Botswana's diamond reserves remain large, its water supply is not, and estimates suggest that the water needed for diamond mining will be insufficient by the mid-twenty-first century.

HIV/AIDS is an additional problem. With approximately 25 percent of its population presently infected, Botswana has one of the highest known incidence rates in the world, and the disease's proliferation caused life expectancy to fall from sixty-five years in 1990 to only forty years in 2005. Although the epidemic continually worsened for two decades after the first case was diagnosed in 1985, there are now signs that the situation is improving, and life expectancy is increasing once again. Thanks primarily to a national program that the state began in 2002, 95 percent of Batswana in need of antiretroviral therapy received it by late 2006, up from almost none only four years previously (Avert 2007). In this way, Botswana's effective state appears to have the infrastructural and organizational capacity to deal with the AIDS epidemic (Avert 2007), although its actions were quite slow to materialize and AIDS remains a difficult and devastating problem.

Given the state's capacity to promote development through the provisioning of goods and sound macroeconomic management, its inability to successfully deal with these problems in a timely manner is somewhat surprising. Inequality, the lack of economic diversification, and AIDS are complex issues that are extremely difficult to overcome. In addition, the state's limited ability to engage the population in active relationships facilitated the rise and persistence of these developmental difficulties by limiting public pressure to address them and preventing collaborative relations between state and society. Indeed, despite several elections and no restrictions on opposition, Botswana has been for all intents and purposes a one-party state over the last four decades.[10] As a consequence, the state has not actively sought societal participation and has become increasingly oligarchic (Picard 1987). In addition, the growing bureaucratic leviathan in Botswana has promoted social complacency by controlling numerous aspects of life and co-opting civil societal organizations, thereby limiting bottom-up demands for change (Maundeni 2004: 32; Rankopo 2004). Thus, a bureaucratic and infrastructurally powerful state can act corporately, create stability, and thereby make possible a seemingly functional democratic system and an expansionary mineral-based economy. In the absence of inclusiveness, however, it can also hinder responsiveness on both sides of the state-society dyad, which threatens the country's continued developmental success (Good 1994, 1996).

Comparisons with Sierra Leone, Mauritius, and Guyana

Botswana's chiefdom institutions were much less despotic than those of colonial Sierra Leone. British officials in Sierra Leone faced strong and violent resistance to colonialism, a factor that caused a divide-and-rule strategy in which precolonial political systems were destroyed and numerous chiefdoms reconstructed. Because the new chiefdoms lacked traditional sanctions against chiefly abuses and because British officials supported the chiefs at almost all times and gave them great institutional powers, the chiefs frequently became local despots. Botswana differs on all accounts—strong opposition to colonialism did not occur, and the colonial response was inactivity instead of destruction. As a consequence, precolonial institutions were left relatively intact, and the local inhabitants maintained greater means of checking chiefly abuses than their Sierra Leonean counterparts. *more direct*

More importantly, the colonies differed because extensive state reforms were attempted in Botswana but not in Sierra Leone. As a result, a territory-wide and highly bureaucratic state was created in Botswana, making the form of rule increasingly direct. By contrast, the state in Sierra Leone remained highly indirect and therefore lacked effective legal-administrative institutions. Comparison of Botswana and Sierra Leone clearly shows that these institutional differences have been an important determinant of their divergent developmental trajectories. In Sierra Leone, the state was incapable of providing developmental goods. In addition, the inability of the Sierra Leonean leaders to pay and control officials resulted in a personalized and predatory state that ultimately collapsed. In stark contrast, Botswana's legal-administrative institutions proved quite capable of providing educational and health services, maintaining law and order, and managing the economy once a more direct form of rule was constructed. In this way, despite being an outlier, Botswana supports the mechanisms highlighted in the Mauritian and Sierra Leonean case studies. *higher capacity*

The different effects of legal-administrative institutions on development are particularly evident when comparing the diamond industries of the two countries. In Botswana, the state effectively controlled the mining and sale of diamonds and used the revenue to implement development projects. The state in Sierra Leone, however, was fissiparous and personalized and therefore unable to either control production or regulate trade. Instead, the trade of diamonds occurred illegally, and state officials received rent for giving select clients control of the diamond market. Such payments were collected as personal revenue, and the diamond industry therefore provided little revenue for state development projects. More importantly, the black market for diamonds caused considerable instability and conflict over the control of diamond production and trade. When combined with the state's inability to either maintain law and order or act corporately, the black market promoted broad-based civil violence and helps explain why the presence of natural resources is related to civil war (Collier 2000; Fearon and Laitin 2003; Reno 1995; Snyder and Bhavnani 2005).

While comparison with Sierra Leone helps highlight why Botswana has been able to avoid state despotism and could therefore successfully implement developmental reforms, comparison with Mauritius offers different

insight. For one thing, it highlights commonalities that have allowed both
to be relatively successful developers. Two interrelated factors stand out:
each former colony's successful development is partially rooted in colonial
reforms, and the state promoted broad-based development in both cases.

In Mauritius, colonial reforms in the 1940s, 1950s, and 1960s expanded
the colonial state, democratized the regime, provided public services
throughout the colony, and embedded the colonial state within society.
The end result was an integrated and effective state able to promote broad-
based development over the past five decades. In Botswana, major reforms
were also implemented during the transitional period. As in Mauritius,
the reforms expanded the state's infrastructural power, increased state
bureaucratization, and democratized the regime. The reforms were more
radical, however, because there was no preexisting structure of direct rule
on which to build. Instead, new state institutions were built, and relatively
autonomous chiefdoms were weakened and integrated into the state. The
reforms were difficult but successful and made possible state-led development despite a history of indirect rule.

Along with these key similarities, there are also important differences
between the cases of Botswana and Mauritius. While both have sustained
relatively democratic regimes throughout the postcolonial period and pos-
sess states that are able to act corporately, Mauritius' political institutions
are more dynamic and capable of engaging the population. In particular,
state inclusiveness helped to prevent the Mauritius political system from
being afflicted by organizational sclerosis, while one-party rule and state
capture of local institutions have limited the Botswanan state's capacity to
engage the population and promote broad-based development.

The comparison of Guyana and Botswana shows that independence
transitions were a critical period during which the legacies of direct and
indirect rule could change. In both outlier cases, conflict between colonizer and colonized sparked institutional transformations that readjusted
the normal developmental trajectories of directly and indirectly ruled colonies. In Botswana, these changes were constructive and resulted in a state
with much greater developmental capacity. After the chiefdom succession
crisis, the chiefs were weakened, transfer to South Africa was no longer
possible, and colonial officials and BDP politicians actively collaborated
to build effective legal-administrative institutions. In Guyana, relations
between colonial officials and PPP politicians never improved, and foreign interference helped spread ethnic violence. As a result, the structure
of the state began to break down, and the ethnicization and militarization
of politics promoted autocratic rule.

Table 7.4 The military and postcolonial governance in British Africa, 1996–2006

	Political stability	Government effectiveness	Rule of law	Lack of corruption	Average
Without military at independence					
Botswana	0.93	0.67	0.62	0.82	0.76
Gambia	0.37	−0.57	−0.07	−0.42	−0.17
Lesotho	0.18	−0.19	−0.12	−0.19	−0.08
Mauritius	0.90	0.54	0.83	0.38	0.66
Swaziland	−0.01	−0.67	−0.39	−0.38	−0.36
Average	0.47	−0.04	0.17	0.04	0.16
With military at independence					
Ghana	0.01	−0.17	−0.24	−0.33	−0.18
Kenya	−1.08	−0.66	−1.03	−0.98	−0.94
Malawi	−0.17	−0.65	−0.44	−0.69	−0.49
Nigeria	−1.62	−1.01	−1.41	−1.25	−1.32
Sierra Leone	−1.21	−1.25	−1.26	−1.06	−1.20
Sudan	−2.20	−1.22	−1.45	−1.14	−1.50
Tanzania	−0.31	−0.44	−0.45	−0.86	−0.52
Uganda	−1.41	−0.48	−0.68	−0.81	−0.85
Zambia	−0.13	−0.83	−0.59	−0.88	−0.61
Zimbabwe	−1.32	−1.04	−1.32	−0.98	−1.17
Average	−0.94	−0.78	−0.89	−0.90	−0.88

Source: World Bank 2007b.

Note: Each governance variable is scored so that the global average is 0, with one standard deviation being equivalent to one point. Based on this scoring, nearly all countries in the world fall between −2.5 and 2.5.

Finally, all four cases point to the developmental significance of the military and militarized states. In both Sierra Leone and Guyana, the military was directly involved in domestic politics and severely hindered state-led development. Most importantly, coercive rule became a substitute for rule through legal-administrative institutions, leaving them subordinate, inactive, and ineffective. Such a coercion-heavy state severely impeded state inclusiveness, created a precedent that might makes right, and promoted state predation.

In both Botswana and Mauritius, military rule never occurred, freeing them from extreme state predation and allowing the legal-administrative institutions to dominate the state. Although one might conclude that the

168 Chapter 7

more effective legal-administrative institutions of each allowed state officials to control the military, neither former colony actually had a military at independence. Three other former British colonies in sub-Saharan Africa also lacked militaries at independence: Gambia, Lesotho, and Swaziland. These five did not experience a single coup between 1956 and 1984 and had only one attempted coup and one reported plot during the same time period. The ten remaining former British colonies in sub-Saharan Africa, on the other hand, had sixteen successful coups, twenty-six attempted coups, and thirty-seven reported plots (McGowan and Johnson 1984). As shown in Table 7.4, the absence of a military at independence is also positively correlated with present levels of governance. In particular, the five former British colonies without a military at independence had much greater political stability between 1996 and 2006 than the other former British colonies, and stability appears to have translated into greater government effectiveness and rule of law and lower corruption. Thus, when states have ineffective legal-administrative institutions, the presence of a military appears to promote instability, increase coercive rule, and limit the expansion of legal-administrative institutions. Under these circumstances, the absence of a military has positive effects on state governance.[11]

Comparing British Colonialism

Testing the Generalizability of Colonial State Legacies

8

One common criticism of comparative historical methods is that the small number of cases under analysis prevents researchers from gaining generalizable insight into their research questions. While a nested-research design helps overcome this problem by using statistical relationships to guide qualitative analysis, the mechanisms highlighted in case studies are not necessarily generalizable and therefore might not underlie the statistical findings. One way to address this potential problem is to test whether the mechanisms highlighted in the previous chapters can be applied to additional cases.

In this chapter, I use abbreviated case studies to check whether the institutional mechanisms discovered in the previous chapters help to explain the postcolonial development levels of several additional former British colonies. Notably, the case studies cannot provide conclusive evidence given their brevity and the fact that they are still only a minority of cases within the entire set. Despite these limitations, they shed important insight into the generalizability of causal mechanisms. If these short case studies consistently highlight institutional mechanisms similar to those in the in-depth case studies and show that the mechanisms help to explain the level of development, they offer evidence that the

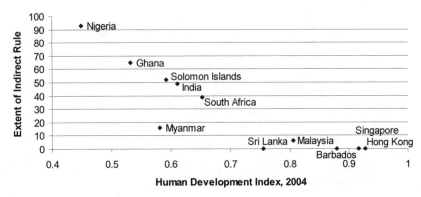

Figure 8.1 Scatter-Plot of Abbreviated Cases

mechanisms discovered in the previous chapters are generalizable. If the institutional mechanisms linked to the form of colonialism do not help to explain development level, the abbreviated case studies provide evidence that the mechanisms do not underlie the statistical findings. Finally, if the case studies provide mixed evidence, the findings are inconclusive.

With this objective, I analyze eleven former British colonies in this chapter: Barbados, Ghana, Hong Kong, India, Malaysia, Myanmar, Nigeria, Singapore, the Solomon Islands, South Africa, and Sri Lanka. Case selection is based on the variable measuring the extent of indirect rule, and the sample includes cases throughout the variable's range. The scatter plot in Figure 8.1 shows this range as well as the relationship between the extent of indirect colonial rule and human development in 2004. It clearly demonstrates that the cases conform to Chapter 3's statistical findings, as the extent of indirect rule is strongly and negatively related to broad-based development. Myanmar is an exception, however, as its human development index score is considerably lower than expected given its relatively direct form of colonialism.

Nigeria

After observing indirect rule first-hand in India, Lord Lugard replicated it while serving as governor of colonial Nigeria and thereby gained renown—somewhat incorrectly—as the inventor of indirect rule. Through the legwork of Lugard and others, Nigeria arguably developed into the most extreme case of indirect rule within the British Empire despite the absence of precolonial chiefs in some parts of the colony. Indeed, given respect for Lugard and the system of rule that he formalized, the colonial government in Nigeria pressured its officials to maintain as indirect a system of domination as possible. In the words of one colonial official, "No more damning remark could be made in the annual secret report on an officer than that he was 'direct' or not sufficiently imbued with the spirit of Indirect Rule" (Crocker 1936: 114).

High levels of indirect rule, in turn, promoted local despotism and general state ineffectiveness. Accordingly, a number of colonial-era observers describe Nigerian chiefs in ways paralleling their counterparts in Sierra Leone.

> The chief is the law, subject to only one higher authority, the white official stationed in his state as advisor. The chief hires his own police . . . he is often the prosecutor and the judge combined and he employs the jailer to hold his victims in custody at his pleasure. No oriental despot ever had greater power than these black tyrants, thanks to the support which they receive from the white officials who quietly keep in the background. (Padmore 1936: 317, quoted in Mamdani 1996: 53)

> As late as 1932, thirty years after our subjugation of the country, it was found amongst the Gwari chiefdoms that forcible seizure of girls for the harims of chiefs, continuous and heavy exaction of both goods and money from the commoners, embezzlement of tax, arbitrary imprisonment and other persecutions, forced labour on a scale whereby in some cases half the able-bodied male population were conscripted to work in construction camps for the benefit of the chief and against the will of the conscripted, and possibly even "palace" murders, were the order in some of the Gwari chiefdoms. Some of these things, as at Kuta, had been going on, unbeknown to the D.O.s [district officers], for nine years, at a distance of only a few hundred yards from the Divisional Headquarters. (Crocker 1936: 114–15)

Noting similar examples of chiefly misconduct, another colonial official declared indirect rule as "Nigeria's curse" (Fitzpatrick 1924).

Consistent with—and, in fact, reinforcing—such chiefly despotism, colonial Nigeria had the smallest number of administrators per capita in all of British Africa (one for every 51,800 Nigerians) (Fisher 1991: 8). As a consequence, the majority of the colonial population was outside the reach of the colonial state, which was completely incapable of implementing policy throughout the territory. Both the colonial state's dependence on chiefs and its Lilliputian size, in turn, made it "a fairly poorly formed state without a central authority, without a national civil service, and without any real capacity to reach down into the society to facilitate even such elementary government functions as systematic taxation" (Kohli 2004: 327).

And, according to Kohli's insightful comparative-historical analysis (2004), this tiny, fragmented, and predatory state has persisted after independence and failed to promote any form of development (363–66). In particular, he shows that the postcolonial state has proved incapable of implementing all sorts of development policy due to its abysmally low levels of infrastructural power, its lack of bureaucratic organization, and the rent-seeking behavior of state officials. As a consequence, the country's rich oil resources have had little if any positive effect on broad-based development, and Nigeria remains one of the poorest and least developed countries in the world. Thus, past colonial claims that indirect rule was Nigeria's curse still appear warranted.

Given that Nigeria's economy is dominated by the exploitation of natural resources, the case also provides insight into the effect of the latter on development. Of interest to this analysis, Nigeria's oil reserves are much more similar to Botswana's kimberlite diamond deposits than Sierra Leone's alluvial diamond deposits in that both oil reserves and kimberlite deposits require deep mines and large infrastructural investments. Alluvial diamond deposits, on the other hand, are located along riverbeds and can be mined by individuals using rudimentary technologies.

Some development experts suggest that the difference between kimberlite and alluvial diamond reserves underlies the Botswanan and Sierra Leonean states' different development records. According to this line of argument, Sierra Leone's alluvial deposits were harder to monopolize than Botswana's kimberlite deposits, and destructive violence over Sierra Leone's diamonds caused state collapse and human misery whereas the Botswanan state was easily able to control the production and trade of diamonds and thereby use this revenue to promote broad-based development. Given the similarity between the form of natural resource reserves in both Nigeria and Botswana, however, a comparison of the two suggests that simply being able to control valuable natural resources does not guarantee resource-based development. Instead, the comparison highlights the centrality of states and provides evidence that states must also have the organizational capacity to manage the economy, control rent-seeking officials, and implement policy throughout the territory if its control of natural resources is to translate into developmental success.

Ghana

Despite the fact that Ghana, Nigeria, and Sierra Leone are all former British colonies located along the west coast of Africa, colonial Ghana (known as the Gold Coast) differed from both colonial Sierra Leone and Nigeria in that it developed a relatively vibrant export economy founded on the production and trade of cocoa. This economic expansion prompted greater colonial involvement in southern Ghana, resulting in a greater extent of direct rule than in Sierra Leone and Nigeria. Coinciding with this difference, Ghana's postcolonial development levels are considerably higher than those of Nigeria and Sierra Leone. At the same time, the overwhelming majority of colonial Ghana was ruled through indirect means; and the nonbureaucratic, infrastructurally weak, and despotic character of the colonial and postcolonial states have negatively affected long-term development in ways that parallel Nigeria and Sierra Leone.

Similar to the cases of Sierra Leone and Nigeria, indirect rule in colonial Ghana transformed local power relations by strengthening chiefs and propping up systems of misrule. A commissioned report in 1932, for example, found that "corruption and oppression are rife" within Ghana's system of indirect rule (Bushe 1932: 1). Boone (2003) finds that the institutional powers bestowed upon chiefs by the British enhanced their "ability to appropriate agricultural wealth not only indirectly in the form of political tribute, but also directly in the form of rent, interest, and profit from their cocoa-growing subjects and peasants" (148). Along the same lines, Newbury (2003) describes how "customary" law allowed Ashanti chiefs to exploit the poor, the landless, and immigrants in order to gain large amounts of money and recognizes that none of this chiefly revenue "filtered down to improvements in roads, education, health" (107). As a consequence of these exploitative relations, tension frequently arose between commoners and chiefs throughout the cocoa belt, and outright rebellion often occurred (Li 2002; Boone 2003: 154; Newbury 2003: 106).

As elsewhere in the British Empire, several state reforms were implemented in Ghana both during and after the independence period. Despite Kwame Nkrumah's efforts to expand central legal-administrative institutions and weaken the chiefs after independence, such transformations proved extremely difficult and "ultimately failed to uproot chiefly authority and prerogative at the micro level, where it remained embedded in relations of production and land access and in deeply personalized structures of obligation, dependency, and authority" (Boone 2003: 177). Berry

(2001), for example, finds that chiefs remain very powerful figures within postcolonial Ghana and suggests that their customary authority—while forcing them to be marginally accountable to their subjects—"has helped to institutionalize chiefly rent-seeking" (196). Thus, despite a charismatic and driven leader, the state remained dependent on chiefly collaborators.

Besides promoting local despotism, Ghana also provides evidence that indirect colonial rule institutionalizes an ineffective central state apparatus. Phillips (1989) recognizes that the colonial state in Ghana was minimalist, infrastructurally weak, and lacked ties to broad segments of society, describing it as "a mere facsimile of a state" (11). Similarly, Chazan (1983) finds that Nkrumah's expansion of the postcolonial state only increased the resources that the state controlled and describes how the continued—and even increasing—ineffectiveness of the state apparatus has been the primary determinant of poor postcolonial development. Not only has the state been completely unable to implement policy needed for national development because of its inability to act corporately and implement policy throughout its territory, but Chazan finds that instability and the absence of corporate coherence have promoted struggles over the state and its resources, something exemplified by a series of coups and two decades of military rule. In this environment, rulers personalized the state and used it to pursue personal interests instead of national development (Dzorgbo 2001).

Solomon Islands

Although most indirectly ruled colonies were located in Africa, the British first used indirect rule in Asia and also employed it in the South Pacific. Outside of Africa, however, the British usually combined aspects of indirect and direct rule, creating more hybrid forms of domination. The Solomon Islands, an archipelago national state located in the Pacific Ocean, is one example.

The British established their first colonial outpost in the Solomon Islands in 1897 and ruled it until 1978. During this period, the form of colonialism changed over time and differed from place to place. Throughout the colonial era, however, the British took a very hands-off approach in the Solomon Islands and had as minimal an administration as could be found in the British Empire. A quarter century after colonialism began, for example, the entire administration—which covered numerous islands spread over 770,000 square kilometers—consisted of ten colonial officials and 100 indigenous police officers (Bennett 1987: 112).

To control their subjects with such a minuscule staff, the British depended on missionaries, who helped convince converts to accept British paramountcy and even provided basic services to much of the population (Bennett 1987). The administration also collaborated with a small group of European settlers, many of whom owned and ran plantations (Bennett 1987).[1] The plantations were never very large, and their owners were nowhere as powerful as those in the Caribbean or Mauritius. Their presence in the Solomon Islands, however, gave the colonial administration loyal collaborators who employed and thereby helped control much of the population. More importantly, they provided most of the colonial government's revenue, which reduced the need to extract resources from the indigenous population and therefore allowed the colonial state to maintain a very limited presence throughout the colony.

Along with these informal imperial agents, locals collaborated with the British and thereby facilitated foreign domination. During the first decades of British rule, the collaborators were recognized as village headmen, their traditional powers were not formalized, and they were under the direct authority of the district officers to a greater extent than their chiefly counterparts in sub-Saharan Africa. By the 1930s, however, the colonial administrators slowly began to heed calls for more indirect forms of rule, and a colony-wide system of rule through "native" institutions was finally formalized in the early 1940s. As a consequence, the colonial state gained the telltale trademarks of indirect rule (customary courts and "native" authorities with formal legal-administrative powers), and the indigenous population was governed through more indirect means during the final three and a half decades of British rule (Belshaw 1950: 118–26). Unlike in Africa, however, the traditional institutions were controlled by native councils instead of individual chiefs, and the positions of the councilors were not hereditary. Given these differences, the traditional authorities in the Solomon Islands were considerably weaker and less autocratic than chiefs in British Africa.

Although the rulers were less despotic than those in Africa, the Solomon Islands still suffered from a colonial state with very limited levels of bureaucratization, infrastructural power, and inclusiveness. Since independence, the situation has hardly improved. According to the World Bank (2007b), the Soloman Islands currently has one of the least effective governments in the world, and different institutional analyses corroborate such claims. As Dauvergne (1998) writes, "The state has trouble providing basic services, including adequate roads, medical facilities, and public schools. It has even more problems handling macro-economic plans, monitoring multinational investors, and collecting taxes" (142). Turnbull (2002) adds an inability to maintain law and order to the list of developmentally destructive state defects and claims that the state's ineffectiveness is caused by low infrastructural power, nonbureaucratic and personalized rule, and the near complete absence of relations between the state and the rural population.

Given this defective state and the eruption of ethnic violence in 1998, other commentators refer to the Solomon Islands as the "the Pacific's first failed state" and compare the country to the likes of Congo (Economist 2003: 39; Reilly 2004). Although such claims and comparisons have proved exaggerated, foreign intervention was the most important factor that prevented the Solomon Islands from joining the ranks of Africa's failed states. In this way, the Solomon Islands shows that the negative state institutional legacy of indirect rule is not limited to sub-Saharan Africa.

India

Historians and social scientists commonly disagree about the form of colonial rule in India, with some claiming it was direct and others insisting that it was indirect. In fact, the country experienced a mixed form of colonial domination, as there were several variations of both direct and indirect rule within the administrative hodgepodge of colonial India. Supporting this book's previous findings, the more directly ruled regions of India currently have higher levels of development than the more indirectly ruled regions, and the country as a whole has had a mediocre developmental record over the past fifty years.

The Indian colonial state attracted many of the best administrators from the United Kingdom, a supposedly incorruptible group of Cambridge and Oxford graduates who had a common esprit de corps and formed the apex of the state bureaucratic machine. While relatively large in absolute terms, the central state was minuscule in relation to the size of the population—per capita, colonial India had one-fifth of the colonial officials of colonial Nigeria, which had the smallest number of administrators per capita in all of British Africa (Fisher 1991: 8). The central state's tiny size, in turn, prevented it from reaching down to the local level and often required additional tiers of colonial control that depended on local intermediaries. Notably, some of these collaborative forms of rule were formally recognized as indirect rule, while others were categorized as direct despite some telltale signs of indirect rule (e.g., administrative dependence on patrimonial collaborators). Whether classified by colonial officials as direct or indirect, all forms of local collaboration severely limited the state's infrastructural power and level of bureaucratization and empowered local intermediaries.

In the areas that were formally categorized as indirectly ruled, the colonial administration recognized some 600 princely states that made up approximately two-fifths of the area of colonial India and possessed one-quarter of the population (Misra 1990: 15). The princely states had British residents who assisted and influenced the princes, yet the princes were given considerable autonomy, especially during the twentieth century as a reward for their opposition to Indian nationalists (Smith 1995: 20). As a consequence, the colonial state's presence was often very limited and based more on patrimonial relations than bureaucratic organization. Although several scholars view the princes as effective traditional rulers, others claim that such a position is overly romantic and nationalistic and overlooks a reality of exploitative relations. Along these lines, Kulkarni (1964) describes the Indian princely states as a "wilderness of oppression and misrule" (154): "By guaranteeing protection to its feudatories from internal rebellion and external attack, British paramountcy made it impossible for the ninety-three million people of the states to launch any such struggle for emancipating themselves from capricious and oppressive rule" (153).

The small size and infrastructural weakness of the colonial state forced the British to employ local intermediaries in much of the supposedly directly ruled territories as well. Zamindars, taluqdars, and other tax-collecting landlords are the most notable examples. These colonial agents were supposedly carried over from precolonial times and were employed in approximately 20 percent of colonial India, including all of Bihar, Rajasthan, and present-day Bangladesh. In order to exploit their services, the colonial state gave them personal possession of large tracts of land, the power to collect taxes from the peasants living on the land, and the right to keep the majority of the revenue for personal use. In order to perform their duties, the landlords managed their own patrimonial administrations, which sometimes had as many as twenty layers of assistants and possessed many formal and informal powers. While this personal system of administration severely limited state bureaucratization, infrastructural power, and inclusiveness, several scholars agree that the formal and informal powers of the landholders in combination with colonial backing institutionalized their control of hierarchical relations of dependence at the local level, which obstructed the ability of the peasants to pursue their well-being (Gopal 1963; Kohli 1987; Kumar 1989; Moore 1966).

Analyses of postcolonial India find that the strength of local intermediaries has not disappeared despite the fact that they lost formal powers
at independence (Kohli 1987; Moore 1966; Reeves 1991). Furthermore, a
comparison of India's states provides evidence that rule through indirect
collaborators left a negative developmental legacy. Using the percentage
of each state's total territory that was ruled by either princes or landlords during colonialism as a measure of indirect colonial rule, the extent
of indirect rule is negatively related to each state's literacy rate (−0.47)
and per capita GDP (−0.43) and positively related to infant mortality
rate (0.48).[2] Banerjee and Iyer (2005) use multivariate statistics to analyze the determinants of uneven development within postcolonial India
and provide similar findings. They calculate the percentage of district
territory that was controlled by intermediary landlords during British
rule, use several different modeling strategies, and continually find that
regions with landlords during colonialism have had significantly lower
levels of economic and human development during the postcolonial
period. Although the authors suggest that these differences are primarily
caused by the effects of property right enforcement on policy and investment, this analysis suggests something different: colonial rule through
zamindars, princes, and other local intermediaries created a minuscule
state that was dependent on local elites; the absence of indigenous intermediaries in other regions required a larger legal-administrative system
to collect taxes, register property, and enforce property rights; and these
more directly ruled regions therefore had states with greater capacities to
promote development.

Kerala, a state within postcolonial India, is an exceptional case that
ultimately supports the general rule about the developmental effects of
indirect colonialism. The state stands out as having the highest levels of
human development in India and among the highest in the Third World,
with life expectancy rates that approach Western levels, nearly universal
literacy for both men and women, and active and democratic politics at the
local level. Heller (1999) finds that Kerala's developmental success was
made possible by a sustained social movement that empowered lower-
class/caste Indians and allowed them to dismantle hierarchical relations
of dependency, force land reforms, restructure local state institutions,
and provide the population with a variety of developmental goods. Such
actions were necessary because the colonial practice of collaborating with
local elites greatly increased the power of the elites and created a minimal
state with very limited presence locally. Development in Kerala was therefore made possible by the destruction of the Indian form of decentralized

despotism and the construction of a direct local state that expanded infrastructural power and inclusiveness (Heller 1999).[3]

All in all, evidence suggests that the proportionally tiny administration in colonial India in combination with the institutionalized practice of dominating large areas through indigenous collaborators hindered development through state incapacity and local despotism. Although these findings parallel those of Sierra Leone and other indirectly ruled colonies, a comparison of colonial India and the more indirectly ruled colonies of sub-Saharan Africa points to important differences as well. Despite the use of indirect rule, large parts of India—especially in the south and west—were ruled through relatively direct means. Additionally, the central legal-administrative institutions in both colonial and postcolonial India were much larger in absolute terms and much more bureaucratic than their counterparts in sub-Saharan Africa (Kohli 2004: 286). As a result of these differences, the Indian state has had considerably greater organizational capacity, which, in turn, has made possible superior development. Indeed, of the sixteen former British colonies in sub-Saharan Africa, only Mauritius and South Africa—both of which experienced more direct forms of colonial rule than India—had higher Human Development Index scores in 2004 (0.800 and 0.653 respectively), while the remaining British African countries averaged only 0.436 versus India's more modest 0.611.

One reason for the difference between India and British Africa is simply that the Indian state did not promote developmental catastrophes à la Sierra Leone. In addition, it proved moderately successful at promoting development in different ways. Most importantly, the relatively capable central legal-administrative institutions helped stabilize national politics and social relations, an impressive feat given the size and diversity of the Indian population and the extreme ethnic violence that coincided with the partition of India and Pakistan (including Bangladesh) at independence. The central state's bureaucratic structure, for example, enforced a strict organizational hierarchy, which limited coups by keeping the military under state control. The relatively effective central state also provided an institutional foundation that facilitated central control over all regions, democratic participation, and a moderately effective enforcement of a unified system of law. Finally, the Indian state proved moderately capable of managing the national economy (Kohli 2004). Along with maintaining reasonable macroeconomic stability, the Indian state's promotion of high-tech industries provides a much-celebrated example of successful state intervention that spurred growth (Evans 1995; Kohli 2004).

South Africa

In a few African colonies, South Africa being the most notable example, Europeans settled in areas with large indigenous populations and constructed a mixed form of colonialism. Here, both direct and indirect institutions were built, with the Europeans living within a direct system of rule and the African population inhabiting either African enclaves within the directly ruled areas or indirectly ruled African reserves. Although South Africa is somewhat exceptional given its racialized form of domination,[4] it still points to the general tendency of legal-administrative effectiveness and development through direct rule and despotism and underdevelopment through indirect rule.

British colonial rule in South Africa began with the capture of the Cape Colony from the Dutch in 1795 and expanded over the next century through the conquest of adjacent lands: Natal in 1843 and the Boer Republics between 1899 and 1902. Only a few years after British South Africa had reached its geographic limits, the British attempted to reconcile differences between the Boer and British communities by granting self-rule in 1910, thereby ending for all intents and purposes British rule (Marx 1998). Throughout the colonial period, the Cape Colony was ruled primarily through centralized and bureaucratic legal-administrative institutions. In areas that were added to the Cape in the late nineteenth century, however, indirectly ruled native reserves were created for the African population. Here, the chiefdom-level political structures were dismantled out of fear that they would provide a strong basis for revolt, and the British ruled through village headman, thereby creating a more localized form of indirect rule than elsewhere in British Africa (Mamdani 1996: 68). In Natal and the former Boer Republics, this combination of direct rule in territories inhabited by European settlers and indirect rule in officially designated native reserves was also present, yet indirect rule took the more common form of rule through chiefs rather than headman.

Between 1890 and 1924, large-scale state reforms occurred in South Africa (Terreblanche 2002: 239). Although the African reserves remained largely unchanged, the state in the directly ruled areas expanded rapidly, took a more active role in the provisioning of developmental goods, and began to manage economic expansion. The South African state proved very successful at promoting development, and white South Africans quickly attained living standards that were among the highest in the world. For example, the South African state's provisioning of developmental goods in the directly ruled areas led to marked improvements in education and health care. In addition, state intervention helped South Africa become one of the few countries with a mineral-based economy to successfully industrialize. Specifically, the state created several public corporations and worked closely with local capitalists to wrestle the South African market from foreign companies and to expand economic production beyond the mining sector (Fine and Rustomjee 1996; Terreblanche 2002: 343–46). With this developmental state, South Africa's average annual GDP growth rate was an impressive 5.3 percent between 1919 and 1970, and the percentage of South Africa's GDP derived from industry increased from less than 7 percent in 1912 to 30 percent in 1970 (Lewis 1990: 24–25).

Although the black South Africans living in the directly ruled townships received some benefits from this impressive development, they faced numerous hardships resulting from institutionalized discrimination. Despite such difficulties, their lot was considerably better than that of their brethren in the indirectly ruled reserves, which were renamed Bantustans during the apartheid period. Both colonial and postcolonial regimes used little of their resources to assist those living in the reserves, making the areas extremely impoverished. For example, although having 40 percent of South Africa's population in 1980, the Bantustans received less than 10 percent of government expenditure and produced less than 4 percent of South Africa's total GDP (Lewis 1990: 43). Moreover, the infant mortality rate in the Bantustans was among the highest in the world in the late 1970s (227 per 1,000) and nearly three times as high as that of Africans living outside of them (Packard 1989: 274).

Segregation and the unequal use of state resources undoubtedly caused much of the hardships suffered in the Bantustans. In addition, the continuation of indirect forms of rule within the Bantustans promoted government ineffectiveness and tyranny at the hands of chiefly collaborators (Mamdani 1996; Rogers 1976). Describing local politics in the Ciskei Bantustan, for example, Evans (1997) writes:

> [C]hiefs were confident that any infraction of rules already heavily weighted in their favor would be condoned by their administrative superiors in the department. In the event that their authority was challenged from below, they also knew that the state had much riding on the viability of Bantu Authorities. They were confident, therefore, that departmental officials and the police would regularly intervene on their behalf. Thus, many chiefs strutted about like resurrected peacocks, generally creating a climate of intimidation and terror that discouraged commoners from questioning even the most flagrant violation of their rights. (272)

Thus, reminiscent of the colonial backing of despotic chiefs in the Sierra Leone Protectorate, patrimonial rule at the local level promoted depravity and predation and—in combination with a racist central administration—made the Bantustans developmental basket cases (Moerdijk 1981).

Myanmar

Although modern India was easily the largest component of the British subcontinent, colonial India also included present-day Bangladesh, Myanmar, and Pakistan. Similar to India, Bangladesh and Pakistan appear to support this book's findings given their mixed forms of colonial rule and poor to moderate postcolonial development records. Myanmar, on the other hand, has a much poorer developmental record than expected given its relatively direct form of colonial rule. The case therefore provides a check on the findings of the previous chapters.

Known as Burma throughout the colonial period, Myanmar was conquered by the British in three stages during the nineteenth century. Given its geographic proximity, the region was incorporated into and ruled as part of colonial India until 1937, at which time it was governed as a separate colony until its independence in 1948. Throughout the colonial period, Burma was controlled through both direct and indirect methods, although the former predominated. The "Scheduled" or "Frontier" Areas were ruled through indirect means. They comprised half of the colony's territory yet contained only one-fifth of its total population, and the majority of the people living in these areas were ethnic minorities (House of Commons 1947). The remainder of the colony was directly ruled and populated primarily by ethnic Burmans. Colonial Myanmar therefore had an ethnically and organizationally bifurcated state, with minorities ruled indirectly and the Burman majority ruled directly (Smith 1994: 22).

Despite its relatively high levels of direct colonial rule, Myanmar is presently one of Asia's poorest countries, with a per capita GDP of only $1,900 (Maddison 2007). It also has relatively high levels of infant mortality, with nearly 8 percent of all infants dying before their first birthday (World Bank 2007a). One important reason for such a poor development record is the country's ineffective state. Indeed, based on World Bank data, governance in Myanmar is among the very poorest in the world: its global percentile rankings of government effectiveness, rule of law, and lack of corruption are third, fourth, and first respectively (World Bank 2007b).

In comparison to other British colonies in the region, Myanmar had lower levels of development, even during colonialism, a situation that appears to be related to its integration into colonial India, little or no investment by either public or private actors, and its rice-based monocrop economy (Booth 2007). Similar to Guyana and Botswana, its colonial transition also helps to explain the country's ineffective state and unexpectedly low levels of development. During World War II, the Japanese captured colonial Myanmar with the active assistance of tens of thousands of ethnic Burmans and ruled it for two years. After regaining control of Myanmar, the British found a nearly stateless society and—given logistical difficulties and their unwillingness to collaborate with the ethnic Burmese elite who they saw as traitors—made only limited progress rebuilding the state before granting Myanmar independence in 1948 (Callahan 2003: 51, 106–8; Taylor 1987: 250–51, 265–67). According to Callahan (2003), "During the brief return of British rule, what passed for the 'state' was a constantly moving target. At no point during this period did any single group or individual establish unchallenged authority over any significant territory, resources, or persons" (113).

In addition to the collapsed colonial state and the very limited attempts to reconstruct it, two additional factors made Myanmar a powder keg ready to explode at independence. First, several minority groups opposed the prospect of Burman rule because of their special autonomy under the British and the brutality that some experienced at the hands of ethnic Burmans during the Japanese occupation (Selth 1986). And given that many ethnic minorities collaborated militarily with the British and Americans during World War II, they were well armed. Second, Burmese communists had also fought Japanese rule, resisted the reestablishment of British rule, and even opposed rule by other ethnic Burmans (Callahan 2003).

Thus, with the near absence of a state, minorities unwilling to accept Burman rule, and communists ready to fight whoever ruled Myanmar, the British granted independence in 1948, an event that immediately resulted in a violent, multi-sided, and long civil war that led to extremely coercive military rule and had devastating effects on development (Callahan 2003: 114–44). In this way, the case parallels Guyana, as both experienced ethnic violence, conflict between indigenous politicians and colonial officials, very limited state reforms in preparation for independence, militarized rule, and thus poor development. Myanmar appears to have been an even more extreme case, however, as the state was all but collapsed at independence and the country experienced much more violent and prolonged civil conflict.

Malaysia

Colonial rule in what is now Malaysia was very eclectic and combined direct and indirect forms of rule (Brown and Ampalavanar 1986: xxvii; Heussler 1981; Ibrahim 1998: 12–13; Ryan 1976). British colonialism on the Malay Peninsula began with the construction of three directly ruled trade-focused city-colonies in the late eighteenth and early nineteenth centuries (Malacca, Penang, and Singapore).[5] With continued British colonial expansion during the late nineteenth and early twentieth centuries, the remainder of Malaya was divided into nine Malay states that were incorporated into the British Empire in two phases (the Federated Malay States in 1895 and the Unfederated Malay States between 1909 and 1914), and each group had a different political status. Among the Federated Malay States, the sultans allied with the British and were allowed to maintain their titles and some privileges, although the colonial powers usurped nearly all of their legal-administrative powers and ruled them through a centralized and bureaucratic state based in Kuala Lumpur. In the Unfederated States, the same process occurred although the sultans maintained greater autonomy, resulting in a slightly more indirect form of colonial rule. Finally, both Sarawak and North Borneo were separate colonies until their merger with independent Malaya in the 1960s and experienced eclectic forms of colonial rule, the latter being a British protectorate governed by a company (the British North Borneo Company) and the former being ruled privately for over a century by British subjects who were recognized locally as white rajas. Thus, with city-states, federated states, unfederated states, and separate colonies that were either company dominated or privately controlled, colonial rule in Malaysia was extremely heterogeneous.

An analysis of the different forms of rule within colonial Malaya provides evidence that colonialism shaped long-term developmental trajectories. The former Straits Settlement colonies—Penang and Malacca—and the former Federated Malay States—Selangor, Perak, Negri Sembilan, and Pahang—experienced more direct forms of colonial rule and, in turn, have been the most developmentally dynamic regions within Malaysia over the last century. The Unfederated States, on the other hand, experienced more indirect forms of rule and have less impressive development records. As shown in Table 8.1, for example, the more directly ruled regions of Malaysia had higher levels of economic development and educational expenditure and lower rates of infant mortality during the late colonial and early independence periods. These relationships appear to be causal, as several

Table 8.1 Regional development within peninsular Malaysia, 1955–70

	Per capita GDP, 1965	Per capita education expenditure, 1955	Infant mortality rate, 1970
Federated Malay States	1,053	14.4	36.2
Straits Settlements (excluding Singapore)	754	16.3	36.1
Unfederated Malay States	522	8.0	44.8

Sources: Abdul Karim 1985: 79; Government of Malaya 1956: 245; Shafruddin 1987: 108.

analyses find that the more direct form of rule in the Straits Settlements and Federated Malay States promoted three factors that made possible developmental improvements: state infrastructural investment in transportation and health, state promotion of economic investment and production, and state enforcement of a rule of law (Baker 1999: 149, 179–80; Jomo 1986: 157, 184–85; Kaur 1985; Welsh 2001: 104).

Besides looking at uneven development within Malaysia, the country also supports this book's basic findings when taken as a whole, as colonial rule in Malaysia became increasingly direct during late colonialism, and the country has had very impressive development since independence. Despite the administrative diversity of colonial Malaysia and the state's use of indirect rule in many areas, legal-administrative institutions became increasingly centralized and bureaucratic throughout the colonial period. In fact, by 1953, 94 percent of court cases were heard in magistrate courts, suggesting a relatively high level of direct rule. Harper (1999) finds that British officials pursued four policy objectives that weakened indirect forms of rule prior to World War II: (1) the construction of a technically trained administration, (2) transformations in land tenure, (3) the creations of new centers of administrative power that rapidly eclipsed the traditional court centers, and (4) the expansion of state involvement into education, social reform, irrigation, transportation, sanitation, and town planning (23). He claims that these policies caused indirect forms of rule to be replaced by a new colonial "Leviathan":

> The mechanisms of indirect rule which had largely absorbed Europeans in Asian polities were changing: Asians were now to be encapsulated in European systems. The colonial state embraced areas of government untouched by the Malay *ancien régime*, services supernumerary to protection. It was a new kind of state entirely. Its power was not negotiable. Its law reflected a new concept of the person that challenged old notions of status and community. It

possessed new systems of administrative accounting in the field of revenue, and laid a host of new charges upon the people. (22–23)

In addition, although British rule broke down in Malaysia during World War II because of the Japanese occupation, the British quickly reestablished the colonial state after regaining control, and direct rule expanded even further during the final decade of colonialism. For one thing, British efforts to control postwar labor disturbances promoted state expansion. In addition, a communist and anticolonial insurgency known as "the Emergency" forced the territorial and administrative expansion of the state (Stubbs 1997). The Emergency began in 1948, lasted for twelve years, and pitted the colonial state against a few thousand communist insurgents, the overwhelming majority of whom were Chinese Malays. In their efforts to combat this threat, which hid in the jungles and mountains, a British-run military force of approximately 100,000 troops was formed. The communist forces were greatly inferior in numbers and therefore resorted to hit-and-run attacks on plantations, public infrastructure, and rural villages, which prompted the administration to expand from 48,000 people in 1948 to 140,000 people in 1959 in an attempt to monitor and protect the population more effectively (Harper 1999: 359).

Thus, colonialism in Malaysia became increasingly direct throughout the colonial period. The end result was a relatively large, infrastructurally powerful, and bureaucratic state, something Milton Esman (1972) describes as an "administrative state" bent on promoting national development. State efforts to promote human development and industrialization during the postcolonial period, in turn, proved very successful, allowing the country to have phenomenal improvements in education, health, economic growth, and income inequality over the past forty years (Ali 1992: 95–111; Bowie 1991: 82–152; Harper 1999: 366–68; Heng and Hoey 1997; Ramesh and Holliday 2001; Stubbs 1997; White 2004: 197). Overall, the case provides evidence that direct rule promotes development.

Given the institutional changes that occurred during the late colonial period, Malaysia is similar to Botswana, Guyana, and Myanmar. Myanmar provides a particularly insightful contrast to Malaysia, as their very different colonial transitions differentially affected state capacity and pushed the two countries down divergent developmental trajectories. Unlike in Myanmar, the British worked closely with the ethnic Malays to build a larger, more centralized, and territory-wide state in the aftermath of Japanese occupation and in order to defeat the communist insurgents. These efforts proved very successful and resulted in the construction of a much more direct and effective state. In Myanmar, on the other hand, the colonial administrators did little to rebuild the state after regaining the colony from Japan and left it as soon as possible with a state with extremely limited organizational capacities. Furthermore, the colonial government did little to mitigate communist and ethnic insurgents who were armed and ready to fight for control of the country, resulting in chaotic violence once the British pulled out. In fact, some renegade British officers were sympathetic to the minorities and helped organize the ethnic insurgencies.

Barbados and the Caribbean Plantation Colonies

Although a large literature on slavery and indentured servitude blames British colonialism for extreme human hardship and the underdevelopment of its sugar-producing colonies, British plantation colonies in the Caribbean currently have more impressive development levels than most other former colonies. As shown in Table 8.2, Bahamas, Barbados, Belize, Guyana, Jamaica, and Trinidad and Tobago all have Human Development Index scores and rankings that are similar to those of Mauritius, with Barbados atop the list, Guyana at the bottom, and Mauritius in the middle. In addition, all of the countries except Guyana have been successful democracies since independence. The postcolonial developmental success of Mauritius is therefore quite representative of other British plantation colonies, with Guyana being a notable underachiever.

Consistent with this book's findings, all of these plantation colonies were directly ruled. Several historical analyses describe how British colonialism in the Caribbean after World War II usually created inclusive and bureaucratic states that had relatively high capabilities to implement a rule of law, promote development, and enforce democratic procedures (Hurwitz and Hurwitz 1971: 181–86; Ledgister 1998: 38–41; Rueschemeyer, Stephens, and Stephens 1992: 239–42). Barbados, which gained its independence in 1966, is the most successful example. Its state has actively and very effectively promoted broad-based developmental improvements beginning during late colonialism and continuing after independence (Bishop, Corbin, and Duncan 1997: 329–36; Howard 1989: 134). Indeed, according to a United Nations (2001) report on the determinants of the country's impressive development, British colonialism laid the foundation for Barbados' developmental success by institutionalizing a state that was not only capable of providing diverse developmental goods in the realm of education, health, housing, and employment but that actually created them during its final two decades. Health care provides one concrete example, and

Table 8.2 Human Development Index scores and rankings among plantation colonies, 2003

Country	Score	Global ranking
Barbados	0.878	30
Bahamas	0.832	50
Trinidad and Tobago	0.801	57
Mauritius	0.791	65
Belize	0.753	91
Jamaica	0.738	98
Guyana	0.720	107

the improvements within this area have an uncanny resemblance to those occurring oceans away in Mauritius:

> The development of health centres in the 1950s had an indelible impact on the health status of Barbadians. Their services included the control of communicable diseases, maternal and child health, nutrition, dental health, ophthalmic and domiciliary services, immunization, and the treatment of venereal disease and tuberculosis. The protection of water supplies, sewerage and solid waste disposal and the protection of food for sale were all integral components of the health centre's services. (United Nations 2001)

These policies rapidly improved public health standards, and Barbadians entered independence with a life expectancy of nearly seventy years, a level equivalent to that of the United States.

Barbados also mirrors Mauritius in that the state's high levels of inclusiveness enhanced its developmental capacity. The state has actively collaborated with a number of social actors to improve the delivery of developmental services and infrastructure and to engage the population. Bishop, Corbin, and Duncan (1997), for example, claim that "[d]uring different phases of social development, governments, colonial and local, have worked together with the Church, concerned citizens, and, more recently, special groups and associations to resolve problems" (329). Similarly, Rueschemeyer, Stephens, and Stephens (1992) note that unions, associations, and parties were very active in colonial and postcolonial Barbados and helped balance the power of the plantation elite, thereby making possible a vibrant democracy (231). More generally, they suggest that state inclusiveness and a balance of power between plantation elite and workers were the norm among British plantation colonies during the late colonial period—although they describe Guyana as an exception—and claim that the colonial state promoted these characteristics (226–68).

City-Colonies: Hong Kong and Singapore

The directly ruled city-colonies—Hong Kong and Singapore—have arguably experienced the most impressive developmental improvements among all former British colonies over the past fifty years. Indeed, Hong Kong and Singapore, respectively, had the world's twenty-second and twenty-fifth highest Human Development Index scores in 2005, placing them right alongside the world's developmental elites.[6] Both also have among the most effective states in the world. As measured by the World Bank's indicators of state effectiveness, political stability, rule of law, and absence of corruption, for example, Singapore is tied with Switzerland for the highest level of governance of all countries in the world, while Hong Kong has the same governance level as the United States.[7]

Hong Kong's and Singapore's extremely effective postcolonial states and remarkable postcolonial development appear to be causally related. Several works provide evidence that Singapore's developmental state actively pursued national industrialization and thereby drove the country's economic success (Baker 1999; Huff 1994, 1999; Krause 1988; Peebles and Wilson 2002). Doner, Ritchie, and Slater (2005), for instance, provide evidence that Singapore's economic development was made possible by a highly effective bureaucratic state with relatively high levels of inclusiveness. High levels of effectiveness allowed the state to successfully manage the country's economic expansion through the Economic Development Board, the Jurong Town Corporation, various state-run companies, and other public organizations. Inclusiveness also promoted development by bringing together the state, labor, and capital in a quasi-corporatist structure that facilitated compromise and combined public and private knowledge and resources in the pursuit of national development. And although they focused largely on industrialization, officials in Singapore have used their high organizational capacity to provide collective and public goods that successfully promoted human development as well (Ramesh and Holliday 2001; Ser 2004).

Hong Kong's state differs from Singapore's in that it did not pursue an active economic role. Despite this difference, it still promoted broad-based development in important ways. According to Krause (1988), the state actively and successfully provided diverse developmental goods—including law and order, clean water, transportation infrastructure, education, and public housing—that ultimately provided the physical infrastructure, legal support, and human capital needed for the region's dramatic economic expansion (S61). Dreze and Sen (1989) recognize that the state's provisioning of means-tested social assistance and other collective goods underlie Hong Kong's equally impressive human development (Dreze and Sen 1989: 192). In fact, Hong Kong presently has an infant mortality rate well below that of the United States, and Ramesh and Holliday (2001) find that an activist state focused on health care provisioning drove Hong Kong's remarkable improvement in public health.

Consistent with this book's findings, both Hong Kong and Singapore were among the most directly ruled colonies within the British Empire, having had extremely large legal-administrative institutions that were organized bureaucratically and present throughout their territories. Even more, a number of their state-led developmental improvements began during colonialism (Ramesh and Holliday 2001), and both emerged from colonialism with relatively developed economies (Krause 1988). Although this is especially true for Hong Kong, which did not gain its independence from Great Britain until 1997, it also holds for Singapore, which emerged from British rule in 1959 with a "legacy of state capability," a factor that Huff (1999) argues provided the foundation for its developmental state (219–20). Thus, direct colonial rule appears to have been a cause of the city-colonies' phenomenal development records.

Sri Lanka

Like Hong Kong and Singapore, colonial Ceylon (present-day Sri Lanka) was ruled relatively directly for nearly 150 years. Unlike the city-colonies, it lacked strategic trade locations, had a much larger territory and indigenous population, and had an agriculture-based economy with several plantations. In this way, it was more similar to colonial Mauritius than to the city-colonies.

Sri Lanka's resemblance to Mauritius also extends to social welfare development. Many recognize that development was largely ignored by the colonial officials in Sri Lanka throughout most of the colonial period but that extensive political and social welfare reforms were implemented during the 1930s and 1940s (de Silva 1997; Jayasuriya 2004; Jeffries 1962; Mills 1933; Nyrop, Benderly, Cort, Parker, Perlmutter, Shinn, and Shivanandan 1971). Similar to the situation in Mauritius, these reforms expanded ties between the colonial state and society and resulted in impressive human development (Jayasuriya 2004). Caldwell (1986) finds that reforms in late-colonial Sri Lanka caused rapid improvements in education rates, the expansion of political participation, greater egalitarianism (especially between men and women), and dramatic improvements in human health. He notes that Sri Lanka had outstanding infant survival rates despite limited economic growth and finds that its impressive levels of societal health are rooted in the aforementioned colonial reforms and the continuation of colonial social welfare policy after independence.[8] Notably, both of these were dependent on a relatively effective state apparatus, which in turn was the outcome of a direct form of colonialism.

Sri Lanka differs markedly from postcolonial Mauritius, however, in that its postcolonial state neither successfully managed the economy nor promoted growth to the same extent. Instead, Sri Lanka's economy has been stagnant over the past few decades due in no small part to an ethnic-based civil war that continues to destabilize and ravage the country (Nithiyanandam 2000). Indeed, Jayasuriya (2004) claims that the state's development policy changed from the colonial precedent of social *welfare* in the 1940s, 1950s, and 1960s to social *warfare* since the 1970s. Despite the horrors of prolonged conflict and a stagnant economy, the country's human development level remains surprisingly high. With a Human Development Index score of 0.755 in 2004, Sri Lanka's level of development is close to that of Mauritius (0.800) and considerably higher than Sri Lanka's more indirectly ruled neighbors: Bangladesh (0.530), India (0.611), and Pakistan (0.539).

Conclusion

This book's comparative-historical analysis of Mauritius and Sierra Leone explores the potential mechanisms underlying the relationship between the form of British colonial rule and long-term developmental trajectories and highlights the impact of legal-administrative institutions. The case studies of Guyana and Botswana, on the other hand, investigate why two former colonies do not conform to the statistical findings linking direct rule to development and indirect rule to despotism. Both outlier cases provide evidence that the institutional legacies of British colonialism sometimes changed during the independence processes and that such transformations readjusted developmental trajectories in accordance with the institutional mechanisms discovered in the Mauritian and Sierra Leonean case studies. Finally, the brief case studies in this chapter test the generalizability of the mechanisms highlighted in the in-depth case studies by applying them to several additional cases. The abbreviated case studies reinforce the findings from the previous chapters and thereby help to integrate the statistical analysis and the in-depth case studies.

Nigeria, Ghana, and the Solomon Islands all experienced relatively indirect forms of colonial rule, and—similar to Sierra Leone—all three suffered from incapacitated central states and had poor development records. At the opposite end of the continuum, colonial control of Hong Kong, Singapore, and Barbados was much more direct, and all three experienced developmental achievements during the postcolonial period that even surpass the likes of Mauritius. As in Mauritius, the state in these former directly ruled colonies was capable of providing developmental goods and promoting economic growth. Sri Lanka is a slightly exceptional directly ruled colony, as the state has been an important instrument promoting human development, but a prolonged civil war and ethnic violence have negatively affected postcolonial development. Between the extremes of direct and indirect rule, the hybrid colonies experienced mixed developmental outcomes. In both India and South Africa, for example, the regions that were more directly ruled have experienced superior development, and, when taken as wholes, both have had mediocre developmental records over the past half century.

Not all cases analyzed in this chapter conform to the statistical relationship, however. In particular, Myanmar has a much lower level of development than expected given its relatively direct form of rule. Similar to Guyana and Botswana, the case shows that the colonial transition was a critical period during which the institutional legacy of British colonialism and the country's developmental legacy transformed in tandem. In colonial Myanmar, Japanese occupation during World War II combined with ethnic and communist insurgencies resulted in a dilapidated and ineffective state, decades of civil war and military rule, and therefore poor development. During the late colonial period, Malaysia also experienced major state institutional changes that readjusted its developmental trajectory, although these changes constructed a more direct form of rule and thereby had positive effects on postcolonial development. The case is not a statistical outlier, however, because most of the reforms occurred during colonialism and are therefore captured by the variable measuring the extent of indirect rule.

Overall, the findings of the abbreviated case studies further support claims that the lineages of both despotism and development lead back to British colonialism. Specifically, they provide additional evidence that the extent of direct and indirect rule and, to a lesser extent, institutional changes during the independence process were critical factors that pushed former British colonies down very different developmental pathways.

Conclusion and Discussion

9

This book begins with a question: Why do former British colonies have such diverse development records? In the subsequent chapters, I employ a three-tiered research design that combines both quantitative and qualitative methods in search of an answer. Each component of the analysis provides consistent, complementary, and powerful evidence pointing to one historical cause: the extent of direct or indirect colonial rule.

To begin the empirical analysis, I operationalize the extent of indirect colonial rule and use multivariate statistical methods to investigate whether the form of colonialism is related to diverse development indicators. Using a number of independent variables and different sets of colonies, I discover that the extent to which British colonial rule was indirect is negatively, significantly, and consistently related to per capita GDP in 1970 and 2000, societal health in 1970 and 2000, average school attainment in 1970 and 1995, and postcolonial political development. Together, these statistical findings suggest that British colonialism began developmental trajectories and that state institutional legacies reinforced these trajectories over extended periods of time. In contrast, the statistical findings lend little support to claims that uneven development among former British colonies was caused either by precolonial or postcolonial factors.

Next, through in-depth case studies of Mauritius, Sierra Leone, Guyana, and Botswana and abbreviated case studies of eleven additional former British colonies, I investigate potential causal mechanisms linking direct rule to development and indirect rule to despotism. The case studies provide evidence that direct rule usually constructed states with effective legal-administrative institutions and thus high capacities to promote development. Indirect rule, on the other hand, institutionalized states with low developmental capacities, and the ineffectiveness of their legal-administrative institutions limited the state's capacity to provide developmental goods and promoted coercive and predatory states that actually impeded development. I find that three state structural characteristics caused these differences.

First, direct and indirect British colonial rule created states with different degrees of bureaucratization, which affected the capacity of states to control officials and act corporately. In directly ruled colonies, bureaucratic states were able to oversee officials and thereby curb their ability to prey on societal actors. In addition, bureaucracy made possible the successful provisioning of complex developmental goods such as health care, law and order, education, economic management, and a social safety net. In contrast, indirect rule institutionalized states with large nonbureaucratic pockets, and these states proved incapable of providing their citizens with basic developmental goods and promoted rampant rent seeking and predation during both colonial and postcolonial periods.

Infrastructural power enhances a state's developmental capacity by allowing it to penetrate society and implement policy throughout its territory, and directly and indirectly ruled colonies also had different levels of infrastructural power. I find that direct rule promoted relatively high levels of infrastructural power, which allowed legal-administrative institutions to provide territory-wide access to a number of developmental goods. In former indirectly ruled colonies, on the other hand, the states had very low levels of infrastructural power. Even more than simply impeding state provisioning of developmental goods, the near absence of the state throughout much of the territory created a fecund environment for state breakdown and civil war.

Third, the book provides evidence that the extent of state inclusiveness has important effects on broad-based development and that direct rule promoted inclusiveness whereas indirect rule obstructed it. Among former directly ruled colonies, relatively high levels of inclusiveness enhanced development during late-colonial and postcolonial periods by making possible collaborative relations between state and societal actors. In particular, state-society relations allowed the successful provisioning of developmental goods in local communities, as the state was able to exploit the information, resources, and energy of the local population. In addition, inclusiveness promoted state accountability to the public and therefore pressured state officials to implement developmental policy. Among former indirectly ruled colonies, however, both the colonial and postcolonial states were far from inclusive. As a consequence, state officials were hardly accountable, and state-society relations were anything but synergistic.

Notably, direct and indirect rule form more of a continuum than a strict dichotomy, and some former colonies found themselves between the extremes. Consistent with the findings on direct and indirect rule, I provide evidence that mixed forms of colonial rule produced middle levels of bureaucratization, infrastructural power, and inclusiveness and thereby mediocre developmental results. In these hybrid cases, the state's legal-administrative capacities were uneven, as some regions of a colony were ruled directly and others indirectly. Consequently, regional variation in development is the norm among former hybrid colonies, with the directly ruled regions having superior development. When taken as a whole, the state in hybrid colonies lacked the legal-administrative capacities of former directly ruled colonies but was considerably more effective than the states of former indirectly ruled colonies.

All in all, the analysis shows that the extent of indirect colonial rule is negatively correlated with development and provides strong evidence that this relationship is causal and driven by state institutional differences in the extent of bureaucratization, infrastructural power, and inclusiveness. I therefore conclude that colonial state legacies are an important cause of uneven development among former British colonies. Thus, contrary to some scholars who praise British rule for promoting development and others who denigrate it for impeding development, these findings suggest that British colonialism should not be characterized as either universally developmental or universally despotic. Instead, its legacy was mixed, being relatively developmental in some places and relatively destructive in others.

That said, I do not claim that the form of colonialism was the only factor affecting the developmental trajectories of former British colonies. Obviously, development is shaped by a number of factors beside states. In addition, I find that postcolonial states usually resemble their colonial precursors but that the state institutional legacies of British colonialism were not set in stone. Most importantly, the independence transition heightened the risk of critical transformations in the state's organizational structure, and major state institutional changes occurred in a few former British colonies during the transition from colony to independent national state. The states in both Botswana and Malaysia, for example, became much more direct during the final years of colonialism and the first decades of independence. Influenced by these changes, both former colonies have experienced very impressive developmental improvements. By contrast, the states in Guyana and Myanmar degenerated during the final years of colonialism and resulted in personalized and militarized rule that was neither bureaucratic nor inclusive. These state institutional changes, in turn, had very negative effects on postcolonial development.

Contributions to the Literature on Colonialism, States, and Development

In showing that British colonialism took different forms and that direct rule had a much more positive effect on long-term development than indirect rule, the analysis contributes to the literature on colonialism, states, and development both by supporting previous findings and by providing new insight. For one thing, the analysis reinforces claims that colonialism was a prolonged event that caused dramatic social transformations and shaped global developmental hierarchies (Polanyi 1957; Wallerstein 1966). Yet unlike scholars who focus on the cleavage between the formerly colonized and the former colonizers, I support Acemoglu, Johnson, and Robinson (2001, 2002), Kohli (2004), Mahoney (2003), and others, finding that former colonies have had very different developmental trajectories and that these differences stem, in no small part, from the form of colonial domination. Thus, to better understand how Malaysia ascended the developmental ladder and why Malawi stagnated or declined, one needs to consider colonial legacies.

In addition to increasing insight into the determinants of global developmental hierarchies, my findings have implications on a subject that is increasingly recognized by diverse scholars as a fundamental problem confronting many of the world's countries: state building (Bates 1989; Evans 2005; Fukuyama 2004; Lange and Rueschemeyer 2005; Wolff 2004). The analysis provides evidence that state structures usually reproduce themselves over extended periods and are therefore difficult to transform. More exactly, state transformations usually build on preexisting structures instead of changing them, and states therefore tend to change in ways that maintain and even strengthen their organizational structures. Similar to Mahoney's (2000) work on the causes of path dependence, I highlight three main mechanisms that enforced state institutional reproduction among former British colonies. First, organizational structures influenced the norms and cognitive frameworks of actors, causing them to act in ways that perpetuated the preexisting structure. Second, an increasing-returns mechanism magnified the costs of major organizational transformations, reduced the costs of reforms that build on preexisting structures, and thereby promoted the reproduction of state structures. Finally, state structures empowered some actors who, in turn, obstructed institutional change in order to protect their positions.

The maintenance of indirect rule in Sierra Leone highlights all three mechanisms. Any attempt to create a territory-wide system of direct rule either during late colonialism or after independence would have been extremely costly given the scale of necessary reforms and the state's limited ability to implement such reforms. In addition, the system of rule through chiefs was hardly questioned because it was accepted and viewed by both officials and the public as appropriate. Indeed, even the Sierra Leoneans who rebelled against the chiefly misrule in the mid-1950s asked for new chiefs, not a new system of rule. Finally, the chiefs and their supporters were powerful figures who adamantly protected their positions, thereby obstructing political reforms.

The fact that Botswana and Guyana do not fit this trend of state institutional continuity shows that major changes were possible. Ultimately, the two outlier cases show that the independence period had the potential to be a critical juncture for institutional transformation by initiating change and obstructing mechanisms of state reproduction. In Botswana, for instance, the chiefdom succession crisis in the Bangwato Territory in combination with impending independence caused preexisting institutions to break down. As a consequence, new forms of rule were considered, the cost of reform was reduced, and the strongest proponents of institutional stasis (the chiefs) were severely weakened. Under these conditions and with sound leadership bent on reforming the state, major institutional changes could and did occur. The case therefore shows that state building is most likely to occur during periods of institutional crisis, as the mechanisms promoting the continuation of state structures are weakened at this time, thereby creating an opening for punctuated change. Contrary to the Botswana case, Guyana shows that such openings need not promote state building and can actually have very negative effects on both state effectiveness and development.

Finally, and most significantly, the findings of this book contribute to the literature on colonial legacies by providing insight into the mechanisms linking states and development. I show that the extent of direct and indirect colonial rule shaped state bureaucratization, infra-structural power, and inclusiveness. All three, in turn, affected whether or not states provided developmental goods or developmental bads, thereby helping to determine whether the states of former British colonies were developmental or despotic.

These institutional mechanisms linking colonialism to postcolonial development differ from past works in important ways and suggest a need to reconsider their findings. For instance, Acemoglu, Johnson, and Robin-son's (2001, 2002) work is arguably the most influential in the field and has inspired considerable interest in the developmental legacies of colo-nialism. They propose that colonialism shaped developmental trajectories through the transfer of effective legal institutions and claim that the extent of European settlement determined whether or not colonial and postcolo-nial states enforced a rule of law. Contrary to their conclusions, I provide evidence that the extent of direct rule had a much stronger and more con-sistent impact on development than the presence of European settlers in former British colonies. Although one might suggest that this difference results from their focus on former overseas colonies from diverse colonial powers, the majority of Europeans settled in the British Empire, includ-ing the four large-scale settler colonies that help drive Acemoglu, Johnson, and Robinson's findings (Australia, Canada, New Zealand, and the United States). In addition to this difference, I find that states can promote broad-based development by constructing and maintaining a variety of collective and public goods. I therefore provide evidence that analyses of colonial leg-acies must expand beyond property right enforcement and recognize the multifaceted ways in which states affect developmental processes. Finally, Acemoglu, Johnson, and Robinson largely overlook the state structures that make possible the provisioning of a rule of law (or other collective and public goods for that matter) and focus instead on policy. My findings pro-vide evidence that bureaucracy, infrastructural power, and inclusiveness are all determinants of a state's developmental capacity and that this capac-ity is necessary for the effective implementation of development policy, suggesting that analyses of colonial legacies must pay close attention to all three state institutional characteristics.

In focusing on the state and direct and indirect rule, the analysis also sheds light on the developmental impact of state decentralization. Contrary to common claims within the democracy literature, I find that decentralized state structures need not promote development. Indeed, consistent with Mamdani's (1996) findings, I show how indirect rule decentralized state power and had very negative effects on development by creating ineffective legal-administrative institutions and encouraging local despotism. Direct rule, on the other hand, promoted much more impressive developmental outcomes, suggesting that centralized state power has more positive effects on development. Yet the decentralization of state power in directly ruled Mauritius during late colonialism made possible a variety of developmental outcomes, offering evidence that direct rule did not necessarily promote development through its high degree of centralization. Instead, the findings suggest that direct rule increased state effectiveness, which was the key to Mauritius' developmental success. In fact, decentralization in Mauritius succeeded largely because it possessed a state that was capable of implementing extensive political reforms, monitoring local government, and interacting with local communities. In contrast, decentralized rule in Sierra Leone promoted despotism and state breakdown because the colonial government proved completely incapable of integrating the state and controlling local officials. In this way, my findings support Heller's (2001) claims that decentralization can promote development in important ways but that developmental decentralization requires a state with great organizational capacity, as decentralization without an effective state can limit state capacity even further while expanding opportunities for state predation.

Beyond the Overseas British Empire?

Within the realm of colonial domination, British overseas colonies are only part of a larger set. It is therefore possible that these findings are peculiar to the British Overseas Empire. In this penultimate section, I apply the findings to non-British and internal colonies in order to explore their potential generalizability.

Japanese, French, Portuguese, and Spanish Overseas Empires

A large literature on colonial legacies compares overseas empires and attempts to assess whether colonialism by one power left a more positive developmental legacy than colonialism by another. A number of works find that the British left a more positive legacy than the French, Portuguese, and Spanish but that Japanese colonialism potentially had the most positive impact on long-term development (Bernhard, Reenock, and Nordstrom 2004; Bertocchi and Canova 2002; Bollen and Jackman 1985; Brown 2000; Crenshaw 1995; Grier 1999; Landes 1998; LaPorta, Lopez-de-Silanes, Shleifer, and Vishny 1999). Given my findings on the determinants of uneven development within the former British Empire, one might expect Japanese colonialism to have been very direct and French, Portuguese, and Spanish colonialism more indirect.

Consistent with this book's findings, Japanese colonialism in South Korea and Taiwan was among the most direct that the world has ever seen, and both South Korea and Taiwan arguably have been the world's most dynamic developers over the past half century. By almost any standard, Japanese colonial states were extremely large, bureaucratic, and territory-wide and did not depend on collaborating intermediaries who controlled indigenous institutions at the local level. Colonial Korea, for example, had one Japanese official for every 400 colonial subjects, a ratio much higher than in any directly ruled British colony (Kohli 2004: 306). Such a direct form of rule was imposed coercively and brutally and therefore had some very negative effects on the Korean and Taiwanese populations. In the long run, however, Japanese colonialism appears to have left some very positive legacies. In particular, numerous studies find that the Korean and Taiwanese states made possible their meteoric development and argue that the legal-administrative legacies of Japanese colonialism helped lay the foundation for their developmental success (Amsden 1985, 1989; Cumings 2005; Ka 1995; Kohli 1994, 2004; Myers and Peattie 1984; Shin 1998; Shin and Han 1999; Wade 1990). Specifically, these works describe how Japanese colonialism helped eliminate the vestiges of patrimonial states and built large, bureaucratic, and effective states that actually kick-started industrialization during the colonial era.

While the Korean and Taiwanese combination of direct rule and developmentalism fits this book's findings, at first glance the literature on French and Portuguese colonialism does not. Indeed, scholars of comparative colonialism commonly assert that colonial rule by these powers was more direct than British colonialism. In light of my findings, former French and Portuguese colonies should therefore have higher levels of development than former British colonies, which—as mentioned previously—is not the case. Colonialism by non-British powers, however, was nothing like direct British rule, and French and Portuguese colonies suffered from many of the same institutional impediments as indirectly ruled British colonies: the states were neither bureaucratic, infrastructurally powerful, nor inclusive and therefore had very limited legal-administrative capacities.

Despite often being described as "direct rule," French colonialism in Africa did not create an integrated form of domination similar to that in directly ruled British colonies. Cohen (1971) finds that French colonialism in sub-Saharan Africa was hardly bureaucratic, being extremely decentralized and dependent on local administrators who had many powers and could not be controlled by their superiors (57–83). In addition, the colonial states in French Africa were minuscule and minimalist by any standard: there were only 751 French administrators and staff in sub-Saharan Africa in 1937—an area the size of Brazil (Aldrich 1996: 151). Even this number is misleading because one third of these officials were not actually physically present in Africa.[1]

As the small number of colonial officials suggests, French rule did not simply employ Europeans. Several analyses of colonial Senegal, for example, find that French colonialism depended heavily on extremely powerful chiefly intermediaries (Boone 1992; Cruise O'Brien 1975; Thomas 2005). This was part of a greater policy of "association," which incorporated indigenous leaders and institutions into the colonial state and was therefore a type of indirect rule (Betts 1961: 106–7; Deschamps 1963). Others make similar statements about all of French Africa (as well as Indochina)[2] but find that French and British forms of indirect rule differed from one another in that the French used village headmen as their key intermediaries instead of chiefdom-level authorities, thereby creating a more localized system of control (Iliffe 1995: 200; Mamdani 1996). Similarly, Firmin-Sellers (2000) analyzes two neighboring villages—one in Cote d'Ivoire, the other in Ghana—and finds that the village chiefs in the former French colony had greater control over land and fewer checks on their powers than those in the former British colony despite similar precolonial political institutions. In this way, French colonialism appears to have institutionalized its own form of decentralized and despotic rule, something Bayart (1993) calls a "rhizome state" and claims has had very negative effects on postcolonial development.

Importantly, most analyses of French colonialism in Africa focus on west Africa and generally overlook French Equatorial Africa, yet French colonialism in central Africa differed markedly from that in west Africa. In the former, the French copied Belgian King Leopold's Congo Free State and ruled through private concessionaire companies that were given rights to land and labor and brutally exploited each in an attempt to make profits. As Coquery-Vidrovitch (1972) and Hochschild (1998) describe, rule through concessionaire companies created a minimalist state based on overt violence and coercion, was extremely predatory, and did not depend on legal-administrative institutions to control vast lands and peoples. Moreover, reforms during the final decade of colonialism failed to either displace previous predatory practices or construct more effective and integrated legal-administrative institutions. French colonialism in Equatorial Africa was therefore different from both direct and indirect British rule, although its developmental legacy was much closer to the latter.

In addition to the fact that French colonialism in sub-Saharan Africa was hardly direct in terms of bureaucratization, infrastructural power, and inclusiveness given the tiny size of the colonial state and the use of both chiefs and private companies, the French did not implement state-building reforms during the independence transition, which also limited state effectiveness. In an analysis of decolonization, Smith (1978) compares British and French rule and finds that Great Britain was much more willing to guide colonial independence processes, had considerable experience with independence transitions by the 1950s, and ultimately was more successful than the French at implementing political reforms that prepared the colonies for self-rule (72–73). Thus, whereas Mauritius and other directly ruled British colonies strengthened their states during the independence process, and while a select few former indirectly ruled and hybrid colonies experienced extensive political reforms prior to independence (Botswana and Malaysia), the large-scale and rapid pullout within the French Empire left nearly all states vulnerable and weakened.

All of these points about French colonialism also apply to former Portuguese colonies in Africa and help to explain their very poor development records. First, although some Africans living in Portuguese colonies were classified as *civilisados* and ruled through more direct institutions (approximately 5,000 in Mozambique and 30,000 in Angola in 1950), the overwhelming majority were ruled indirectly through chiefs (Mamdani 1996: 87). In addition, the Portuguese colonial state was concentrated in settler regions but hardly present elsewhere and depended on concession companies to control large territories (Hall and Young 1997: 3–11). Finally, very little preparation was made to ready Portuguese colonies for independence. In fact, Portuguese colonies experienced full-scale warfare between colonial troops and local freedom fighters during the final years of colonialism. And after a coup in 1974 abruptly changed the Portuguese government's stance on colonial independence, the troops were hastily withdrawn, thereby making possible independence with virtually no attempt to hand over state institutions to local elites. In this way, the initial postcolonial government was little more than a hodgepodge of competing military leaders backed up by their troops, making the ultimate legacy of Portuguese colonialism a divided, incapacitated, and militarized state.

The Spanish Empire was less dependent on local intermediaries than British colonies under indirect rule, and the fact that most former Spanish colonies have levels of development that are higher than those of former indirectly ruled British colonies supports this book's general findings. At the same time, the Spanish Empire also provides evidence that seems to refute this book's general findings. First, only a few former Spanish colonies have levels of postcolonial development that are comparable to those of directly ruled British colonies. Even more problematic, those former Spanish colonies that were ruled most intensively and had the largest colonial states (e.g., Bolivia, Guatemala, Peru) generally have the poorest developmental records during the twentieth century, while those that were colonial backwaters (e.g., Argentina, Chile, Costa Rica, Uruguay) became the most developed regions within the former Spanish Empire.

Despite this apparent incongruence, the Spanish Empire actually conforms to this book's findings when analyzed in greater depth. According to Lange, Mahoney, and vom Hau (2006), intensive colonialism within the British and Spanish Empires had different effects on long-term development because of the different legal-administrative institutions that they constructed. Whereas direct and intensive British colonialism promoted the construction of relatively effective states, intensive Spanish colonialism created more patrimonial states with lower levels of bureaucratic organization and infrastructural power. When the Spanish metropole attempted to implement the Bourbon Reforms in the eighteenth century in order to reduce the power of local elites and create more powerful and effective colonial states, the success of the reforms was inversely related to the intensity of Spanish rule. In the core colonies, the reforms were relatively unsuccessful because the state was more institutionalized and protected by powerful political and economic elites. The reforms in the peripheral colonies, on the other hand, proved more successful because they did not experience the same social and political constraints. In fact, in the Spanish colonial backwaters, the reforms laid the foundation—albeit a flimsy one—for future legal-administrative expansion along nonpatrimonial lines and thereby superior economic and social development (Mahoney and vom Hau 2005). A comparison of the Spanish and British Empires therefore provides evidence that the legal-administrative capacities of former directly ruled British colonies were not caused simply by the greater intensity of direct rule than of indirect rule. Instead, the organizational structure of the state was vital.

All in all, this brief comparison of different colonial empires suggests that colonial state legacies might account for uneven development outside of the Pax Britannica. Japanese colonialism built relatively effective states, and former Japanese colonies have, in turn, been remarkable developers.

French and Portuguese colonialism, on the other hand, usually institu-tionalized more defective states, and most of their former colonies have had relatively poor developmental records. Finally, Spanish colonialism promoted states with varied yet mediocre developmental capacities, and the twentieth-century development records of former Spanish colonies have neither been as poor as former indirectly ruled British colonies nor as impressive as former directly ruled British colonies. Notably, the compari-son of British and other colonial empires also provides insight into past claims about the relative merit of British colonialism and suggests that the positive statistical relationship between British colonialism and devel-opment is driven by two factors: the relatively poor development records of most former non-British colonies and the relatively impressive broad-based development of a dozen former directly ruled British colonies.

Internal Colonialism within Europe

Within early modern Europe, various forms of indirect rule were employed to dominate peripheral yet usually adjacent territories, something Hech-ter (1975) refers to as internal colonialism. Over the centuries, however, national states arose and expanded direct forms of rule over these ter-ritories, forming infrastructurally powerful and bureaucratic national states. In one of his analyses of state building in Europe, for example, Tilly (1992) recognizes that indirect rule was present throughout Europe until recently. He describes how it was a difficult obstacle that had to be overcome for the construction of bureaucratic, territory-wide national states in early modern Europe (103–17). Once completed, however, rapid European development and expansionism were possible. The history of state building and development in Europe therefore coincides with this book's general findings.

Ireland, an internal colony of Great Britain that ultimately gained its independence, provides similar support. As part of Great Britain, Ireland was integrated into the British political and economic systems. It there-fore had a direct form of rule similar to that in Great Britain with one important exception: there was a cultural division of labor between British lords and capitalists and Irish peasants and laborers, and the political and economic institutions were controlled by the former (Fitzpatrick 1999; Hechter 1975). As a result, the government was largely an instrument of British elite interests, which severely limited the extent of state inclusive-ness and caused the government to overlook the well-being of the Irish population. The potato famine provides a devastating example.

With the formation of the Irish Free State in 1922, the state began to lose its instrumental character. The highly bureaucratic and infrastructurally powerful legal-administrative institutions, however, remained largely unchanged: "Under changed masters the same main tasks of administration continued to be performed by the same staff in the same general lines of organization and procedure" (Breen, Hannan, and Rottman 1990: 23). Ninety-eight percent of the British civil service, for example, retained their positions within the Free State administration (Breen, Hannan, and Rottman 1990: 23).

Ireland's state continued a socially and economically conservative orientation for several decades after independence but began to expand its role in social and economic activities by the 1950s and 1960s. In particular, it promoted social welfare development through the expansion of public services, especially health and education. It also tried to promote industrialization through import-substitution industrialization, yet these economic reforms were much less successful. The country's high rates of economic growth over the last few decades, however, suggest that the Irish state was not hindering economic expansion (O'Hearn 1998). Instead, this Celtic tiger appears to diverge from its Asian counterparts in that it was less interventionist and promoted economic growth primarily by enforcing an effective rule of law, increasing human capital, providing health care, and encouraging technological innovation and investments. Thus, the impressive human and economic development in Ireland over the last half century—which has allowed it to have one of the highest Human Development Index scores in the world—was promoted by an effective state focused on domestic well-being. While this focus was absent during British rule, the legal-administrative institutions were present and appear to have had positive effects on postcolonial development.

*   *   *   *

The above discussion provides initial insight into whether the effectiveness of legal-administrative institutions helps explain the developmental trajectories of countries outside of the former British Overseas Empire. Although far from conclusive, it suggests that states are general causes of long-term development. Overseas colonialism by Japan, France, Portugal, and Spain institutionalized states with different developmental capacities, and these different capacities appear to have promoted their levels of postcolonial development. Unlike British colonialism, however, the state capacities of non-British colonies do not always neatly coincide with direct and indirect rule, yet colonialism by all powers appears to have affected development by shaping the levels of state bureaucratization, infrastructural power, and inclusiveness. Similarly, a look at internal colonialism in Europe provides evidence that the fabled "rise of the West" occurred only after internal colonial rule transformed from indirect to direct domination. Even Ireland, an internal colony that suffered under British rule yet ultimately became independent, shows that direct rule helped lay the institutional foundation for postcolonial development.

Two Roads Diverging

In his famous poem contemplating past decisions, Robert Frost concludes that the choice to head down the road less traveled had great consequences and shows concern and remorse about what could have been if the alternative had been chosen instead. In this same way, scholars of colonialism often contemplate what would have been if colonialism never occurred. Although this book provides little insight into the colonial counterfactual, it provides greater inference into what would have been if British colonialism was either more direct or more indirect. Thus, if British colonial officials had contemplated different options and chosen to construct certain systems of rule just as Frost's character chose to head down the road less traveled, the decisions made by a few individuals about how to dominate foreign lands would have had profound and long-term effects. In particular, if they had decided to rule more directly, the inhabitants of former British colonies would likely be better able to pursue their well-being today. If, on the other hand, they had chosen to rule more indirectly, those living in former colonies would likely have inferior capacities to pursue their well-being.

Yet colonial officials might not have been free to make decisions about the form of colonialism. As described in Chapter 3, the extent of indirect rule is significantly and positively related to precolonial population density, and the precolonial population might have caused certain types of rule. For instance, the relationship might show either that the presence of a settled indigenous population with some form of political structure above the village facilitated indirect rule, that large and rebellious populations could not easily be ruled directly, or both. The disease environment is another factor that potentially limited the options of colonial officials. In Sierra Leone, for example, a deadly disease environment helped earn the colony the nickname the "white man's grave," and high death rates of European officials might have prevented direct rule.[3] Third, direct rule was more costly than indirect rule, and British politicians were very wary about using British funds to finance colonial expansion. One of the greatest costs of colonialism, in turn, was the staff, which could also be limiting in its own right. Thus, if a region did not have exploitable natural resources to cover the cost of direct rule or if colonial conquest occurred during the late colonial period when the colonial staff was already overly stretched throughout the empire, direct rule might not have been feasible.

For these reasons and more, it seems likely that British colonial officials were constrained and could not construct whatever system of rule they wanted. At the same time, there are instances in which officials seem to have made choices about the extent of direct and indirect rule. In Sri Lanka, for example, a large population and hazardous disease environment should have promoted indirect rule, but it was ruled directly. Similarly, Cyprus had a very dense population and was colonized at a time when indirect rule was the norm, yet it too was ruled directly. In addition, the form of colonialism in Botswana and Malaysia changed over time, showing that the type of colonial rule was not predetermined and that alternatives were possible. These examples suggest that the range of options available to colonial officials likely differed from colony to colony.

The recognition that the form of colonialism was at least partially dependent on other factors and not simply an arbitrary decision of early colonial officials has implications on the impact of colonialism on long-term development. Specifically, if other factors shaped the form of colonialism, these factors might diminish the overall causal importance of colonial rule. This book's findings, however, suggest that a partial dependence on other factors does not reduce the causal influence of colonialism, as all evidence points to it as *the* dynamic element shaping long-term development. The statistical analysis, for example, finds a strong relationship between the form of colonialism and numerous postcolonial development indicators and even suggests that colonialism sparked a developmental reversal of fortune. The case studies provide additional evidence by highlighting causal mechanisms linked to and instigated by the form of colonial rule, not the factors potentially affecting the form of colonialism.

Counterfactual evidence supports the same conclusion. Indeed, if colonialism had never occurred, the factors that affected the form of British colonial rule would probably not have determined state legal-administrative capacities, as regions with different population densities, with or without exploitable natural resources, and with different disease environments have proved capable of building effective states. In fact, past analyses claim that low population densities—not high—hinder state building (Herbst 2000), that natural resources are more of a curse than a blessing to state building (Snyder and Bhavnani 2005), and that disease and state building can actually go hand in hand (Munck 2005). I therefore conclude that the form of colonialism was the critical determinant of uneven development among former British colonies. Paraphrasing Frost, two colonial roads diverged, both were ultimately taken, and that has made all (or at least much) of the difference, causing despotism in some places and development in others.

Chapter 1

1. Although not focusing on colonialism, Amsden (1985, 1989) is a notable exception, as she highlights the developmental impact of bureaucratic state organization.

2. Residuals measure the extent to which individual cases conform to general statistical findings. Specifically, they measure the difference between a case's actual dependent variable score and the predicted value of the dependent variable based on the independent variables included in the model.

Chapter 2

1. For general histories of the British Empire, see Ferguson 2002; Kirk-Greene 2000; Marshall 1996; Porter 1996.

2. Notably, many early settlers arrived as indentured workers or prisoners. Therefore, these colonies were far from any utopian ideal of freedom and equality yet were much more egalitarian than other former British colonies.

3. Overlooking small outposts that continue to be British colonies (such as Gibraltar and the Falkland Islands), Hong Kong was the last colonial possession to gain its independence from British rule when it did so in 1997.

4. Notably, the settler colonies were simultaneously the most and least exclusionary: white settlers were included, yet the surviving indigenous population was almost completely excluded. Given that the Europeans made up the overwhelming majority of the population, however, colonial rule must be seen as highly inclusive as a whole.

Chapter 3

1. Despite their name, these courts were very influenced by colonialism and not simply based on custom. In fact, Mamdani (1996) suggests that customary courts were often colonial fabrications with little customary basis at all.

2. Compatible data for the extent of indirect rule are not available for Bangladesh, India, Myanmar, Pakistan, and South Africa, all of which experienced mixed forms of rule. For this analysis, data for these cases are estimated differently from Lange (2004). Specifically, scores are estimated by taking the percentage of the total population living in indirectly ruled regions. For Bangladesh, India, and Pakistan, two distinct forms of indirect rule occurred: indirect rule through princely states and indirect rule through landlords such as zamindars and taluqdars. Notably, although rule via landlords fits this book's definition of indirect rule, it was formally recognized by the colonial officials as direct rule. In addition, the landlords usually had fewer formal powers than the princes. Recognizing these differences, the estimates for these three countries are based on a formula that adds the percentage of the total population that was ruled under each form of indirect rule but weights the landlord regions only half as much as the princely states (indirect rule = percentage of total population ruled by princely states + ½ percentage of total population ruled by landlords).

Two means were used to estimate the populations living in indirectly ruled regions of Bangladesh, India, and Pakistan. First, data on the population living in indirectly ruled princely states was taken from House of Commons (1942: 5) and used to estimate the percentage of the population's of Bangladesh, India, and Pakistan that were ruled by princely states: Bangladesh = 0%, India = 26%, and Pakistan = 23%. Second, a map showing the regions that were ruled indirectly via landlords was taken from Schwartzberg (1978: 61) and used to estimate the percentage of the total populations of the three countries that were ruled through this form of indirect rule: Bangladesh = 100%, India = 46%, and Pakistan = 53%. Specifically, a transparency showing the modern districts of all three countries was placed on the map showing the regions that were ruled via landlords during the colonial period, and the regions that were ruled through landlords were then traced onto the transparency. The present populations that live in the districts that were under landlord rule during colonialism were then collected and used to estimate the percentage of the population under landlord rule during British colonialism.

3. Some former British colonies are not included in the State Antiquity Index. Of these, Putterman provides scores for a few in the "introduction and appendix" of the State Antiquity Index (Putterman 2007b). For the remaining two cases with missing values (Bahamas and Belize), I have scored them based on both the technique Putterman uses and the scores of neighboring countries with similar state histories (Guatemala for Belize and Barbados, Dominican Republic, and Haiti for Bahamas).

4. Some former British colonies are not included in the Agricultural Transitions Dataset. Of these, Putterman provides scores for some in the "data description" (Putterman 2007a). For the remaining two countries (Fiji and Solomon Islands), data are taken from Gosden (1992) and Kirch (1996).

5. The data for the variable are from a variety of sources: Australian Bureau of Statistics 2006; Bahamas 1970 Census 1990–93; Bahamas Department of Statistics 2006; Bolland 1986; Central Statistical Office 1968; Central Statistical Office 1985; DeGlopper 1991; Department of Agriculture 1886; Department of Statistics 1968; Government of Egypt 1985a, 1985b, 1985c; Gangulee 1947; Greene and Harrington

1966; Hassan and Benjamin 1973; Hoffman 1948; Hudson and Seyler 1989; Katz 1968; Klein 2004; Knibbs 1908; Koop 1960; Kuczynski 1948; Kuo and Chiew 1984; Meleagrou and Yesilada 1993; Meyerson, Hornbeck, and Haggerty 1989; Nelson and Dobert 1973; New Zealand Registrar General 1908; Neville 1990; Paxton 1970, 1971, 1972, 1975, 1978, 1981; Philosophical Society of Sudan 1958; Rutheiser 1993; Sautman 2004; Slade 1985; Smith 1994; Sullivan 1989; Statistics Canada 1878; Steinberg 1948, 1953, 1954, 1957, 1958, 1959, 1960, 1961, 1962, 1963, 1964, 1966, 1967; Steinberg and Paxton 1968; Toth 1995; Turner 1998; US Bureau of the Census 1975; Union Office of Census and Statistics 1925; Woods, Perry, and Steagall 1997.

6. With the inclusion of these seven independent variables, this analysis' models are similar to those of previous works on the developmental legacies of colonialism. Acemoglu, Johnson, and Robinson (2001, 2002), for example, include variables for European population, latitude, precolonial population density, and ethnolinguistic fractionalization. This analysis differs from their work, however, in a few ways. First, I include variables for precolonial state history, time of onset of settled agriculture, and—most notably—the form of colonial rule. I also exclude variables measuring the identity of the colonizer, which is irrelevant given the restricted sample of my analysis. Finally, I exclude regional dummies because it is uncertain what they measure. In particular, they likely capture precolonial, colonial, and postcolonial factors and therefore provide no insight into the three hypotheses for uneven development within the former British Empire. Notably, my previous work (Lange 2004, 2005a) includes regional controls and finds that the African control is negatively related to different measures of development. Similar to the analysis below, however, they point to the extent of indirect rule as the most important cause of postcolonial development.

7. Data for a few former British colonies are not included in the Penn World Tables. I fill in these missing scores converting data from Maddison (2007) and World Bank (2007).

8. For the educational attainment variable, Bahamas, Belize, Brunei, Egypt, Gambia, Solomon Islands, and Tanzania are missing data in either 1970, 1995, or both. I exclude all from the analysis in order to employ the same set of cases for both 1970 and 1995, which is necessary to check the postcolonial hypothesis.

9. World Bank data on infant mortality rate in 2000 are missing for Canada and Hong Kong. Canada was added using data from UNICEF, and Hong Kong is added using data from the CIA World Factbook.

10. Data for Hong Kong are not available for democracy, so it is not included in the analysis.

11. For all models, previously significant relations retain their direction and significance when influential cases are excluded. In a couple of models, however, variables become significant with the omission of influential cases: for per capita GDP in 1970, the European population variable becomes significant when Hong Kong and Brunei are excluded, and European population and state history variables become significant for infant mortality in 1970 when Egypt, Gambia, Hong Kong, and Sierra Leone are excluded. Without any theoretical justification to exclude these outlying cases, however, all available cases are included in the models below.

12. The only substantive change is that the European population variable became significant.

13. In the results presented here, the European population variable is not significantly related to infant mortality in 2000. Yet as reported in the diagnostic section,

tests suggest that heteroskedasticity might affect the findings for the models of infant mortality in 2000, and the European population variable becomes significant when rerunning the models with robust standard errors.

14. One potential mechanism underlying this relationship is that early state formation promoted more patrimonial forms of authority, which, in turn, impeded democratization.

15. This more limited model was chosen because the qualitative analysis focuses on the effects of direct and indirect rule, not any of the other independent variables. In addition, it is appropriate given that the customary court variable independently explains an average of 51.4 percent of variation in the eight models above and is the only variable that is consistently related to postcolonial development.

Chapter 4

1. These percentages are estimated based on the names of the state employees.

2. In 1954, there were 506 Mauritians for every police officer, while there were 702 citizens for every officer in Great Britain (Colony of Mauritius 1954b).

3. Of the 450,000 Indian indentured workers, 338,000 arrived in the island between 1843 and 1865. Notably, approximately 100,000 Indians returned to India after completing work in Mauritius.

4. The overwhelming majority of Indo-Mauritian farms were quite small: in 1930, 13,312 were less than five acres, 676 were between five and ten acres, 278 were between 10 and 20 acres, 136 were between 20 and 40 acres, and 93 were between 40 and 100 acres (Colony of Mauritius 1930).

5. According to the 1831 constitution, the Council of Government consisted of fourteen persons, half of whom were high-ranking colonial officials (ex officio members) and half of whom were selected by the governor from among the island's chief proprietors and principal merchants. With a new constitution written in 1886, the Council of Government was modified to consist of the governor, eight ex officio members, nine nominated members, and ten members elected from the local population (two from Port Louis and one from each of the island's eight districts). Notably, from 1886 until 1948, suffrage was based on monetary and land holdings, restrictions that empowered the Franco-Mauritians to control the elected seats (Mannick 1979: 49).

6. In 1950 the number of commissioners was increased, with two-thirds now elected (Dukhira 1994: 134).

7. No council could have more than twelve members, eight of whom were elected and four of whom were appointed by the government (Mauritius Legislative Council 1951a). Village councils were endowed with the powers to (1) establish schools; (2) build health care and welfare centers; (3) provide and regulate public markets and places of public activity; (4) construct, repair, and light streets and public places; (5) provide water supplies; and (6) initiate any public works promoting the sanitation of the villages (Mauritius Legislative Council 1951a).

8. These include the Swinden, Ramage, Meacock, Newton, Meade, and Browne reports.

9. The commission comprised six permanent members who appointed 2,700 official-level state employees between 1955 and 1965 and disciplined 240 others between 1957 and 1965 (Weir 1959: 3; Morgan 1961: 6; Morgan 1966: 6).

10. Between 1949 and 1958, the number of state employees receiving special training increased dramatically, from 210 to 1,140, thereafter stabilizing at around 1,000 employees per year (Colony of Mauritius 1950a, 1959a, 1962, 1964a, 1965).

11. Between 1951 and 1962, the only state employees administering local government in each of the four districts were a civil commissioner and five technical assistants (Bazerque 1993: 23).

12. Representatives of the Labour, Health, Forest, Public Assistance, and Education Departments shared the district office; and the Judicial, Public Works, and Police Departments had their own offices next to the district office (Colony of Mauritius 1948a:1–2).

13. Village councils were formally founded with the creation of antimalarial committees (Simmons 1982: 121).

14. Even when accounting for rapid population growth, these figures show that membership to the three types of organizations increased from 14 percent of the total population to 21 percent within a 14-year period. Although this percentage does not take into account individuals with multiple memberships, the actual percentage of individuals participating in local organizations was likely much higher since the calculation uses total population instead of the population of Mauritians old enough to be members. Moreover, these figures provide only a limited scope of local associations in colonial Mauritius, since they exclude local organizations such as churches or mosques as well as those without corporately held assets.

Chapter 5

1. The European slave trade began in the sixteenth century and resulted in the capture and sale of tens of thousands of Africans in Sierra Leone. While Curtin (1975) claims that 143,000 slaves were exported from Sierra Leone between 1731 and 1800, Jones (1983) suggests that the number was actually considerably higher.

2. Abraham (1978) notes that the chiefs were commonly removed until World War I, after which the British only rarely deposed chiefs. For example, between 1916 and 1942, less than ten chiefs were deposed (290).

3. The government's Republic of Sierra Leone Military Force "was officially disbanded in 1998 after seven inglorious years of looting, coup plotting (twice successful) and collusion" with the rebels (Fanthrope 2001: 365).

Chapter 6

1. In 1891, however, the extreme power of the plantocracy and their vehement opposition to colonial policy on several occasions caused the governor to expand suffrage for the election of members of the Combined Court as punishment, legislation that caused the membership of the Combined Court to be increasingly dominated by middle-class Creoles by the early 1920s. At this time, the rise of a middle class that was increasingly opposed to balanced budgets and the interests of sugar was deemed undesirable, and the colonial powers therefore changed the constitution to allow the plantocracy to dominate the government through the expansion of appointed members to the new legislative council as well as through the creation of informal channels of legislation (Lutchman 1974: 211; Rose 1988). It was not until the late 1940s and early 1950s that the expansion of suffrage broke the power of the sugar industry once and for all.

2. Compared to a yearly average of some twenty cases brought to court by laborers against the planters in Guyana between 1876 and 1896, the average in Mauritius between 1860 and 1889 was over 750, and 68 percent of these resulted in convictions.

3. This figure is down from a high of 30 percent in 1875 (Smith 1962: 47).

4. According to Ian Mikardo, a Labour MP in the United Kingdom, the official newsletter of the recognized sugar workers' union (Man-Power Citizen's Association) supported the sugar industry, not the workers: "The main article in this paper is a straightforward defense of two things—of capitalism in general and colonial employers in particular. No where in the paper is there any reference to the low wages and unspeakable living conditions of the workers of British Guiana . . . The article pays a series of warm tributes to the employers. It even gives them credit for the abolition of slavery (which in fact, they fiercely opposed), establishing industrial safety (which in fact, they haven't cared two pence about), and 'nearly abolishing' women and child labour (which in fact, they have struggled to retain)" (Jagan 1997: 137).

5. By the late 1950s and early 1960s, British officials actually believed Jagan was a better option than Burnham but supported the latter under strong American pressure (Rabe 2005).

6. By the mid-1920s, Afro-Guyanese—although only 39 percent of the total population—held 85 percent of all civil administrative posts while the Indians—comprising 42 percent of the total population—held only 4 percent of the positions within the administration (Lutchman 1971a: 3).

Chapter 7

1. According to the Boers, Livingston assisted the Tswana during this war, using his mission to manufacture arms (Ramsay 1991). Without this victory, Botswana would have almost certainly been incorporated into South Africa.

2. These directly ruled regions prevented the form of colonialism in Botswana from being highly indirect. Botswana's score for the extent of indirect rule (43), however, is smaller than expected given the small size of the population living in the directly ruled regions. The score appears to capture some of the institutional changes described below that began after the succession crisis in the Ngwato chiefdom.

3. During the 1909 constitutional convention of the Union of South Africa, a tentative agreement was reached that Botswana, Lesotho, and Swaziland would be transferred to the Union government. Because of strong opposition by chiefs, missionaries, and humanitarians, however, the transfer did not occur. Nevertheless, the final draft of the Union constitution left the door open for transfer at a later date, stating that the British Parliament could ratify the transfer after due consultation with the Africans within the territories.

4. Notably, colonialism did induce political transformations. The three minor Tswana chiefdoms, for example, had historically not been completely autonomous from the major chiefdoms; colonialism recognized the former as completely independent from the latter. Outside of the eight Tribal Territories, the colonial authorities began to create the institution of chieftaincy, as none had previously existed.

5. While studying in London, Khama befriended a young Guyanese student, one Forbes Burnham.

6. The colonial government had neglected education to such an extent that there were only thirty-three established posts within the Department of Education as late as 1950 (Hermans 1974: 103).

7. Prior to 1971, the relationship between the central government and the district councils was undefined. Afterwards, however, the district commissioners—the primary officials in charge of local administration—were made ex officio members of the district councils and became chairmen of the newly created district development committees (DDCs). DDCs were organized as instruments that enabled the central government to (1) coordinate development policy locally, (2) serve as a district planning board, and (3) advise the central administration about local conditions (Temane 1977: 4; Macartney 1978: 238). The DDCs consisted of between twenty-five and thirty representatives from all relevant government departments and NGOs and, although under the chairmanship of the district commissioner, were managed by the district officer development (DOD), who acted "as a communications link between District Councils, departmental field staff and the District Administration" (Picard 1977: 1, 14). While providing a medium through which diverse actors from local and central government could meet, the DDCs were dominated by government officials and were sometimes limited to unelected officials. Besides the DDC, the central administration increased its ties and control of local government by enacting the Unified Local Government Service in 1973, which removed the power to appoint the executive staff of the district councils from the councils themselves and gave it to the central administration.

8. Consequently, in 1972—six years after independence—44 percent of all middle and senior grade posts were filled by expatriate officers, a number that declined to 34 percent by 1977 (Macartney 1978: 421; Republic of Botswana 1977b: appendix 2).

9. For example, although the 1946 census claims that all Africans in the Tlokwa Reserve were ethnic Tlokwa, Schapera (1952) notes that only 216 of the 442 African tax returns from the Tlokwa Reserve in the mid-1930s were from ethnic Tlokwa (116).

10. At the time of writing, it appears that one-party domination might end given a growing rift between different factions in the BDP and the possibility that the party will split before the next election.

11. Military rule in South Korea did not have the same effect. Along with the fact that South Korea's military rulers were concerned with an external threat and did not use the military as a tool to regulate domestic social relations, South Korea's much larger and relatively effective state appears to have promoted this difference: legal-administrative institutions in Korea restrained the use of military coercion domestically, promoted greater accountability, and provided rulers with noncoercive means of implementing policy.

Chapter 8

1. There were 150 European settlers in the Solomon Islands in 1950 (Belshaw 1950: 15).

2. The state-level development indicators are taken from Census of India (2001), Chandigarh Administration (2007), and Government of India (2007). The following calculations of the percentage of territory under the control of either princes or landlords were made by the author based on Schwartzberg (1978: 61, 66). The scores for each state are:

Andhra Pradesh	48
Bihar	100
Chhatisgarh	100
Gujarat	89
Haryana	100
Jharkhand	100
Kerala	54
Karnataka	61
Madhya Pradesh	100
Maharashtra	39
Orissa	100
Punjab	100
Rajasthan	100
Tamil Nadu	3
West Bengal	100
Uttarkhand	100
Uttar Pradesh	100

Notably, Assam was an outlier in all three relationships, a finding that coincides with other analyses, and appears to have been caused by its high levels of social, political, and economic isolation as well as political violence and instability. I therefore removed it from the set. When the case is included, the relationships fall to –0.24 for GDP, 0.35 for infant mortality, and –0.38 for literacy.

3. Kohli (1987) makes a similar argument for West Bengal, claiming that relatively successful social welfare reforms in the state were made possible by the weakening of the landed classes.

4. Notably, Mamdani (1996) argues that indirect rule was always racialized, with whites running the central colonial administration and nonwhites running the peripheral chiefdoms. He therefore claims that South Africa was simply the extension of the bifurcated state, having a white settler population and therefore a larger central administration to rule over them directly.

5. Singapore was a separate colony for most of the colonial period; merged with Malaya, North Borneo, and Sarawak in 1963; yet separated from Malaysia once and for all in 1965.

6. Germany is ranked twentieth, Spain twenty-first, Israel twenty-third, and Greece twenty-fourth.

7. The data are from 1996–97 and therefore prior to Hong Kong's independence.

8. After the colonial reforms, average life expectancy in Sri Lanka increased by twelve years in only seven years.

Chapter 9

1. For example, all of French Equatorial Africa had 366 administrators and civil servants in 1928, yet only 250 of these were actually in the colony (Suret-Canale 1971: 312).

2. Consistent with this book's findings, the most directly ruled region of French Indochina was southern Vietnam, and it has subsequently enjoyed greater development than the other regions.

3. Mamdani (1996) notes that the presence of educated Africans could have served—and actually did for a while—as officials in the central administration, which would have made possible a more direct form of rule in Sierra Leone despite its disease environment. Notably, the use of the indigenous population as officials within the central state did occur in colonial Cyprus, India, Malaya, and elsewhere and thereby made possible more direct forms of rule despite a paucity British officials.

BIBLIOGRAPHY

Abdul Karim, Muhammad Rai. 1985. *Regionalization and Access to Primary Health Services in Malaysia.* Ph.D. Dissertation, University of Pittsburgh.

Abernethy, David. 2000. *The Dynamics of Global Dominance: European Overseas Empires, 1415–1980.* New Haven: Yale University Press.

Abraham, Arthur. 1978. *Mende Politics and Government under Colonial Rule.* New York: Oxford University Press.

———. 2001. "Dancing with the Chameleon: Sierra Leone and the Elusive Quest for Peace." *Journal of Contemporary African Affairs,* 19 (2): 205–28.

Acemoglu, Daron, Simon Johnson, and James Robinson. 2001. "Colonial Origins of Comparative Development: An Empirical Investigation." *American Economic Review,* 91 (5): 1369–1401.

———. 2002. "Reversal of Fortune: Geography and Institutions in the Making of the Modern World Income Distribution." *Quarterly Journal of Economics,* 117 (4): 1231–94.

Ackbarally, Nasseem. 2002. "Mauritius: A Cyber-Island in the Making." *Contemporary Review,* 281 (1640): 160–62

Adamson, Alan. 1970. "Monoculture and Village Decay in British Guiana, 1854–1872." *Journal of Social History,* 3 (4): 386–405.

———. 1972. *Sugar without Slaves: The Political Economy of British Guiana, 1838–1904.* New Haven: Yale University Press.

Aldrich, Robert. 1996. *Greater France: A History of French Overseas Expansion.* New York: St. Martin's Press.

Ali, Anuwar. 1992. *Malaysia's Industrialization: The Quest for Technology.* New York: Oxford University Press.

Allen, Christopher. 1978. "Sierra Leone." *West African States: Failure and Promise.* John Dunn ed. New York: Cambridge University Press, 189–211.

Allen, Richard. 1999. *Slaves, Freedmen, and Indentured Laborers in Colonial Mauritius.* New York: Cambridge University Press.

Allgoo, Rajpalsingh. 1985. *Le Movement Syndical à L'Ile Maurice.* Port Louis: Artisans and General Workers Union.

Amsden, Alice. 1985. "The State and Taiwan's Economic Development." *Bringing the State Back In.* Peter Evans, Dietrich Rueschemeyer, and Theda Skocpol eds. New York: Cambridge University Press, 78–106.

———. 1989. *Asia's Next Giant: South Korea and Asian Industrialization.* New York: Oxford University Press.

———. 2001. *The Rise of "The Rest": Challenges to the West from Late-Industrializing Economies.* New York: Oxford University Press.

Anderson, Lars-Gunnar, and Tore Janson. 1997. *Languages in Botswana.* Gaborone: Longman-Botswana.

Anonymous. 1956a. "Seretse Strangles Tribalism." Kew: Public Records Office, DO119/1358.

Anonymous. 1956b. "What Is Happening on Our Border?" *Die Transvaler,* 27 October. Kew: Public Records Office, DO119/1358.

Australian Bureau of Statistics. 2006. "A Snapshot of Australia, 1901." http://www .abs.gov.au/Websitedbs/D3110124.NSF/24e5997b9bf2ef35ca2567fb00299c59/ c4abd1fac53e3df5ca256bd8001883ec!OpenDocument (accessed 1 July 2007).

Avert. 2007. "HIV & AIDS in Botswana." http://www.avert.org/aidsbotswana.htm (27 December 2007).

"Bahamas 1970 Census." 1990–1993. *International Population Census, post 1967, Latin America and the Caribbean* [microform]. Woodbridge, CT: Research Publications.

Bahamas Department of Statistics. 2006. "Population and Growth Rate for Census Years 1838 to 2000." http://www.bahamas.gov.bs/bahamasweb2/home.nsf/ vContentW/9C7DE759B4AEFBEA06256ED10071AF8C (accessed 1 September 2007).

Baker, Jim. 1999. *Crossroads: A Popular History of Malaysia and Singapore.* Singapore: Times Books International.

Banerjee, Abhijtit, and Lakshmi Iyer. 2005. "History, Institutions, and Economic Performance: The Legacy of Colonial Land Tenure Systems in India." *American Economic Review,* 95 (4): 1190–1213.

Barro, Robert, and Jong-Wha Lee. 2000. "International Data on Educational Attainment: Updates and Implications." CID Working Paper No. 042.

Bates, Robert. 1981. *Markets and States in Tropical Africa.* Berkeley: University of California Press.

———. 1989. *Beyond the Miracle of the Market.* New York: Cambridge University Press.

Bayart, Jean-François. 1993. *The State in Africa: The Politics of the Belly.* New York: Longman.

Bazerque, Bernarde. 1993. "The Evolution of Personnel in Rural Local Government." B.A. Thesis, University of Mauritius.

Beckford, George. 1983. *Persistent Poverty: Underdevelopment in Plantation Economies of the Third World*. London: Zed Books.

Belshaw, Cyril. 1950. *Island Administration in the South West Pacific: Government and Reconstruction in New Caledonia, the New Hebrides, and the British Solomon Islands*. London: Royal Institute of International Affairs.

Benedict, Burton. 1965. *Mauritius: Problems of a Plural Society*. New York: Praeger.

Bennett, Judith. 1987. *The Wealth of the Solomons: A History of a Pacific Archipelago, 1800–1978*. Honolulu: University of Hawai'i Press.

Bernhard, Michael, Christopher Reenock, and Timothy Nordstrom. 2004. "The Legacy of Western Overseas Colonialism on Democratic Survival." *International Studies Quarterly*, 48: 225–50.

Berry, Sara. 2001. *Chiefs Know Their Boundaries: Essays on Property, Power, and the Past in Asante, 1896–1996*. Portsmouth, NH: Heinemann.

Bertocchi, Graziella, and Fabio Canova. 2002. "Did Colonization Matter for Growth?: An Empirical Exploration into the Historical Causes of Africa's Underdevelopment." *European Economic Review*, 46: 1851–71.

Betts, Raymond F. 1961. *Assimilation and Association in French Colonial Theory, 1890–1914*. New York: Columbia University Press.

Bhagirutty, Chandersendsing. 1988. *50 Ans de Lutte Syndicale, 1938–1988*. Port Louis: Plantation Workers Union.

Bishop, Myrtle, Rosalyn Corbin, and Neville Duncan. 1997. "Barbados: Social Development in a Small Island State." *Development with a Human Face*. Santosh Mehrotra and Richard Jolly eds. Oxford: Clarendon Press, 323–54.

Blackburn, Robin. 2005. "Imperial Margarine." *New Left Review*, 35. http://newleft review.org/A2584 (13 November 2007).

Bolland, O. Nigel. 1986. *Belize: A New Nation in Central America*. Boulder, CO: Westview Press.

Bollen, Kenneth, and Robert Jackman. 1985. "Political Democracy and the Size Distribution of Income." *American Sociological Review*, 50 (4): 438–57.

Boone, Catherine. 1992. *Merchant Capital and the Roots of State Power in Senegal, 1930–1985*. New York: Cambridge University Press.

———. 1994. "States and Ruling Classes in Postcolonial Africa: The Enduring Contradictions of Power." *State Power and Social Forces: Domination and Transformation in the Third World*. Joel Migdal, Atul Kohli, and Vivienne Shue eds. New York: Cambridge University Press, 108–40.

———. 2003. *Political Topographies of the African State: Territorial Authority and Institutional Choice*. New York: Cambridge University Press.

Booth, Anne. 2007. *Colonial Legacies: Economic and Social Development in East and Southeast Asia*. Honolulu: University of Hawai'i Press.

Bowie, Alasdair. 1991. *Crossing the Industrial Divide: State, Society, and the Politics of Economic Transformation in Malaysia*. New York: Columbia University Press.

Brady, Henry, and David Collier. 2004. *Rethinking Social Inquiry: Diverse Tools, Shared Standards*. New York: Rowan and Littlefield Publishers.

Brautigam, Deborah. 1997. "Institutions, Economic Reform, and Democratic Consolidation in Mauritius." *Comparative Politics*, 30 (1): 45–62.

———. 2004. "The People's Budget? Politics, Participation and Pro-Poor Policy." *Development Policy Review*, 22 (6): 653–68.

Breen, Richard, Damian Hannan, David Rottman, and Christopher Whelan. 1990. *Understanding Contemporary Ireland: State, Class and Development in the Republic of Ireland*. New York: St. Martin's Press.

Brewer, I. G. 1974. "Sources of the Criminal Law of Botswana." *Journal of African Law*, 18 (1): 24–36.

British Colonial Office. 1943. "Brief for Sir Cosmo Parkinson." Kew: Public Records Office, CO167/921/5.

———. 1947. *Annual Colonial Report* (Malaya). London: HMSO.

———. 1951. *Annual Colonial Report* (Kenya). London: HMSO.

———. 1953. *Annual Colonial Report* (Gold Coast). London: HMSO.

———. 1955a. *Annual Colonial Report* (Basutoland, Bechuanaland, the Gambia, Kenya, Nyasaland, Nigeria, Northern Rhodesia, Sierra Leone, Singapore, Swaziland, Tanganyika, Uganda, Zanzibar). London: HMSO.

———. 1955b. *Annual Colonial Report* (the Bahamas, Barbados, Basotholand, British Guiana, British Honduras, Cyprus, Fiji, the Gambia, Hong Kong, Jamaica, Mauritius, North Borneo, Northern Rhodesia, Nyasaland, Sarawak, Sierra Leone, Singapore, Southern Rhodesia, Swaziland, Tanganyika, Trinidad and Tobago, Uganda, Zanzibar). London: HMSO.

———. 1956. *Annual Colonial Report* (Brunei, the Solomon Islands). London: HMSO.

———. 1958. *Annual Colonial Report* (Bechuanaland). London: HMSO.

Brotherson, Festus. 1988. "The Politics of Permanent Fear: Guyana's Authoritarianism in the Anglophone Caribbean." *Caribbean Affairs*, 1 (3): 57–76.

Brown, David. 2000. "Democracy, Colonization, and Human Capital in Sub-Saharan Africa." *Studies in Comparative International Development*, 35 (1): 20–40.

Brown, Ian, and Rajeswary Ampalavanar. 1986. *Malaysia*. Denver: Clio Press.

Burgess, G., and J. K. Hunn. 1966. *Report on Public Administration in Guyana*. Georgetown, British Guiana: Government Printers.

Burrowes, Reynold. 1984. *The Wild Coast: An Account of Politics in Guyana*. Cambridge, MA: Schenkman Publishing Company.

Burt, Ronald. 1992. *Structural Holes: The Social Structure of Competition*. Cambridge, MA: Harvard University Press.

Bushe, H. G. 1932. "Report by Mr. H. G. Bushe on his Tour in West Africa." Kew: Public Records Office, CO554/90/13.

Caldwell, John. 1986. "Routes to Low Mortality in Poor Countries." *Population and Development Review*, 12 (2): 171–220.

Callaghy, Thomas. 1984. *The State-Society Struggle: Zaire in Comparative Perspective*. New York: Columbia University Press.

Callahan, Mary. 2003. *Making Enemies: War and State Building in Burma*. Ithaca, NY: Cornell University Press.

Carroll, Barbara Wake, and Terrance Carroll. 1999. "Civic Networks, Legitimacy and the Policy Process." *Governance*, 12 (1): 1–28.

———. 2000. "Trouble in Paradise: Ethnic Conflict in Mauritius." *Commonwealth and Comparative Politics*, 38 (2): 25–50.

Carter, Marina. 1995. *Servants, Sirdars and Settlers: Indians in Mauritius, 1834–1874*. Delhi: Oxford University Press.

Cartwright, John. 1970. *Politics in Sierra Leone, 1947–67*. Buffalo: Toronto University Press.

Census of India. 2001. "State Wise Population Totals with Percentage of Urban Population (Provisional)." http://cyberjournalist.org.in/census/cenindia.html (9 September 2007).

Central Statistical Office. 1985. *Report on the 1976 Swaziland Population Census, Vol. 1: Administrative and Statistical Reports*. Accessed from *International Population Census, post-1967, Africa* [microform]. Woodbridge, CT: Research Publications

Central Statistical Office. 1968. *Pakistan Statistical Yearbook*. Karachi: Government of Pakistan Press.

Chandigarh Administration. 2007. "Table 7. Per Capita Income of All States." http://sampark.chd.nic.in/images/statistics/SDP2005R6.pdf (9 September 2007).

Chanock, Martin. 1985. *Law, Custom, and Social Order : The Colonial Experience in Malawi and Zambia*. New York: Cambridge University Press.

Chazan, Naomi. 1983. *An Anatomy of Ghanaian Politics: Managing Political Recession, 1969–1982*. Boulder, CO: Westview Press.

Chibber, Vivek. 2002. "Bureaucratic Rationality and the Developmental State," *American Journal of Sociology*, 107 (4): 951–89.

Clapham, Christopher. 1982. "The Politics of Failure: Clientelism, Political Instability, and National Integration in Liberia and Sierra Leone." *Private Patronage and Public Power*. Christopher Clapham ed. New York: St. Martin's Press, 71–97.

Clifford, Bede. 1938. "Letter to Malcolm MacDonald, 14 October." Kew: Public Records Office, CO167/902/5.

Cohen, William. 1971. *Rulers of Empire: The French Colonial Service in Africa*. Stanford, CA: Hoover Institute Press.

Collier, Paul. 2000. "Economic Causes of Civil War and Their Implications for Policy." http://go.worldbank.org/8G8VEO9RJ1 (21 March 2006).

Collins, B. A. N. 1969. *The Public Services of Guyana: Report of the Commission of Inquiry*. Georgetown: Government Printers.

Colony of British Guiana. 1936. "Report of the Committee Appointed to Enquire into the Administration and General Organization of the Medical Services of the Colony, Legislative Council Paper No. 9." Georgetown: Guyana National Archives, AB4/44.

Colony of Fiji. 1955. "Legislative Council Paper 29: Annual report of the Secretary of Fijian Affairs." Kew: Public Records Office.

Colony of Kenya. 1952. "African Affairs Department Annual Report, 1951." Kew: Public Records Office.

Colony of Mauritius. 1887. *Blue Book of the Colony of Mauritius*. Port Louis: Government Printers. University of Mauritius, Mauritius Collection.

———. 1901. *Blue Book of the Colony of Mauritius*. Port Louis: Government Printers. University of Mauritius, Mauritius Collection.

———. 1912. *Blue Book of the Colony of Mauritius*. Port Louis: Government Printers. University of Mauritius, Mauritius Collection.

———. 1921. *Blue Book of the Colony of Mauritius.* Port Louis: Government Printers. University of Mauritius, Mauritius Collection.

———. 1930. *Blue Book of the Colony of Mauritius.* Port Louis: Government Printers. University of Mauritius, Mauritius Collection.

———. 1932. *Staff List.* Port Louis: Government Printers. Mauritius National Archives.

———. 1934. *Staff List.* Port Louis: Government Printers. Mauritius National Archives.

———. 1939. *Blue Book of the Colony of Mauritius.* Port Louis: Government Printers.

———. 1947. *Annual Colonial Report.* Port Louis: Government Printers.

———. 1947–53. *Annual Report of the Mauritius Police Force and on Crime.* Port Louis: Government Printers. Mauritius National Archives.

———. 1948a. *Annual Report on the District Administration (North) for 1948.* Kew: Public Records Office, CO167/944/7.

———. 1948b. *Blue Book of the Colony of Mauritius.* Port Louis: Government Printers. University of Mauritius, Mauritius Collection.

———. 1948–59. *Yearbook of Statistics.* Port Louis: Government Printers. University of Mauritius, Mauritius Collection.

———. 1950a. *Annual Report of the Labour Department.* Port Louis: Government Printers. Mauritius National Archives.

———. 1950b. *Staff List.* Port Louis: Government Printers. Mauritius National Archives.

———. 1951. *Annual Report of the Labour Department.* Port Louis: Government Printers. Mauritius National Archives.

———. 1951–1968. *Annual Colonial Report.* Port Louis: Government Printers.

———. 1954a. *Annual Report of the Education Department.* Port Louis: Government Printers. Mauritius National Archives.

———. 1954b. "Letter from the Inspector General of the Colonial Police Force, September 21." Kew: Public Records Office, CO1036/3.

———. 1954c. "Report on District Administration in Mauritius for 1954." Kew: Public Records Office.

———. 1955. *Annual Report of the Social Welfare Department.* Port Louis: Government Printers. Mauritius National Archives.

———. 1956. *Annual Colonial Report.* Port Louis: Government Printers.

———. 1957. *Annual Report of the Labour Department.* Port Louis: Government Printers. Mauritius National Archives.

———. 1959a. *Annual Report of the Labour Department.* Port Louis: Government Printers. Mauritius National Archives.

———. 1959b. *Yearbook of Statistics.* Port Louis: Government Printers. University of Mauritius, Mauritius Collection.

———. 1960. *Staff List.* Port Louis: Government Printers. Mauritius National Archives.

———. 1962. *Annual Report of the Ministry of Labour and Social Security.* Port Louis: Government Printers. Mauritius National Archives.

———. 1962–68. *Annual Report of the Labour Department.* Port Louis: Government Printers. Mauritius National Archives.

———. 1963. *Annual Report of the Registrar of Associations.* Port Louis: Government Printers. Mauritius National Archives.

————. 1964a. *Annual Report of the Ministry of Labour and Social Security*. Port Louis: Government Printers. Mauritius National Archives.

————. 1964b. *Annual Colonial Report*. Port Louis: Government Printers.

————. 1965. *Annual Report of the Ministry of Labour*. Port Louis: Government Printers. Mauritius National Archives.

————. 1967a. *Annual Report of the Ministry of Labour*. Port Louis: Government Printers. Mauritius National Archives.

————. 1967b. *Staff List*. Port Louis: Government Printers. Mauritius National Archives.

Colony of Mauritius 1939, 1951–68, 1955, 1959a, 1968a; Koenig 1931; Mauritius Economic Commission 1948; Mauritius Legislative Council 1956b; Titmuss 1968.

————. 1968a. *Annual Report of the Ministry of Labour*. Port Louis: Government Printers. Mauritius National Archives.

————. 1968b. *Annual Colonial Report*. Port Louis: Government Printers.

Colony of Nigeria. 1953. "Native Courts Commission of Inquiry, 1949–1952." Kew: Public Records Office, CO554/652.

Colony of Northern Rhodesia. 1955. "Judiciary: Annual Report, 1955." Kew: Public Records Office, CO799/35.

Colony of Sierra Leone. 1955. *Report of the Administration of the Provinces*. Freetown: Government Printers.

Colony of Southern Rhodesia. 1955. "Report of the Secretary for Justice, Internal Affairs and Housing." Kew: Public Records Office.

Colony of Sudan. 1949. "Report on the Administration of Sudan." Kew: Public Records Office, FO371/96845.

Colony of Uganda. 1955. "Annual Reports of the Eastern Province, Western Province, Northern Province, and Kingdom of Buganda, 1955." Kew: Public Records Office.

Commonwealth Relations Office. 1956. "Councils in the Bechuanaland Protectorate, November 1 1956." Kew: Public Records Office, DO119/1358.

Coquery-Vidrovitch, Catherine. 1972. *Le Congo au Temps des Grandes Compagnies Concessionaires, 1898–1930*. Paris: Mouton.

Crenshaw, Edward. 1995. "Democracy and Demographic Inheritance: The Influence of Modernity and Proto-Modernity on Political and Civil Rights, 1965 to 1980." *American Sociological Review*, 60 (5): 702–18.

Crocker, Walter. 1936. *Nigeria: A Critique of British Colonial Administration*. London: G. Allen and Unwin.

Crowder, Michael, Jack Parson, and Neil Parsons. 1990. "Legitimacy and Faction." *Succession of High Office in Botswana*. Jack Parson ed. Athens: Ohio University Press, 1–32.

Cruise O'Brien, Donal. 1975. *Saints and Politicians: Essays in the Organization of Senegalese Peasant Society*. New York: Cambridge University Press.

Cumings, Bruce. 2005. "State Building in Korea: Continuity and Crisis." *States and Development: Historical Antecedents of Stagnation and Advance*. Matthew Lange and Dietrich Rueschemeyer eds. New York: Palgrave Macmillan, 211–35.

Curtin, Philip. 1975. "Measuring the Atlantic Slave Trade." *Race and Slavery in the Western Hemisphere: Quantitative Studies*. Stanley Engerman and Eugene Genovese eds. Princeton: Princeton University Press, 107–28.

Dachs, A. J. 1998. "Missionary Imperialism: The Case of Bechuanaland." *Botswana: Politics and Society.* W. A. Edge and M. H. Lekorwe eds. Pretoria: J. L. van Schaik Publishers, 32–42.

Danns, George. 1978. "Decolonization and Militarization in the Caribbean: The Guyanese Example." Presented at Inter-American Politics Seminar Series. University of Guyana, Caribbean Collection: JL 689 A15 D3.

Dauvergne, Peter. 1998. "Weak States and the Environment in Indonesia and the Solomon Islands." *Weak and Strong States in Asia-Pacific Societies.* Peter Dauvergne ed. St. Leonards, Australia: Allen & Unwin, 135–57.

Davis, Mike. 2001. *Late Victorian Holocausts: El Niño Famines and the Making of the Third World.* New York: Verso.

DeBroglio, R., and R. Neerunjun. 1961. "Notes on the Laws of Mauritius and on the Judicial and Legal System." Kew: Public Records Office, CO1036/977.

DeGlopper, Donald R. 1991. "The Society and Its Environment." *Singapore: A Country Study.* Louis R. Mortimer ed. Washington, DC: Library of Congress, 65–117.

Department of Agriculture. 1886. *Canada: Statistical and Abstract and Record.* Ottawa: Maclean, Roger & Co.

Department of Statistics. 1968. *Annual Abstract of Statistics 1968, no. 27.* Kingston, Jamaica: Government Printer.

Deschamps, Hubert. 1963. "Et Maintenant, Lord Lugard?" *Africa,* 33 (4): 293–305.

de Silva, Chandra Richard. 1997. *Sri Lanka: A History.* New Delhi: Vikas Publishing House.

Despres, Leo. 1967. *Cultural Pluralism and Nationalist Politics in British Guiana.* Chicago: Rand McNally.

Diamond, Jared. 1997. *Guns, Germs, and Steel: The Fates of Human Societies.* New York: W. W. Norton.

Dommen, Edward, and Bridget Dommen. 1997. "Mauritius: The Roots of Success 1960–1993." *Development with a Human Face: Experiences in Social Achievement and Economic Growth.* Santosh Mehrotra and Richard Jolly eds. New York: Clarendon Press, 148–78.

Doner, Richard, Bryan Ritchie, and Dan Slater. 2005. "Systemic Vulnerability and the Origins of Developmental States: Northeast and Southeast Asia in Comparative Perspective." *International Organizations,* 59: 327–61.

Dorjahn, Vernon. 1960. "The Changing Political System of the Temne." *Africa,* 30 (2): 110–40.

Dorman, Maurice. 1957. "Letter to C. G. Eastwood, 16 February." Kew: Public Records Office, CO554/1993.

———. 1959. " Letter 1 April 1959." Kew: Public Records Office, MS/105/1.

———. 1960. "Letter from 8 January 1960." Kew: Public Records Office, CO554/2146.

Doyle, Michael. 1986. *Empires.* Ithaca, NY: Cornell University Press.

Dreze, Jean, and Amartya Sen. 1989. *Hunger and Public Action.* New York: Oxford University Press.

D'Souza, Dinesh. 2002. "Two Cheers for Colonialism." *Chronicle Review: The Chronicle of Higher Education,* 45: B7–B12.

Dukhira, Chit. 1994. *Grass Roots Democracy for National Development*. Stanley, Mauritius: Editions de l'Océan Indien.

Durbarry, Ramesh. 2001. "The Export Processing Zone." *The Mauritian Economy*. Rajen Dabee and David Greenaway eds. New York: Palgrave, 105–29.

Dzorgbo, Dan-Bright. 2001. *Ghana in Search of Development: The Challenge of Governance, Economic Management and Institution Building*. Burlington, VT: Ashgate.

Easterly, William, and Ross Levine. 1997. "Africa's Growth Tragedy: Policies and Ethnic Divisions." *Quarterly Journal of Economics*, 112: 1203–50.

———. 2002. "Tropics, Germs, and Crops: How Endowments Influence Economic Development." Working Paper 9106. National Bureau of Economic Research.

Economist. 2003. "The Pacific's First Failed State?" 366 (8311): 39.

Edge, W. A. 1998. "Botswana: A Developmental State." *Botswana: Politics and Society*. W. A. Edge and M. H. Lekorwe eds. Pretoria: J. L. van Schaik Publishers, 333–48.

Egner, E. B. 1979. "Review of Socio-Economic Development in Botswana, 1966–1979." Botswana National Archives, Micro 472.

Engerman, Stanley, and Kenneth Sokoloff. 1997. "Factor Endowments, Institutions, and Differential Paths of Growth among New World Economies." *How Latin America Fell Behind*. S. H. Haber ed. Stanford: Stanford University Press, 260–304

Esman, Milton. 1972. *Administration and Development in Malaysia: Institution Building and Reform in a Plural Society*. Ithaca, NY: Cornell University Press.

Esman, Milton, and Norman Uphoff. 1984. *Local Organizations: Intermediaries in Local Development*. Ithaca, NY: Cornell University Press.

Evans, Ivan. 1997. *Bureaucracy and Race: Native Administration in South Africa*. Berkeley: University of California Press.

Evans, Peter. 1995. *Embedded Autonomy: States and Industrial Transformation*. Princeton: Princeton University Press.

———. 1996. "Government Action, Social Capital, and Development: Reviewing the Evidence on Synergy." *World Development*, 24 (6): 1119–32.

———. 2005. "Harnessing the State: Rebalancing Strategies for Monitoring and Motivation." *States and Development: Historical Antecedents of Stagnation and Advance*. Matthew Lange and Dietrich Rueschemeyer eds. New York: Palgrave Macmillan, 26–47.

Evans, Peter, and James Rauch. 1999. "Analysis of 'Weberian' State Structures and Economic Growth." *American Sociological Review*, 64 (5): 748–65.

Fanthrope, Richard. 2001. "Neither Citizen nor Subject? 'Lumpen' Agency and the Legacy of Native Administration in Sierra Leone." *African Affairs*, 100: 363–86.

Fawcus, Peter, and Alan Tilbury. 2000. *Botswana: The Road to Independence*. Gaborone, Botswana: Pula Press.

Fearon, James. 2003. "Ethnic and Cultural Diversity by Country." *Journal of Economic Growth*, 8: 195–222.

Fearon, James, and David Laitin. 2003. "Ethnicity, Insurgency, and Civil War." *American Political Science Review*, 97 (1): 75–90.

Ferguson, Niall. 2002. *Empire: The Rise and Demise of the British World Order and the Lessons for Global Power*. New York: Basic Books.

———. 2004. *Colossus: The Price of America's Empire*. New York: Penguin.

Feyrer, James, and Bruce Sacerdote. (Forthcoming). "Colonialism and Modern Income: Islands as Natural Experiments." *Review of Economics and Statistics.*

Fine, Ben, and Zavareh Rustomjee. 1996. *The Political Economy of South Africa: From Minerals-Energy Complex to Industrialization.* Boulder, CO: Westview.

Finnegan, Ruth, and David Murray. 1970. "Limba Chiefs." *West African Chiefs.* Michael Crowder and Obaro Ikime eds. New York: Africana.

Firmin-Sellers, Kathryn. 2000. "Institutions, Context, and Outcomes: Explaining French and British Rule in West Africa." *Comparative Politics,* 32 (3): 253–72.

Fisher, Michael. 1991. *Indirect Rule in India: Residents and the Residency System, 1764–1858.* Delhi: Oxford University Press.

Fitzpatrick, David. 1999. "Ireland and the Empire." *The Oxford History of the British Empire: Volume III, The Nineteenth Century.* Andrew Porter ed. New York: Oxford University Press, 495–521.

Fitzpatrick, J. F. J. 1924. "Nigeria's Curse: The Native Administration," *National Review,* 84 (502): 617–24.

Fukuyama, Francis. 2004. *State-Building: Governance and World Order in the 21st Century.* Ithaca, NY: Cornell University Press.

Fyfe, Christopher. 1962. *A History of Sierra Leone.* London: Oxford University Press.

Gangulee, N. 1947. *Indians in the Empire Overseas: A Survey.* London: New India Publishing House Limited.

Gann, L. H., and Peter Duignan. 1978. *The Rulers of British Africa, 1870–1914.* Stanford: Stanford University Press.

Gillet, Simon. 1973. "The Survival of Chieftaincy in Botswana." *African Affairs,* 72 (2): 179–85.

Glasgow, Roy. 1970. *Guyana: Race and Politics among Africans and East Asians.* The Hague: Martinus Nijhoff.

Goldsmith, Arthur. 1999. "Africa's Overgrown State Reconsidered: Bureaucracy and Economic Growth." *World Politics,* 51 (7): 520–46.

Goldsworthy, David. 1971. *Colonial Issues in British Politics, 1945–1961: From "Colonial Development" to "Winds of Change."* Oxford: Clarendon Press.

Good, Kenneth. 1993. "At the Ends of the Ladder: Radical Inequalities in Botswana." *Journal of Modern African Studies,* 31 (2): 203–31.

———. 1994. "Corruption and Mismanagement in Botswana: A Best-Case Example?" *Journal of Modern African Studies,* 32 (3): 499–521.

———. 1996. "Towards Popular Participation in Botswana." *Journal of Modern African Studies,* 34 (1): 53–77.

———. 2005. "Resource Dependency and Its Consequences: The Costs of Botswana's Shining Gems." *Journal of Contemporary African Studies,* 23 (1): 27–50.

Good, Kenneth, and Skye Hughes. 2002. "Globalization and Diversification: Two Cases in Southern Africa." *African Affairs,* 101 (402): 39–60.

Gopal, Ram. 1963. *British Rule in India: An Assessment.* New York: Asia Publishing House.

Gosden, Chris. 1992. "Production Systems and the Colonization of the Western Pacific." *World Archaeology,* 24 (1): 55–69.

Government of the Bechuanaland Protectorate. 1905. *Bechuanaland Protectorate Blue Book, 1904/05.* Botswana National Archives, S.602/1.

———. 1931. *Annual Medical and Sanitary Report, 1930*. Botswana National Archives, S.88/9.

———. 1934. "Letter No. 38, 16/3/34." Botswana National Archives, S.439/5 1934.

———. 1941. "Letter Kg.276, 3 April, 1941, District Commissioner, Tsabong." Botswana National Archives, S.439/5 1934.

———. 1945. *Bechuanaland Protectorate Staff List, 1945*. Botswana National Archives, S.L. 1945.

———. 1951a. *Annual Medical and Sanitary Report for the Year 1950*. Botswana National Archives, BNB 1195.

———. 1951b. *Annual Report of the Education Department, 1950*. Botswana National Archives, BNB 513.

———. 1956. *Annual Report of the Education Department, 1955*. Botswana National Archives, BNB 518.

———. 1957a. *Bechuanaland Protectorate Junior Staff List*. Botswana National Archives, S.L. 1957/2.

———. 1957b. *Bechuanaland Protectorate Police, Junior Staff List*. Botswana National Archives, S.L. 1957/2 Pol.

———. 1957c. *Bechuanaland Protectorate Senior Service Staff List*. Botswana National Archives, S.L. 1957/1.

———. 1963. "Health and Medical Position in the B.P." Botswana National Archives, S. 393/3/1.

———. 1964. *Annual Report of the Education Department, 1958*. Botswana National Archives, BNB 527.

———. 1965. *Bechuanaland Protectorate: The Development of the Public Service*. Botswana National Archives, BNB 497.

Government of Egypt. 1985a. "Egypt 1917 Census." *International Population Census, pre-1945, Africa* [microform]. Woodbridge, CT: Research Publications.

———. 1985b. "Egypt 1927 Census." *International Population Census, pre-1945, Africa* [microform]. Woodbridge, CT: Research Publications

———. 1985c. "Egypt 1937 Census." *International Population Census, pre-1945, Africa* [microform]. Woodbridge, CT: Research Publications

Government of India. 2007. "State-Wise Infant Mortality Rate." http://indiabudget .nic.in/es2005<h>06/chapt2006/tab95. pdf (11 October 2007).

Government of Malaya. 1956. *Federation of Malaya Annual Report: 1955*. Kuala Lumpur: Government Press.

Government of Mauritius. 1969. *Annual Report of the Registry of Associations*. Port Louis: Government Printers. University of Mauritius, Mauritius Collection.

Government of Sierra Leone. 1920. *Sierra Leone Blue Book, 1919*. Freetown: Government Printers.

———. 1947. *Colonial Annual Reports: Sierra Leone*. London: HMSO.

———. 1953. "Sessional Paper No. 2 of 1953: Report of the Commission on the Civil Service of Sierra Leone, 1952–3." Kew: Public Records Office.

———. 1954. *Sessional Paper No. 2 of 1954: The Duties and Functions of the Provincial Administration under the Ministerial System, 1954*. Kew: Public Records Office.

———. 1955a. *1955 Report on the Administration of the Provinces*. Freetown: Government Printers. Kew: Public Records Office, CO270/90.

————. 1955b. "Protectorate Disturbances: Sierra Leone." Kew: Public Records Office, CO554/1329.

————. 1955c. "Sierra Leone Political Intelligence Report." Kew: Public Records Office, CO554/1329.

————. 1956a. "Letter: s.f. 9236/6/11." Kew: Public Records Office, CO554/1331.

————. 1956b. *Sierra Leone: Report of Commission of Inquiry into Disturbances in the Provinces (Nov. 1955 to March 1956)* (the Cox Report). London: HMSO.

————. 1957–59. *Enquiry into the Conduct of Certain Chiefs, Sub-Chiefs, and Headmen in Sierra Leone: Decisions and Subsequent Action*. Kew: Public Records Office, CO554/1993.

————. 1959. "Sessional Paper No. 4 of 1959: Government Statement on Africanization." Kew: Public Records Office.

————. 1960. "Application of Report by the Sierra Leone Intelligence Committee, May 1960." Kew: Public Records Office, WAF103/37/1.

Greene, Evarts B., and Virginia D. Harrington. 1966. *American Population before the Federal Census of 1790*. Gloucester, MA: Peter Smith.

Grier, Robin M. 1999. "Colonial Legacies and Economic Growth." *Public Choice*, 98: 317–35.

Gulhati, Ravi, and Raj Nallari. 1990. *Successful Stabilization and Recovery in Mauritius*. Washington, DC: World Bank.

Gunderson, Gifford. 1970. "Nation-Building and the Administrative State: The Case of Botswana." University of California, Berkeley, Ph.D, Department of Political Science.

Gupta, Partha. 1975. *Imperialism and the British Labour Movement, 1919–1964*. New York: Holmes and Meier.

Hadenius, Axel, and Frederick Uggla. 1996. "Making Civil Society Work, Promoting Democratic Development: What Can States and Donors Do?" *World Development*, 24: 1621–39.

Hailey, William. 1938. *An African Survey*. New York: Oxford University Press.

————. 1951. *Native Administration in the British African Territories, Part III*. London: HMSO.

Hall, Margaret, and Tom Young. 1997. *Confronting Leviathan: Mozambique since Independence*. Athens: Ohio University Press.

Hall, R. 1954. "Political Situation in Sierra Leone." Kew: Public Records Office, CO554/1179.

Harper, T. A. 1999. *The End of Empire and the Making of Malaya*. Cambridge, UK: Cambridge University Press.

Harrigan, Walter. 1949. *Report of the Judicial Enquiry Re Seretse Khama of the Bamangwato Tribe*. Kew: Public Records Office.

Harvey, Charles, and Stephen Lewis. 1990. *Policy Choice and Development Performance in Botswana*. New York: St. Martin's Press.

Hassan, Riaz, and Geoffrey Benjamin. 1973. "Ethnic Outmarriage Rates in Singapore: The Influence of Traditional Socio-Cultural Organization." *Journal of Marriage and the Family*, 35 (4): 731–38.

Hayward, Fred. 1989. "Sierra Leone: State Consolidation, Fragmentation, and Decay." *Contemporary West African States*. Donal Cruise O'Brien, John Dunn, and Richard Rathbone eds. New York: Cambridge University Press, 165–80.

Hechter, Michael. 1975. *Internal Colonialism: The Celtic Fringe in British National Development, 1536–1966*. Berkeley: University of California Press.

———. 2000. *Containing Nationalism*. New York: Oxford University Press.

Hechter, Michael, and Nika Kabiri. 2004. "Attaining Social Order in Iraq." http://faculty.washington.edu/hechter/AttainingSocialOrderInIraq.pdf (13 September 2007).

Heller, Patrick. 1999. *The Labor of Development*. Ithaca, NY: Cornell University Press.

———. 2001. "Moving the State: The Politics of Democratic Decentralization in Kerala, South Africa, and Porto Alegre," *Politics and Society*, 29 (1): 121–63.

Heng, Leong Choon, and Tan Siew Hoey. 1997. "Malaysia: Social Development, Poverty Reduction, and Economic Transformation." *Development with a Human Face*. Santosh Mehrotra and Richard Jolly eds. Oxford: Clarendon Press.

Herbst, Jeffrey. 2000. *States and Power in Africa*. Princeton: Princeton University Press.

Hermans, Quill. 1974. "Towards Budgetary Independence: A Review of Botswana's Financial History, 1900–1973." *Botswana Notes and Records*, 6: 89–115.

Heston, Alan, Robert Summers, and Bettina Aten. 2006. "Penn World Table Version 6.2." Center for International Comparisons at the University of Pennsylvania (CICUP): http://pwt.econ.upenn.edu/ (04 May 2007).

Heussler, Robert. 1981. *British Rule in Malaya: The Malayan Civil Service and Its Predecessors, 1867–1942*. Westport, CT: Greenwood Press.

Hintzen, Percy, and Ralph Premdas. 1982. "Guyana: Coercion and Control in Political Change." University of Guyana, Caribbean Collection, JL 685 A1 H55.

———. 1983. "Race, Ideology, and Power in Guyana." *Journal of Commonwealth and Comparative Politics*, 11 (2): 175–94.

Hochschild, Adam. 1998. *King Leopold's Ghost: A Story of Greed, Terror, and Heroism in Colonial Africa*. Boston: Houghton Mifflin.

Hoffman, Lawrence A. 1948. "India: Main Population Concentrations." *Geographical Journal*, 111 (3): 89–100.

Hollet, David. 1999. *Passages from India to El Dorado: Guyana and the Great Migration*. Madison: Fairleigh Dickinson University Press.

Hollup, Oddvar. 1994. "The Disintegration of Case and Changing Concepts of Indian Ethnic Identity in Mauritius." *Ethnology*, 33 (4): 297–316.

Hooper, Charles. 1938a. *Report of the Commission of Inquiry into the Unrest on Sugar Estates in Mauritius*. Port Louis: Government Printers. University of Mauritius, Mauritius Collection.

———. 1938b. "Summary Report on the Administration of Justice and the Working of the Legal System." Kew: Public Records Office, CO167/902/5.

House of Commons. 1939. *Statistical Abstract for British India*. London: HMSO.

———. 1942. *Statistical Abstract for British India and Certain Indian States*. London: HMSO.

———. 1947. *Burma: Frontier Areas Committee of Enquiry, 1947*. London: HMSO.

———. 1951. *Report on the Administration for the Sudan for the Year 1948*. London: HMSO.

Howard, Michael. 1989. *Dependence and Development in Barbados, 1945–1985*. Bridgetown, Barbados: Carib Research and Publications.

Howe, Stephen. 1993. *Anticolonialism in British Politics: The Left and the End of Empire, 1918–1964.* Oxford: Clarendon Press.

Huber, Evelyne, and John Stephens. 2001. *Development and Crisis of the Welfare State: Parties and Policies in Global Markets.* Chicago: University of Chicago Press.

Hudson, R. S. 1956. "Letter from 14 May, 1956." Kew: Public Records Office, CO554/1329.

Hudson, Rex A., and Daniel J. Seyler. 1989. "Jamaica." *Islands of the Commonwealth Caribbean: A Regional Study.* Sandra W. Meditz and Dennis M. Hanratty eds. Washington, DC: Library of Congress, 43–160.

Huff, W. G. 1994. *The Economic Growth of Singapore: Trade and Development in the Twentieth Century.* New York: Cambridge University Press.

———. 1999. "Turning the Corner in Singapore's Developmental State?" *Asian Survey,* 39 (2): 214–42.

Hurwitz, Samuel, and Edith Hurwitz. 1971. *Jamaica: A Historical Portrait.* New York: Praeger Publishers.

Ibrahim, Zawawi. 1998. *The Malay Labourer: By the Window of Capitalism.* Singapore: Stamford Press.

Iliffe, John. 1995. *Africans: The History of a Continent.* Cambridge: Cambridge University Press.

Imrie, John, and Thomas Young. 1990. "South Africa and Botswana: Case of Destabilization?" *International Affairs Bulletin,* 14 (1): 4–21.

Ince, Basil. 1974. *Decolonization and Conflict at the United Nations: Guyana's Struggle for Independence.* Cambridge, MA: Schenkman Publishers.

Inger, I. 1985. "Constraints to Popular Participation in Rural Development." *Theory and Practice of People's Participation in Rural Development.* B. D. Tsiane and F. Youngman eds. Botswana National Archives, BNB 9787, 31–39.

Ireland, W. 1897. *Demerarian.* Georgetown, Guyana: Baldwin and Company.

Jagan, Cheddi. 1997. *The West on Trial.* Glasgow: Hansib Caribbean.

Janson, Tore and Joseph Tsonope. 1991. *Birth of a National Language: The History of Setswana.* Gaborone: Heinemann.

Jayasuriya, Laksiri. 2004. "Social Policy and the Sri Lankan Welfare State: The British Colonial Legacy." *Social Policy and the Commonwealth: Prospects for Social Inclusion.* C. Jones Finer and P. Smyth eds. New York: Palgrave Macmillan, 109–24.

Jeffries, Charles. 1938. *The Colonial Empire and Its Civil Service.* New York: Cambridge University Press.

———. 1962. *Ceylon: The Path to Independence.* London: Pall Mall Press.

Jeffries, K. 1998. "Botswana and Diamond-Dependent Development." *Botswana: Politics and Society.* W. A. Edge and M. H. Lekorwe eds. Pretoria: J. L. van Schaik Publishers, 300–318.

Johnson, Chalmers. 1982. *Miti and the Japanese Miracle: The Growth of Industrial Policy, 1925–1975.* Stanford: Stanford University Press.

Jomo, Kwame Sundaram. 1986. *A Question of Class: Capital, the State, and Uneven Development in Malay.* New York: Oxford University Press.

Jones, Adam. 1983. *From Slaves to Palm Kernels.* Wiesbaden: Franz Steiner Verlag.

Ka, Chih-ming. 1995. *Japanese Colonialism in Taiwan: Land Tenure, Development, and Dependency, 1985–1945.* Boulder: Westview Press.

Kandeh, Jimmy. 2002. "Subaltern Terror in Sierra Leon." *Africa in Crisis: New Challenges and Possibilities.* Tunde Zack-Williams, Diane Frost, and Alex Thomson eds. Sterling, VA: Pluto Press, 179–95.

Kann, U., and D. Taylor. 1989. "Manpower Development and Education Since Independence." *Pula,* 6: 38–62.

Katz, William Loren ed. 1968. *Negro Population in the United States: 1790–1915.* New York: Arno Press.

Kaur, Amarjit. 1985. *Bridge and Barrier: Transport and Communications in Colonial Malaya, 1870–1957.* New York: Oxford University Press.

Kilson, Martin. 1966. *Political Change in a West African State: A Study of the Modernization Process in Sierra Leone.* Cambridge: Harvard University Press.

Kirch, Patrick. 1996. "Lapita and Its Aftermath: The Austronesian Settlement of Oceania." *Transactions of the American Philosophical Society,* 86 (5): 57–70.

Kirk-Greene, Anthony. 2000. *Britain's Imperial Administrators, 1858–1966.* New York: St. Martin's Press.

Klein, Herbert S. 2004. *A Population History of the United States.* New York: Cambridge University Press.

Knibbs, G.H. 1908. *Official Year Book of the Commonwealth of Australia: No. 1—1901–1907.* Melbourne: McCarron, Bird & Co.

Koenig, M. 1931. *Final Report of the Census Enumeration Made in the Colony of Mauritius.* Port Louis: Government Printers. Mauritius National Archives.

Kohli, Atul. 1987. *The State and Poverty in India: The Politics of Reform.* New York: Cambridge University Press.

———. 1994. "Where Do High Growth Political Economies Come From? The Japanese Lineage of Korea's 'Developmental State.'" *World Development,* 22 (9): 1269–93.

———. 2004. *State-Directed Development: Political Power and Industrialization in the Global Periphery.* New York: Cambridge University Press.

Koop, John Clement. 1960. *The Eurasian Population in Burma.* New Haven, CT: Yale University Press.

Kpundeh, Sahr. 1999. "The Fight Against Corruption in Sierra Leone." *Curbing Corruption: Toward a Model for Building National Integrity.* Rick Stapenhurst and Sahr Kpundeh eds. Washington, DC: World Bank, 207–34.

Krause, Lawrence. 1988. "Hong Kong and Singapore: Twins or Kissing Cousins?" *Economic Development and Cultural Change,* 36 (3): S45–S66.

Kuczynski, Robert. 1948. *Demographic Survey of the British Colonial Empire, Volume I.* New York: Oxford University Press.

———. 1949. *Demographic Survey of the British Colonial Empire, Volume II.* New York: Oxford University Press.

———. 1953. *Demographic Survey of the British Colonial Empire, Volume III.* New York: Oxford University Press.

Kulkarni, V. B. 1964. *British Dominion in India and After.* Bombay: Bharatiya Vidya Bhavan.

Kumar, Anand. 1989. *State and Society in India: A Study of the State's Agenda-Making, 1917–1977.* New Delhi: Radiant Publishers.

Kuo, Eddie C.Y., and Seen-Kong Chiew. 1984. *Ethnicity and Fertility in Singapore.* Singapore: Institute of Southeast Asian Studies.

Laitin, David. 1986. *Hegemony and Culture: Politics and Religious Change among the Yoruba*. Chicago: University of Chicago Press.

Lamusse, Roland. 2001. "Macroeconomic Policy and Performance." *The Mauritian Economy*. Rajen Dabee and David Greenaway eds. New York: Palgrave, 11–44.

Land, Anthony. 1987. "The Role of the State in the Provision of Domestic Water Supply and Sanitation in Rural Botswana." Ph.D. Dissertation, Loughborough University of Technology. Botswana National Archives, BNB 11,700.

Landes, David. 1998. *The Wealth and Poverty of Nations: Why Some Are So Rich and Some So Poor*. New York: W. W. Norton.

Lange, Matthew. 2003a. "Embedding the Colonial State: A Comparative-Historical Analysis of State Building and Broad-Based Development in Mauritius." *Social Science History*, 27 (3): 397–423.

———. 2003b. "Structural Holes and Structural Synergies: A Comparative-Historical Analysis of State-Society Relations and Development in Colonial Sierra Leone and Mauritius." *International Journal of Comparative Sociology*, 44 (4): 372–407.

———. 2004. "British Colonial Legacies and Political Development." *World Development*, 32 (6): 905–22.

———. 2005a. "British Colonial State Legacies and Development Trajectories: A Statistical Analysis of Direct and Indirect Rule." *States and Development: Historical Antecedents of Stagnation and Advance*. Matthew Lange and Dietrich Rueschemeyer eds. Palgrave Macmillan, 117–39.

———. 2005b. "The Rule of Law and Development: A Weberian Framework of States and State-Society Relations." *States and Development: Historical Antecedents of Stagnation and Advance*. Matthew Lange and Dietrich Rueschemeyer eds. Palgrave Macmillan, 48–65.

Lange, Matthew, James Mahoney, and Matthias vom Hau. 2006. "Colonialism and Development: A Comparative Analysis of Spanish and British Colonies." *American Journal of Sociology*, 111 (5): 1412–62.

Lange, Matthew, and Dietrich Rueschemeyer. 2005. *States and Development: Historical Antecedents of Stagnation and Advance*. New York: Palgrave Macmillan.

LaPorta, Rafael, Florencio Lopez-de-Silanes, Andrei Shleifer, and Robert Vishny. 1999. "The Quality of Government." *Journal of Law, Economics, and Organization*, 15 (1): 222–82.

Latin American Bureau. 1984. *Guyana: Fraudulent Revolution*. London: Latin American Bureau.

Ledgister, F. S. J. 1998. *Class Alliances and the Liberal Authoritarian State: The Roots of Post-Colonial Democracy in Jamaica, Trinidad and Tobago, and Surinam*. Trenton, NJ: Africa World Press.

Lee, J. M. 1967. *Colonial Development and Good Government: A Study of the Ideas Expressed by the British Official Classes in Planning Decolonization, 1939–1964*. Oxford: Clarendon Press.

Leftwich, Adrian. 2000. *States and Development*. London: Polity Press.

Lenski, Gerhard. 1970. *Human Societies: A Macrolevel Introduction to Sociology*. New York: McGraw-Hill.

Lewis, Stephen. 1990. *The Economics of Apartheid*. New York: Council on Foreign Relations Press.

———. 1993. "Policymaking and Economic Performance: Botswana in Comparative Perspective." *Botswana: The Political Economy of Democratic Development*. Stephen John Stedman ed. Boulder: Lynne Rienner Publishers, 11–27.

Li, Anshan. 2002. *British Rule and Rural Protest in Southern Ghana*. New York: Peter Lang.

Lieberman, Evan. 2003. "Nested Analysis in Cross-National Research." *Newsletter: American Political Science Association--Comparative Politics*, 14 (1): 17–20.

———. 2005. "Nested Analysis as a Mixed-Method Strategy for Comparative Research." *American Political Science Review*, 99 (3): 435–52.

Lieberson, Stanley. 1985. *Making It Count: The Improvement of Social Research and Theory*. Los Angeles: University of California Press.

Lipset, Seymour Martin, Martin Trow, and James Coleman. 1956. *Union Democracy: The Inside Politics of the International Typographical Union*. New York: Free Press.

Low, D. Anthony, and R. Cranford Pratt. 1960. *Buganda and British Overrule, 1900–1955: Two Studies*. New York: Oxford University Press.

Lugard, Frederick. 1922. *The Dual Mandate in British Tropical Africa*. London: W. Blackwood and Sons.

Lutchman, Harold. 1970. "The Problems of Political Change and Administrative Adaptation in Guyana." University of Guyana, Caribbean Collection: JL 685 A L88.

———. 1971a. "Race and the Public Service in Guyana." University of Guyana, Caribbean Collection: JL 686 Z13 R24.

———. 1971b. "Some Administrative Problems of the Cooperative Republic of Guyana." *Journal of Administrative Overseas*, 10 (2): 87–99.

———. 1974. *From Colonialism to Co-operative Republic: Aspects of Political Development in Guyana*. Rio Piedras, Puerto Rico: Institute of Caribbean Studies.

———. 1979. "Fascism or Socialism? History Will Judge." University of Guyana, Caribbean Collection: JL 683 A6 L88.

Macartney, William. 1978. "Local Government and the Politics of Development in Botswana." Ph.D. Dissertation, University of Edinburgh, Department of Political Science.

Maddison, Angus. 2007. *Historical Statistics for the World Economy: 1–2003 AD*. http://www.ggdc.net/maddison/ (3 November 2007)

Mahoney, James. 2000. "Path Dependence in Historical Sociology." *Theory and Society*, 29: 507–48.

———. 2003. "Long-Run Development and the Legacy of Colonialism in Spanish America." *American Journal of Sociology*, 109 (1): 51–106.

Mahoney, James, and Matthias vom Hau. 2005. "Colonial States and Economic Development in Spanish America." *States and Development: Historical Antecedents of Stagnation and Advance*. Matthew Lange and Dietrich Rueschemeyer eds. New York: Palgrave Macmillan, 92–116.

Malinowski, Bronislaw. 1929. "Practical Anthropology." *Africa*, 2 (1): 22–38.

Mamdani, Mahmood. 1996. *Citizen and Subject*. Princeton: Princeton University Press.

———. 2001. *When Victims Become Killers*. Princeton: Princeton University Press.

Mandle, Jay. 1973. *The Plantation Economy: Population and Economic Change in Guyana, 1838–1960*. Philadelphia: Temple University Press.

———. 1974. "The Plantation States as a Sub-region of the Post-bellum South." *Journal of Economic History*, 34 (3): 732–38.

———. 1982. *Patterns of Caribbean Development: An Interpretive Essay on Economic Change*. New York: Gordon and Breach Science Publishers.

Mann, Michael. 1984. "The Autonomous Power of the State: Its Origins, Mechanisms, and Results." *Archives Européennes de Sociologie*, 25: 185–213.

Mannick, A. R. 1979. *Mauritius: The Development of a Plural Society*. Nottingham: Spokesman.

Mars, Perry. 2001. "Ethnic Politics, Mediation, and Conflict Resolution: The Guyana Experience." *Journal of Peace Research*, 38 (3): 353–72.

Marshall, A. H. 1955. *Report on the Local Government in British Guiana*. Georgetown, British Guiana: Government Printers.

Marshall, P. J. 1996. *British Empire*. New York: Cambridge University Press.

Marx, Anthony. 1998. *Making Race and Nation: A Comparison of the United States, South Africa, and Brazil*. New York: Cambridge University Press.

Maundeni, Zibani. 1998. "The Struggle for Political Freedom and Independence." *Botswana: Politics and Society*. W. A. Edge and M. H. Lekorwe eds. Pretoria: J. L. van Schaik Publishers, 118–33.

———. 2004. *Civil Society, Politics and the State in Botswana*. Gaborone, Botswana: Medi Publishing.

Mauritius Economic Commission. 1948. *Health and Welfare: Report of the Committee No. 3*. Port Louis: Government Printer. Mauritius National Archives.

Mauritius Legislative Council. 1951a. "Ordinance No. 75: An Ordinance to Provide for the Constitution of Village Councils." Port Louis: Government Printers. Mauritius National Archives.

———. 1951b. "Ordinance No 76: An Ordinance to Provide for the Constitution of District Councils." Port Louis: Government Printers. Mauritius National Archives.

———. 1956a. "Sessional Paper No. 2: The Development of Rural Local Government in Mauritius." Port Louis: Government Printers. Mauritius National Archives.

———. 1956b. "Sessional Paper No. 5: Mauritius Development and Welfare Ten-Year Plan." Port Louis: Government Printers. Mauritius National Archives.

———. 1956c. "Sessional paper No. 9: Report of the Commission Appointed to Examine the Possibility of Subsidizing Religions Which Are Not Being Subsidized at Present in Mauritius." Port Louis: Government Printers. Mauritius National Archives.

Mayput, Vedita. 1993. "Development and Activities of the Arya Samaj Movement in Mauritius, 1900–1968." B.A. Thesis, University of Mauritius.

McEvedy, Colin, and Richard Jones. 1978. *Atlas of World Population History*. New York: Facts on File.

McGowan, Pat, and Johnson, Thomas. 1984. "African Military Coups d'Etat and Underdevelopment: A Quantitative Historical Analysis. *Journal of Modern African Studies*, 22: 633–66.

Meacock, D. W. 1955. "Mauritius Legislative Council Paper No. 7: Final Report of the Organization and Methods Adviser." Port Louis: Government Printers. Mauritius National Archives.

Meade, J. E. 1961. *The Economic and Social Structure of Mauritius*. London: Methuen.

Meisenhelder, Thomas. 1997. "The Developmental State in Mauritius." *Journal of Modern African Studies*, 35 (2): 279–97.

Meleagrou, Eleni, and Birol Yesilada. 1993. "The Society and Its Environment." *Cyprus: A Country Study*. Eric Solsten ed. Washington, DC: Library of Congress, 47–103.

Mendez, Juan, Guillermo O'Donnell, and Paul Pinheiro. 1999. *The (Un)Rule of Law and the Underprivileged in Latin America*. Notre Dame, IN: University of Notre Dame Press.

Merry, Sally Engle. 1991. "Law and Colonialism." *Law and Society Review*, 25 (4): 889–922.

Meyerson, Beatrice Berle, John F. Hornbeck, and Richard A. Haggerty. 1989. "Barbados." *Islands of the Commonwealth Caribbean: A Regional Study*. Sandra W. Meditz and Dennis M. Hanratty eds. Washington, DC: Library of Congress, 385–425.

Migdal, Joel. 1988. *Strong Societies and Weak States: State-Society Relations and State Capabilities in the Third World*. Princeton: Princeton University Press.

———. 1994. "The State in Society: An Approach to Struggles of Domination." *State Power and Social Forces: Domination and Transformation in the Third World*. Joel Migdal, Atul Kohli, and Vivienne Shue eds. New York: Cambridge University Press, 7–36.

Mills, Lennox. 1933. *Ceylon Under British Rule, 1795–1932*. London: Oxford University Press.

Misra, B. B. 1990. *The Unification and Division of India*. Delhi: Oxford University Press.

Moerdijk, Donald. 1981. *Anti-Development: South Africa and Its Bantustans*. Paris: UNESCO Press.

Moody, Sydney. 1945. *Report of the Commission of Enquiry into the Disturbances Which Occurred in the North of Mauritius in 1943*. London: Colonial Office. University of Mauritius, Mauritius Collection.

Moore, Barrington. 1966. *Social Origins of Dictatorship and Democracy: Lord and Peasant in the Making of the Modern World*. Boston: Beacon Press.

Morgan, W. S. 1961. "Eighth Progress Report of the Public Service Commission." Mauritius Legislative Council Paper. Port Louis: Government Printers. Mauritius National Archives.

———. 1966. "Twelfth Progress Report of the Public Service Commission." Mauritius Legislative Council Paper. Port Louis: Government Printers. Mauritius National Archives.

Morrison, Andrew. 1998. *Justice: The Struggles for Democracy in Guyana 1952–1992*. Georgetown, Guyana: Red Thread Womens' Press.

Munck, Thomas. 2005. *Seventeenth-Century Europe: State, Conflict, and the Social Order in Europe*. New York: Palgrave Macmillan.

Myers, Ramon H., and Mark R. Peattie. 1984. *The Japanese Colonial Empire, 1895–1945*. Princeton: Princeton University Press.

Nath, Shyam. 2001. "Government Expenditure and Economic Development." *The Mauritian Economy*. Rajen Dabee and David Greenaway eds. New York: Palgrave, 150–65.

N'Diaye, Boubacar. 2004. *The Challenge of Institutionalizing Civilian Control: Botswana, Ivory Coast, and Kenya in Comparative Perspective.* New York: Lexington Books.

Nelson, Harold D., and Margarita Dobert. 1973. *Area Handbook for the Democratic Republic of Sudan.* Washington, DC: US Government Printing Office.

Nepal, D. 1982. *The Development of Local Government in Mauritius.* Moka: Mahatma Gandhi Institute.

———. 1984. *British Mauritius, 1810–1948.* Moka: Mahatma Gandhi Institute.

Neville, Warwick. 1990. "The Population Composition of Brunei." *Singapore Journal of Tropical Geography,* 11 (1): 27–42.

Newbury, Colin. 2003. *Patrons, Clients, and Empire: Chieftaincy and Over-rule in Asia, Africa, and the Pacific.* New York: Oxford University Press.

New Zealand Registrar General. 1908. *Statistics of the Dominion of New Zealand for the Year 1907,* vol. 1. Wellington: Government Printer.

Nithiyanandam, V. 2000. "Ethnic Politics and Third World Development: Some Lessons from Sri Lanka's Experience." *Third World Quarterly,* 21 (2): 283–311.

North, Douglass. 1990. *Institutions, Institutional Change and Economic Performance.* Cambridge: Cambridge University.

Nyrop, Richard, Beryl Benderly, Ann Cort, Newton Parker, James Perlmutter, Rinn-Sup Shinn, and Mary Shivanandan. 1971. *Area Handbook for Ceylon.* Washington, DC: United States Government Printing Office.

Odell, Malcolm. 1985. "Local Government." *Politics and Rural Development in Southern Africa: The Evolution of Modern Botswana.* Louis Picard ed. Lincoln: University of Nebraska Press, 61–83.

O'Donnell, Guillermo. 1993. "On the State, Democratization, and Some Conceptual Problems." *World Development,* 21 (8): 1355–69.

O'Hearn, Denis. 1998. *Inside the Celtic Tiger: The Irish Economy and the Asian Model.* Sterling, VA: Pluto Press.

Olson, Mancur. 1965. *The Logic of Collective Action: Public Goods and the Theory of Groups.* Cambridge, MA: Harvard University Press.

Onis, Ziya. 1991. "The Logic of the Developmental State." *Comparative Politics,* 24 (1): 109–26.

Oodiah, M. 1988. *Histoire du Syndicalisme Mauricien.* Port Louis: Royal Printing.

Otlhogile, Bojosi. 1975. "Aspects of Administration of Justice in Colonial Bechuanaland: From the Resident Commissioner's Court to the High Court." University of Botswana, Botswana Collection, BDSC Pamphlets 91/230.

Packard, Randall. 1989. *White Plague, Black Labor: Tuberculosis and the Political Economy of Health and Disease in South Africa.* Berkeley: University of California Press.

Padmore, George. 1936. *How Britain Rules Africa.* New York: Lothrop, Lee & Shepard.

Parsons, Neil. 1998. *King Khama, Emperor Joe, and the Great White Queen: Victorian Britain Through African Eyes.* Chicago: University of Chicago Press.

Parsons, Neil, Willie Henderson, and Thomas Tlou. 1995. *Seretse Khama, 1921–1980.* Gaborone: Botswana Society.

Paul, Louis Jose. 1997. *Deux Siècles d'Histoire de la Police á l'Ile Maurice, 1768–1968.* Paris: Editions L'Harmattan.

Paxton, John. 1970. *The Statesman's Yearbook,* vol. 107. New York: St. Martin's Press.

———. 1971. *The Statesman's Yearbook,* vol. 108. New York: St. Martin's Press.

———. 1972. *The Statesman's Yearbook*, vol. 109. New York: St. Martin's Press.

———. 1975. *The Statesman's Yearbook*, vol. 112. New York: St. Martin's Press.

———. 1978. *The Statesman's Yearbook*, vol. 115. New York: St. Martin's Press.

———. 1981. *The Statesman's Yearbook*, vol. 118. New York: St. Martin's Press.

Peebles, Gavin, and Peter Wilson. 2002. *Economic Growth and Development in Singapore: Past and Future*. Northampton, MA: Edward Elgar.

Peters, Pauline. 1994. *Dividing the Commons*. Charlottesville: University Press of Virginia.

Phillips, Anne. 1989. *The Enigma of Colonialism: British Policy in West Africa*. Bloomington: Indiana University Press.

Philosophical Society of Sudan. 1958. *The Population of Sudan: Report on the Sixth Annual Conference*. Khartoum: Government of the Republic of Sudan.

Picard, Louis. 1977. "Working Paper No. 14: Rural Development in Botswana: The District Administration and the Creation of District Development Committees, 1966–1973." Botswana National Archives, BNB 3738.

———. 1984. "Administration Reorganisation—A Substitute for Policy? The District Administration and Local Government in the Bechuanaland Protectorate, 1949–1966." *Botswana Notes and Records*, 16: 85–96.

———. 1987. *The Politics of Development in Botswana: A Model for Success?* Boulder, CO: Lynne Rienner Publishers.

Pierson, Paul. 2003. "Big, Slow-Moving, and . . . Invisible: Macrosocial Processes in the Study of Comparative Politics." James Mahoney and Dietrich Rueschemeyer eds. *Comparative Historical Analysis in the Social Sciences*. New York: Cambridge University Press, 177–207.

———. 2004. *Politics in Time: History, Institutions, and Social Analysis*. New York: Cambridge University Press.

Pochun, Malati. 2001. "Population and Demographics." *The Mauritian Economy*. Rajen Dabee and David Greenaway eds. New York: Palgrave, 258–88.

Polanyi, Karl. 1957. *The Great Transformation*. Boston: Beacon Press.

Porter, Bernard. 1996. *The Lion's Share: A Short History of British Imperialism, 1850–1995*. New York: Longman.

Premdas, Ralph. 1995. *Ethnic Conflict and Development: The Case of Guyana*. Brookfield, VT: Avebury.

Proctor, J. H. 1968. "The House of Chiefs and the Political Development of Botswana." *Journal of Modern African Studies*, 6 (1): 59–79.

Putterman, Louis. 2000. "Can an Evolutionary Approach to Development Predict Post-war Economic Growth?" *Journal of Development Studies*, 36 (3): 1–30.

———. 2007a. "Agricultural Transition Data." http://www.econ.brown.edu/fac/ Louis_Putterman/ (10 September 2007).

———. 2007b. "State Antiquity Index." http://www.econ.brown.edu/fac/Louis_ Putterman/ (12 January 2007).

Rabe, Stephen G. 2005. *U.S. Intervention in British Guiana: A Cold War Story*. Chapel Hill: University of North Carolina Press.

Ramesh, M., and Ian Holliday. 2001. "The Health Care Miracle in East and Southeast Asia: Activist State Provision in Hong Kong, Malaysia, and Singapore." *Journal of Social Policy*, 30 (4): 637–51.

Ramsay, Jeff. 1991. "The Batswana-Boer War of 1852–53: How the Batswana Achieved Victory." *Botswana Notes and Records*, 23: 193–207.

———. 1998a. "20th Century Antecedents of Decolonising Nationalism in Botswana." *Botswana: Politics and Society*. W. A. Edge and M. H. Lekorwe eds. Pretoria: J. L. van Schaik Publishers, 101–17.

———. 1998b. "The Establishment and Consolidation of the Bechuanaland Protectorate, 1870–1910." *Botswana: Politics and Society*. W. A. Edge and M. H. Lekorwe eds. Pretoria: J. L. van Schaik Publishers, 62–98.

Rankopo, Morena J. 2004. "Three Decades of Community Development in Botswana: Is There Social Inclusion?" *Social Policy and the Commonwealth: Prospects for Social Inclusion*. C. Jones Finer and P. Smyth eds. New York: Palgrave Macmillan, 68–80.

Reddi, Sada. 2005. "Fighting Malaria in the 1940s." *Mauritius Times*. http://www.fightingmalaria.org/news.php (22 June 2006).

Reeves, Peter. 1991. *Landlords and Governments in Uttar Pradesh: A Study of Their Relations Until Zamindari Abolition*. Bombay: Oxford University Press.

Reilly, Benjamin. 2004. "State Functioning and State Failure in the South Pacific." *Australian Journal of International Affairs*, 58 (4): 479–93.

Reno, William. 1995. *Corruption and State Politics in Sierra Leone*. New York: Cambridge University Press.

Republic of Botswana. 1968. *Staff List, 1968*. Botswana National Archives, S.L. 1968/2.

———. 1973a. *Annual Statement of Accounts, 1972/3*. Botswana National Archives, BNB 2091.

———. 1973b. *Report of the Department of Health for the Year 1973*. Botswana National Archives, BNB 2495.

———. 1974. *Annual Statement of Accounts, 1973/4*. Botswana National Archives, BNB 2671, 2672.

———. 1975a. *Annual Statement of Accounts, 1974/5*. Botswana National Archives, BNB 3074, 3098.

———. 1975b. *National Accounts and Selected Indicators, 1966–1976*. Botswana National Archives, BNB 3408.

———. 1976a. *Annual Statement of Accounts, 1975/6*. Botswana National Archives, BNB 3705, 3706.

———. 1976b. *Establishment Register, 1975/76*. Botswana National Archives, BNB 2828.

———. 1977a. *Annual Statement of Accounts, 1976/7*. Botswana National Archives, BNB 4948, 4949.

———. 1977b. *Report of the Presidential Commission on Localisation and Training in the Botswana Public Service*. Gaborone: Government Printers.

———. 1978. *Annual Statement of Accounts, 1977/8*. Botswana National Archives, BNB 4950.

———. 1979. *Annual Statement of Accounts, 1978/9*. Botswana National Archives, BNB 4350.

———. 1980. *Annual Statement of Accounts, 1979/80*. Botswana National Archives, BNB 4799.

———. 1981a. *Annual Statement of Accounts, 1980/1*. Botswana National Archives, BNB 6439.

———. 1981b. *Medical Statistics, 1978/79*. Botswana National Archives, BNB 5097.

———. 1982a. *Annual Statement of Accounts, 1981/2*. Botswana National Archives, BNB 8237.

———. 1982b. *National Accounts of Botswana, 1973/4–1981/2*. Botswana National Archives, BNB 7763.

———. 1983. *Annual Statement of Accounts, 1982/3*. Botswana National Archives, BNB 8102.

———. 1984a. *Annual Statement of Accounts, 1983/4*. Botswana National Archives, BNB 9131.

———. 1984b. *Health Statistics Report 1984*. Botswana National Archives, BNB 11,005.

———. 1984c. *The Structure and Operation of Health Services in Botswana*. Botswana National Archives, BNB 9300.

———. 1985a. *Education Statistics*. Botswana National Archives, BNB 9463.

———. 1985b. *National Accounts of Botswana, 1984/5*. Botswana National Archives, BNB 10,710.

———. 1985c. *Report of the Auditor-General on the Accounts of the Botswana Government, 1985*. Botswana National Archives, BNB 9734.

———. 1985d. *Report on the National Food Strategy*. Botswana National Archives, BNB 10,821.

———. 1986a. *Annual Statement of Accounts, 1985/6*. Botswana National Archives, BNB 11,538.

———. 1986b. *National Accounts, 1985/6*. Botswana National Archives, BNB 11,707.

Rey, Charles. 1988. *Monarch of All I Survey: Bechuanaland Diaries 1929–37*. Neil Parsons and Michael Crowder eds. Gaborone: Botswana Society.

Richards, Paul. 1996. *Fighting for the Rain Forest: War, Youth, and Resources in Sierra Leone*. London: International African Institute.

Ridley, S. 1941. *Report on the Condition of Indians in Mauritius*. New Delhi: Government of India Press. Kew: Public Records Office.

Roberts, Richard, and Kristin Mann. 1991. "Law in Colonial Africa." *Law in Colonial Africa*. Kristin Mann and Richard Roberts eds. Portsmouth, NH: Heinemann.

Robertson, Harold. 1979. "From Protectorate to Republic: The History of Botswana, 1926–1966." Ph.D. Dissertation, Dalhousie University, Department of History.

Robertson, J. H. 1959. "Letter from 2 October." Kew: Public Records Office, CO1036/572.

Robinson, Ronald. 1972. "Non-European Foundations of European Imperialism: Sketch for a Theory of Collaboration." *Studies in the Theory of Imperialism*. Roger Owen and Bob Sutcliffe eds. London: Longman, 117–40.

Rodney, Walter. 1981. *A History of Guyanese Working People, 1881–1905*. London: Heinemann Educational Books.

Rogers, Barbara. 1976. *Divide and Rule: South Africa's Bantustans*. London: International Defense and Aid Fund.

Rolison, William. 1974. *British Colonial Policy and the Independence of Guyana*. Ph.D. Dissertation, University of Missouri-Columbia, Department of Political Science.

Rose, Euclid. 2002. *Dependency and Socialism in the Modern Caribbean: Superpower Intervention in Guyana, Jamaica, and Grenada, 1970–1985*. New York: Lexington Books.

Rose, James. 1988. "From Oligarchy to Bureaucracy: The Coming of Crown Colony Government to British Guiana in 1928." Presented at Conference of Caribbean Historians. University of Guyana, Caribbean Collection: JL 683 A7 R684.

Roy, Jay Narain. 1960. *Mauritius in Transition*. Allahabad, India: Ram Pratap Tripathi.

Rueschemeyer, Dietrich, Evelyne Stephens, and John Stephens. 1992. *Capitalist Development and Democracy*. Chicago: University of Chicago Press.

Rueschemeyer, Dietrich, and John Stephens. 1997. "Comparing Social Historical Sequence: A Powerful Tool for Causal Analysis." *Comparative Social Research*, 17: 55–72.

Rutheiser, Charles C. 1993. "Belize: Its Society and Environment." *Guyana and Belize: Country Studies*. Tim Merrill ed. Washington, DC: Library of Congress, 187–220.

Ryan, N. J. 1976. *A History of Malaysia and Singapore*. New York: Oxford University Press.

Sallahuddin. 1994. *Guyana: The Struggle for Liberation, 1945–1992*. Georgetown, Guyana: Guyana National Printers Limited.

Samatar, Absi Ismail. 1999. *An African Miracle: State and Class Leadership and Colonial Legacy in Botswana Development*. Portsmouth, NH: Heinemann.

Sautman, Barry. 2004. "Hong-Kong as a Semi-Ethnocracy: 'Race,' Migration, and Citizenship in a Globalized Region." *Remaking Citizenship in Hong Kong: Community, Nation and the Global City*. Agnes S. Ku and Ngai Pun eds. New York: RoutledgeCurzon, 115–138.

Schapera, Isaac. 1952. *The Ethnic Composition of Tswana Tribes*. London: London School of Economics and Political Science. Botswana National Archives, BNB 599.

———. 1962. *The Tswana*. London: International African Institute.

Schlesinger, Arthur. 1965. *A Thousand Days: John F. Kennedy in the White House*. New York: Houghton Mifflin.

Schwartzberg, Joseph ed. 1978. *A Historical Atlas of South Asia*. Chicago: University of Chicago Press.

Scott, James. 1972. "The Erosion of Patron-Client Bonds and Social Change in Rural Southeast Asia." *Journal of Asian Studies*, 31 (1): 5–37.

Scott, Robert. 1955. Letter from 29 June. Kew: Public Records Office, CO1036/53.

———. 1959. "Mauritius: Political and Economic Development." Kew: Public Records Office, CO1036/381.

Seawar, Lloyd. 1957. "Topic for Tonight, June 19." Kew: Public Records Office, CO1031/2531.

Seidman, Robert. 1978. *The State, Law, and Development*. New York: St. Martin's.

Selth, Andrew. 1986. "Race and Resistance in Burma, 1942–1945." *Modern Asian Studies*, 20 (3): 483–500.

Sen, Amartya. 1999. *Development as Freedom*. New York: Knopf.

Ser, Tan Ern. 2004. "Balancing State Welfarism and Individual Responsibility: Singapore's CPF Model." *Social Policy and the Commonwealth: Prospecwts for Social Inclusion*. C. Jones Finer and P. Smyth eds. New York: Palgrave Macmillan, 125–37.

Shafruddin, B. H. 1987. *The Federal Factor in the Government and Politics of Peninsular Malaysia*. Singapore: Oxford University Press.

Shin, Gi-Wook. 1998. "Agrarian Conflict and the Origins of Korean Capitalism." *American Journal of Sociology*, 103 (5): 1309–51.

Shin, Gi-Wook, and Do-Hyun Han. 1999. "Colonial Corporatism: The Rural Revitaliza-
tion Campaign, 1932–1940." *Colonial Modernity in Korea.* G. Shin and M. Robinson
eds. Cambridge: Harvard University Press.

Siddle, D. J. 1968. "War Towns in Sierra Leone: A Study in Change." *Africa,* 37: 47–55.

Sillery, Anthony. 1952. *The Bechuanaland Protectorate.* Oxford: Oxford University Press.

Silverman, Marilyn. 1980. *Rich People and Rice: Factional Politics in Rural Guyana.*
Leiden: E. J. Brill.

Simmons, Adele Smith. 1976. "Class or Communalism? A Study of the Politics of
the Creoles of Mauritius." *African Diaspora: Interpretive Essays.* M. Kilson and
R. Rosberg eds. Cambridge: Harvard University Press.

———. 1982. *Modern Mauritius: The Politics of Decolonization.* Bloomington: Indiana
University Press.

Singh, Chaitram. 1988. *Guyana: Politics in a Plantation Society.* New York: Praeger.

Skogland, Anton. 1977. *Botswana: The Development of Basic Health Services in the Rural
Areas.* Botswana National Archives, Micro 173.

Slade, E.H. 1985. *Census of Pakistan, 1951, Vol. 1.* Government of Pakistan: Karachi.
Accessed from *International Population Census, 1945–1967, Asia [microform].* Woodbridge, CT: Research Publications.

Smith, Martin. 1994. *Ethnic Groups in Burma: Development, Democracy and Human
Rights.* London: Anti-Slavery International.

Smith, Raymond. 1962. *British Guiana.* New York: Oxford University Press.

Smith, Simon C. 1995. *British Relations with the Malay Rulers from Decentralization to
Malayan Independence, 1930–1957.* Singapore: Oxford University Press.

Smith, Tony. 1978. "A Comparative Study of French and British Decolonization."
Comparative Studies in Society and History, 20 (1): 70–102.

Snyder, Richard, and Ravi Bhavnani. 2005. "Diamonds, Blood, and Taxes: A Revenue-
Centered Framework for Explaining Political Order." *Journal of Conflict Resolution,*
49 (4): 563–97.

Sokoloff, Kenneth, and Stanley Engerman. 2000. "Institutions, Factor Endowments, and
Paths of Development in the New World." *Journal of Economic Perspectives,* 14: 217–32.

Statistics Canada. 1878. *Censuses of Canada: 1608–1876,* vol. 5. Ottawa: Maclean,
Roger, & Co.

Steinberg, S.H. 1948. *The Statesman's Yearbook,* vol. 85. New York: St. Martin's Press.

———. 1953. *The Statesman's Yearbook,* vol. 90. New York: St. Martin's Press.

———. 1954. *The Statesman's Yearbook,* vol. 91. New York: St. Martin's Press.

———. 1957. *The Statesman's Yearbook,* vol. 94. New York: St. Martin's Press.

———. 1958. *The Statesman's Yearbook,* vol. 95. New York: St. Martin's Press.

———. 1959. *The Statesman's Yearbook,* vol. 96. New York: St. Martin's Press.

———. 1960. *The Statesman's Yearbook,* vol. 97. New York: St. Martin's Press.

———. 1961. *The Statesman's Yearbook,* vol. 98. New York: St. Martin's Press.

———. 1962. *The Statesman's Yearbook,* vol. 99. New York: St. Martin's Press.

———. 1963. *The Statesman's Yearbook,* vol. 100. New York: St. Martin's Press.

———. 1964. *The Statesman's Yearbook,* vol. 101. New York: St. Martin's Press.

———. 1966. *The Statesman's Yearbook,* vol. 103. New York: St. Martin's Press.

———. 1967. *The Statesman's Yearbook,* vol. 104. New York: St. Martin's Press.

Steinberg, S.H., and John Paxton. 1968. *The Statesman's Yearbook*, vol. 105. St. Martin's Press: New York.

Stiglitz, Joseph. 2002. *Globalization and Its Discontents*. New York: W. W. Norton.

Stinchcombe, Arthur L. 1995. *Sugar Island Slavery in the Age of Enlightenment: The Political Economy of the Caribbean World*. Princeton: Princeton University Press.

———. 1999. "Ending Revolutions and Building New Governments." *Annual Review of Political Science*, 2: 49–73.

Storey, William. 1995. "Small-Scale Sugar Cane Farmers and Biotechnology in Mauritius: The 'Uba' Riots of 1937." *Agricultural History*, 69 (2): 161–75.

Stubbs, Richard. 1997. "The Malayan Emergency and the Development of the Malaysian State." *The Counter-insurgent State: Guerrilla Warfare and State Building in the Twentieth Century*. Richard Stubbs ed. New York: St. Martin's Press, 50–71.

Sullivan, Mark P. 1989. "The Northern Islands: The Bahamas." *Islands of the Commonwealth Caribbean: A Regional Study*. Sandra W. Meditz and Dennis M. Hanratty eds. Washington, DC: Library of Congress, 519–559.

Suret-Canale, Jean. 1971. *French Colonialism in Tropical Africa, 1900–1945*. London: C. Hurst and Company.

Taylor, Robert H. 1987. *The State in Burma*. London: C. Hurst & Company.

Temane, B. K. 1977. "Rural Development, Industrial Innovation and Planning for Rural Development." Botswana National Archives, Micro 793.

Tendler, Judith. 1993. "Tales of Dissemination in Small-Farm Agriculture: Lessons for Institution Builders." *World Development*, 21 (10): 1567–82.

Tendler, Judith, and Sara Freedheim. 1994. "Trust in a Rent-Seeking World: Health and Government Transformed in Northeast Brazil." *World Development*, 22 (12): 1771–91.

Tennassee, Paul Nehru. 1986. *Guyana: A Nation-State Disintegrates*. Georgetown: Guyana National Library.

Terreblanche, Sampie. 2002. *A History of Inequality in South Africa, 1652–2002*. Scottsville, South Africa: University of Natal Press.

Thomas, Martin. 2005. *The French Empire Between the Wars: Imperialism, Politics, and Society*. New York: Manchester University Press.

Tilly, Charles. 1984. *Big Structures, Large Processes, Huge Comparisons*. New York: Russell Sage Foundation.

———. 1992. *Coercion, Capital, and European States, AD 990–1992*. Cambridge, MA: Blackwell.

———. 2005. *Trust and Rule*. New York: Cambridge University Press.

Titmuss, Richard. 1968. *Social Policies and Population Growth in Mauritius*. London: Frank Cass and Co.

Toth, Anthony. 1995. "Mauritius." *Indian Ocean: Five Island Countries*. Helen Chapin Metz ed. Washington, DC: Library of Congress, 89–135.

Turnbull, Jane. 2002. "Solomon Islands: Blending Traditional Power and Modern Structures in the State." *Public Administration and Development*, 22: 191–201.

Turner, Barry. 1998. *The Statesman's Yearbook*, vol. 135. New York: St. Martin's Press.

Union Office of Census and Statistics. 1925. *Official Yearbook of the Union of South Africa and of Basutoland, Bechuanaland Protectorate, and Swaziland, Statistics Mainly for the Period 1910–1924, No. 7*. Pretoria: Government Printing and Stationery Office.

Union of South Africa. 1956. *Official Year Book of the Union of South Africa*. Pretoria: Government Printers.

United Nations. 2001. *An Analysis of Economic and Social Development in Barbados: A Model for Small Island Developing States*. http://www.eclac.org/publicaciones/ xml/2/7812/G0652.html (11 October 2007).

———. 2003. *Human Development Report*. New York: Oxford University Press.

Uphoff, Norman, and Milton Esman. 1979. *Local Organization for Rural Development: Analysis of Asian Experience*. Ithaca, NY: Cornell University.

US Bureau of the Census. 1975. *Historical Statistics of the United States, Colonial Times to 1970, Bicentennial Edition, Part 2*. Washington, DC: US Government Printing Office.

Visawasam, C. 1973. *Sierra Leone: Local Government in the Chiefdom*. Freetown, Sierra Leone: United Nations Development Programme.

Wade, Robert. 1990. *Governing the Market: Economic Theory and the Role of Government in East Asian Industrialization*. Princeton: Princeton University Press.

Wallerstein, Immanuel. 1966. *Social Change: The Colonial Situation*. New York: Wiley.

———. 1974. *The Modern World System*. New York: Academic Press.

Walter, A. 1926. *Final Report on the Census Enumeration Made in the Colony of Mauritius*. Port Louis: Government Printers. Mauritius National Archives.

Wang, Xu. 1999. "Mutual Empowerment of State and Society: Its Nature, Conditions, Mechanisms, and Limits." *Comparative Politics*, 31 (2): 231–49.

Weber, Max. 1968. *Economy and Society*. New York: Bedminster Press.

———. 1992. *The Protestant Ethic and the Spirit of Capitalism*. New York: Routledge.

Weir, Neil. 1955. "Progress report of the Service Commission." Mauritius Legislative Council Sessional Paper No. 8. Port Louis: Government Printers. Mauritius National Archives.

———. 1959. "Fifth Progress Report of the Public Service Commission." Mauritius Legislative Council Paper No. 2. Port Louis: Government Printers. Mauritius National Archives.

Welsh, Bridget. 2001. "Taxing Malaya: Revenue Generation, Political Rights, and State Power." Ph.D. Dissertation, Columbia University.

White, Nicholas. 2004. *British Business in Post-colonial Malaysia, 1957–70: "Neo-Colonialism" or "Disengagement."* New York: RoutledgeCurzon.

Wolff, Martin. 2004. "State Building is the Greatest Problem." *Financial Times*, November 3.

Woods, Louis A., Joseph M. Perry, and Jeffrey W. Steagall. 1997. "The Composition and Distribution of Ethnic Groups in Belize: Immigration and Emigration Patterns, 1980–1991." *Latin American Research Review*, 32 (3): 63–88.

World Bank. 2002. *World Development Indicators* (CD-ROM). ESDS International, University of Manchester.

———. 2007a. *World Development Indicators On-Line* (9 July 2007).

———. 2007b. *Worldwide Governance Indicators, 1996–2006*. http://web.worldbank .org/WBSITE/EXTERNAL/WBI/EXTWBIGOVANTCOR0,,contentMDK:20771165 ~menuPK:1866365~pagePK:64168445~piPK:64168309~theSitePK:1740530,00 .html (17 September 2007).

World Health Organization. 2006. *Coverage Estimates: Improved Drinking Water.* http://www.wssinfo.org/pdf/country/BWA_wat.pdf (27 December 2007).

Wray, M. O. 1956. Letter H.152C19, 27 October. Kew: Public Records Office, DO119/1358.

Wylie, Diane. 1990. *A Little God: The Twilight of Patriarchy in a Southern African Chiefdom.* Middletown, CT: Wesleyan University Press.

Wylie, Kenneth. 1977. *The Political Kingdoms of the Temne: Temne Government in Sierra Leone 1825–1910.* New York: African Publishing Company.

Yeldman, C. 1948. "Report of Civil Commissioner, North." Kew: Public Records Office, CO167/944/8.

Young, Allen. 1958. *The Approaches of Local Self-Government in British Guiana.* London: Longmans, Green and Company.

INDEX

Page references followed by t or f refer to tables and figures, respectively.